T0386124

CALIFORNIA NATURAL HISTORY GUIDES

FIELD GUIDE TO
GRASSES OF CALIFORNIA

California Natural History Guides

Phyllis M. Faber and Bruce M. Pavlik, General Editors

Field Guide to
GRASSES of
CALIFORNIA

James P. Smith, Jr.

Illustrated by Kathy Simpson

UNIVERSITY OF CALIFORNIA PRESS

To the students in my agrostology classes at Humboldt State University
(1970–2005)

_____

University of California Press, one of the most distinguished university presses in the
United States, enriches lives around the world by advancing scholarship in the humanities,
social sciences, and natural sciences. Its activities are supported by the UC Press
Foundation and by philanthropic contributions from individuals and institutions. For
more information, visit www.ucpress.edu.

California Natural History Guide Series No. 110

University of California Press
Oakland, California

Library of Congress Cataloging-in-Publication Data

Smith, J. P. (James Payne), 1941–
    Field guide to grasses of California / James P. Smith, Jr. ; illustrated by Kathy Simpson.
    pages cm. — (California natural history guide series ; no. 110)
    Includes bibliographical references and index.
    ISBN 978-0-520-27567-6 (cloth : alk. paper).—ISBN 978-0-520-27568-3 (pbk. : alk. paper)
    1. Grasses—California—Identification.   I. Title. II. Title: Grasses of California.
    QK495.G74S623 2014
    584'.74—dc23   2013040442

23
10   9   8   7   6   5   4   3

The paper used in this publication meets the minimum requirements of ANSI/NISO
Z39.48-1992 (R 1997) (*Permanence of Paper*). ♾

Cover photograph: *Pleuropogon californicus*

The publisher gratefully acknowledges
the generous support of
Gordon E. and Betty I. Moore,
members of the Laureate Circle of the
University of California Press Foundation.

The publisher gratefully acknowledges the generous
support of the August and Susan Frugé Endowment
Fund in California Natural History of the University
of California Press Foundation.

The publisher also gratefully acknowledges
the generous support of
the General Endowment Fund of the
University of California Press Foundation.

CONTENTS

PREFACE

My interest in the grass family began over fifty years ago during a botany course I was taking from Harriet Barclay at the University of Tulsa. In discussing the grasses, she told us that they grew just about everywhere, were probably the most important plants economically to humans, and yet were so difficult that only a relatively small number of botanists were able to identify them. Who would not find that an intriguing combination? I decided that grasses would be the focus of my graduate school studies. This led me to Iowa State University, where I studied under Richard W. Pohl, the pre-eminent American expert on the grass family. I am grateful to both of these distinguished and inspiring professors for setting me on this path that would become a life-long preoccupation.

I began teaching a course in agrostology, the identification and systematics of the family, when Pohl was away on sabbatical. I then accepted a position at Humboldt State College (now Humboldt State University), where I remained throughout my professional career as a faculty member and as an administrator. During those decades, I taught agrostology to a few hundred students. Our course at HSU was probably the largest on that topic in the United States. I always looked forward to offering the class because it was so rewarding to see the students get interested in this group of plants that I found so fascinating and to watch them develop their competence and confidence as the term progressed. A number of them have sent me notes through the years explaining how they had been hired for a position because they had taken a class in grass identification. I like to think that my years of teaching students about grasses, especially how to recognize the genera of common grasses of the United States, provided me with a perspective that has been useful in writing this book. There is something to be said for having to stand before a class of undergraduates and attempting to explain grass structure, evolution, classification, and identification. That experience also suggested the need for an introduction to the family intended for readers with little or no background in botany. An extensive syllabus and a key to California grasses that I wrote for the class and revised several times form the basis of some of the sections of this book.

While I have collected grasses wherever my travels have taken me, I have concentrated on the California grass flora, especially in recent years as retirement has allowed me more time for field work. I served as the editor for the grass family in both editions of *The Jepson Manual* and I contributed generic treatments to the *Flora of North America North of Mexico*. I am also the author of *A Key to the Genera of the Grasses of the Conterminous United States*.

In closing, allow me to acknowledge and extend my gratitude to the students in my agrostology classes at Humboldt State, especially to Joseph DiTomaso, Jennifer Whipple, and Teresa Prendusi, all three of whom now have distinguished careers. Their enthusiasm and gentle prodding ("What did you mean by this?" "This step in the key won't work") were invaluable. A special thanks to the late John Sawyer, my colleague at HSU and field companion for over four decades. He often insisted that we go to places I might not have otherwise, and on numerous occasions he saw grasses I had missed. His constant badgering about "How do you tell this grass from that other one?" probably served some useful purpose. Jane Cole, drawing on both her botanical knowledge and computer skills, converted color transparencies and put them in final form for submission. Finally, I am very much indebted to Kathy Simpson for the fine illustrations that appear in this book and to Lloyd Simpson for the map that he prepared.

INTRODUCTION

This book is about the most frequently encountered plants in California. For many of us, grasses are also the least known and perhaps the most intimidating component of our flora. My purpose in writing this book is to provide you with the background and tools that you need to identify the more common **native** and **naturalized** grasses and thereby to cast doubt on the notion that only a small group of experts who have spent many decades of study are able to tell one grass from another. This will take some time and effort on your part. Most worthwhile projects do. I begin with the assumption that, although you want to know more about our grass flora, you have no special background—such as a university course in botany or plant systematics—in the subject. You may well know corn, wild oat, pampas grass, and Bermuda grass when you see them, but the rest of the family may still be a mystery. Although you are the primary audience, I hope that other readers with more extensive background and experience will also find this book useful for its commentary and information not readily available from other sources.

SCOPE AND ORGANIZATION. Will this book allow you to identify every grass found in California? No, only the more common ones. Our "official" state flora, *The Jepson Manual: Vascular Plants of California,* and the treatment of the family in *Flora of North America North of Mexico* come much closer to satisfying that goal. There is certainly an element of subjectivity involved in determining which grasses are common enough to be included here. I began by looking at the grasses found in Beecher Crampton's *Grasses in California.* I modified that list based on my own field experience. I have been collecting grasses in California for over 40 years. If I have not seen a particular grass in the field, I have presumed that you were not likely to have found it either. Finally, I used the specimen collection data from the Consortium of California Herbaria as a check on how often, how widely, and how recently particular grasses had been collected. I have also included a few weedy grasses that are not as yet a problem, as well as a few rare grasses and some conspicuous grasses, such as maize and wild-rice, even though they are not technically naturalized.

This book is in five parts. Part 1 sets the stage by describing the grass family and its close relatives and explaining the scientific and common names of grasses and their classification. Part 2 explains grasses' vegetative and reproductive structure, their **spikelet** structure, and their arrangement into **inflorescences**. Part 3 presents an overview of the California grass flora, first in terms of major taxonomic groupings, then a numerical tally and a discussion of their occurrence in various habitats. This part also includes a compilation of grasses that are found only in California as well as those that are rare and endangered, weedy, toxic, or have ethnobotanical uses. Part 4 explains how to collect grasses and make scientifically useful specimens, how to identify grasses using a dichotomous key, and the key itself. That key is modified from one that I wrote for the second edition of *The Jepson Manual.* Once you have keyed an unknown grass to **genus**, you are ready to turn to Part 5, where you will find a description of the genera arranged alphabetically, with keys to the more commonly encountered representatives.

FORMAT OF TREATMENTS. The standard format begins with the generic name, common name, whether the plant is an **annual** or **perennial**, and its height, a notation if the **stem** is woody, the length of the inflorescence, the spikelet size and features as well as features of the **palea** (other than the standard 2-veined or 2-**keeled**). The **stamen** and **stigma** number are noted only when they are other than 3 and 2, respectively, which is the pattern for almost all of our temperate grasses.

The second paragraph begins with three numbers, as in 1 • 12 • 60. These tell you the number of **species** in that genus found in California, in the conterminous United States (the "lower 48"), and in the world. This is followed by a statement of where the grasses are native, and a comment on their economic importance, if any.

Next comes the key to species. Each is identified by its scientific name followed by the common name of the grass, whether it is native or naturalized and annual or perennial (unless that is already stated in the generic description), as well as a brief description, typical habitat, and its distribution. I have included additional commentary for many species. The combination of the features I use in the key itself and the descriptive material that follows is intended to give a more complete picture of what this particular grass looks like and where it is found. Various measurements are based on specimens, monographs, and standard references, especially *The Jepson Manual* and *Flora of North America North of Mexico.* Unusual character states are shown in brackets, as in "**lemma** veins 1–3 [5]," which indicates that the lemma typically has one to three veins, but sometimes you will see five of them.

TAXONOMIC PHILOSOPHY. A. Tindell Hopwood, the British geologist, once described the urge to classify objects around us as a fundamental human instinct, comparing it to the predisposition to sin. Our prehistoric ancestors developed very practical classifications of the plants around them: These were good to eat, but those will make you sick; this one will cure a fever; that one will allow you to commune with the gods. Although our modern approach to classification is more sophisticated, it remains fundamentally an effort to deal with the vast array of objects in our universe—plants, animals, rocks, stars, and so on. We continue to struggle with a central question in classifying plants and animals: Do orders, families, genera, and even species exist in nature or are they constructs of the human intellect? I begin with the fundamental belief that in the plant kingdom only individual plants have an objective existence and that all the taxonomic framework that we have created is exactly that—a product of the human intellect. Some populations of plants do indeed appear to be biologically isolated by the forces of natural selection. In many other cases the boundaries are much less clear.

Is the diversity that we see around us best captured by recognizing genera and species that emphasize overall similarities or significant differences? Do we lump or do we split? I am an unrepentant lumper. My view derives from the oft-quoted advice of William of Occam, "One should not increase, beyond what is necessary, the number of entities required to explain anything." I believe that all too often we have named new grass species based on one or a handful of specimens, rather than on naturally occurring populations in the field where the uniqueness may not be so clear when more plants are observed. W. J. Beal, in 1896 in his *Grasses of North America*, put it very succinctly: "It is a pity some of these forms ever received distinct names." We have also been far too eager to elevate subgenera and sections of well-known genera to generic status. Sir Joseph Dalton Hooker (1817–1911) expressed this clearly when he wrote, ". . . elevating every minor group, however trifling the characters by which it is distinguished, to the rank of genus, evinces, we think, a want of appreciation of the true value of classification. The genus is the group which . . . is kept most prominently before the mind, and which has therefore the most importance attached to it." Mary Barkworth, in a treatment in the *Flora of North America,* offered the view that although some grasses have sometimes been placed in two genera, and although they may ". . . differ consistently in some morphological characters, their overall similarity is striking. There seems little value in promoting each to generic rank." Other contemporary botanists have cautioned against defining genera on the basis of evolutionary patterns that compromise their usefulness to us. I heartily endorse the view of Aljos Farjon that "taxonomy should be a science that earns its respect from users as well as fellow scientists." I also have great sympathy for the advice offered by B. K. Simon, ". . . conservatism in making nomenclatural changes is probably advisable, until it is possible to demonstrate some diagnosable features that can be observed fairly readily and simply."

Accordingly, I have retained broad, traditional concepts of a number of genera (e.g., *Agrostis, Bromus, Elymus, Festuca, Panicum,* and *Stipa*), where dismemberment has often been justified on the basis of DNA-RNA content, chromosome number, and distinctiveness of chromosome sets, along with anatomical and chemical features. These features are, of course, valuable and assist us in understanding the possible relationships and origins of grasses. Once you resort to these more subtle features, the recognition of segregate genera can begin to cascade. Is a genus defined solely on a different base chromosome number a useful concept? What about a series of **transverse** thickening bars on the inner wall of the **dorsal** epidermal cells of the lemma?

A CONCERN. Our knowledge of the California grass flora is far from complete. One of the reasons for this deficiency is that far too few of us are going out into the field and documenting the occurrence of our grasses, including some of the most common weedy species. I collected one of these "common as sin" grasses the other day in Arcata. It was last collected here in 1929! As you learn how to identify grasses and how to construct herbarium-quality specimens, I ask that you develop the habit of reporting unusual finds to the botanist at your local campus or state/federal agency and documenting that occurrence with a specimen when appropriate. Or send me an e-mail at jps2@humboldt.edu.

THE GRASS FAMILY AND ITS RELATIVES

Of all plants grasses are the most important to man. The different kinds are known by a very few, even among botanists. This is largely because they are supposed to be very difficult.

Agnes Chase, 1959

What Are Grasses?

The word "grass" itself has a complex etymology. In the broad sense, it has been applied to small **herbaceous** plants in general, particularly those whose leaves and stems are eaten by wild or domesticated animals. It may trace back to the Indo-Iranian word "ghra," which means "to grow," and to the concepts of green and grain. In this sense, grasses are more or less nondescript greenery.

Our focus is much narrower. All true grasses belong to a single family of flowering plants, *Gramineae*. I use the phrase "true grasses" because there are many plants that have "grass" as part of their common name that are not actually grasses. Some common examples drawn from the California flora include blue-eyed-grass (an iris), bear-grass (a lily), cotton-grass (a sedge), snake-grass (a horsetail), sugar-grass (a rush), and nut grass (a sedge). Grass, the common name of one of California's leading agricultural products, is not a grass but a member of the hemp family.

Although the grass family was not formally named until 1789, our recognition of this group of plants goes back to prehistoric times, no doubt in part because of their ubiquitous nature and their usefulness to us. Theophrastus and other early students of natural history clearly recognized them as a distinct group. We now have a much clearer understanding of the limits of the family and where it fits into the plant kingdom. Grasses are flowering plants, which comes as a surprise to many people who think of flowers in terms of lilies, orchids, sunflowers, roses, and so on, with their attractive bright colors. Plants with inconspicuous, greenish, wind-pollinated flowers often go unnoticed and unappreciated.

Although grasses are the most frequently encountered higher plants, they do not constitute the largest plant family. The grass family ranks fourth in number of genera and fifth in number of species. See table 1.

A Description of a Typical Member of the Family

What follows is a more detailed description of typical members of the family. If some of the terms are unfamiliar, you can refer to the discussion of vegetative structure, inflorescence types, and spikelets or to the glossary for assistance.

TABLE 1. Comparative size of the grass family

Family	Number of Genera	Family	Number of Species
Sunflower or daisy family	1,590	Sunflower or daisy family	23,600
Orchid family	779	Orchid family	22,500
Bean or legume family	720	Bean or legume family	19,500
Grass family	715	Madder or coffee family	10,900
		Grass family	10,500

Source: Data from Mabberley, 2008

Grasses are annual or perennial **herbs** that are sometimes more or less woody in the case of canes, reeds, and bamboos. Their roots are generally fibrous and often extensive. The stems (also called **culms**) are generally round, sometimes flattened, erect to **prostrate**; their **nodes** are swollen and solid, but the **internodes** are generally hollow; **rhizomes** and **stolons** are frequent; some stem bases are enlarged and **bulb**-like. Leaves are alternate, two-ranked, simple, generally elongate, and differentiated into a **blade** with **parallel** veins, a **sheath** (typically open with its edges meeting or overlapping slightly) that encircles the stem, and a **ligule** (a **membranous** flap or series of hairs at inner **apex** of sheath).

The grass flowers are found in spikelets that are themselves tiny **spikes** of flowers and associated **bracts**. The spikelets, in turn, are typically borne in branched or unbranched arrangements called inflorescences. Spikelets may be round or flattened in cross-section. A generalized spikelet consists of the lower and upper **glumes**, which are two **sterile**, overlapping, basal bracts. They may be equal or unequal in size and shape, and may bear conspicuous hairs or **bristles** (**awns**). Spikelets typically break apart at maturity either below or above the glumes. Above the glumes are one or more **florets** (a flower and two associated bracts) attached to an internal **axis** (**rachilla**). The typically more prominent bract, the lemma, may be similar to glumes in appearance and texture or quite dissimilar, and may be awned or awnless. The lemma more or less encloses the second bract, the palea. It is generally thin, transparent, awnless, and two-veined. The base of the floret sometimes forms a sharp-pointed and/or hairy structure, the **callus**.

Grass flowers are generally **bisexual**, **minute**, wind-pollinated, the **perianth** reduced to two or three structures (**lodicules**). Most of the grasses of the temperate regions have three **stamens** with comparatively large **anthers**. **Stigmas** are generally two, typically dissected and feather-like; the **ovary** has a single chamber. The characteristic fruit of the grass family is the **grain** or **caryopsis**, with the fruit wall more or less completely fused to the seed coat of the single seed inside; less often it is an **achene** where the seed is free from the fruit wall.

Unique Features

The features that I have just cited are characteristic of plants of the family, but none is both unique and universal. The fruit type comes very close. Although single-seeded fruits are found in a number of other families, the caryopsis is not. It is the fusion of the inner layer of the fruit wall with the outer layer of the seed that is unique. The grass embryo is also unique. Its single cotyledon, called a **scutellum**, produces enzymes that digest the typically starchy component in the seed. The family has also evolved a unique system to prevent self-pollination based on genetic incompatibility of the surface of the stigma and pollen grains.

Distribution

Grasses are the most **cosmopolitan** of all vascular plants; they occur on all continents, including Antarctica. Fully two-thirds of all of the higher plants of the southernmost continent are grasses, a fact that does not sound quite so impressive when you learn that the flora consists of three species. Plant communities dominated by grasses make up almost one-quarter of the world's vegetation, and they cover a similar percentage of California. Grasses are also the most frequently encountered vascular plants. There may well be more individual grass plants than there are all other vascular plants combined! Grasses are found from the polar regions to the equator, from the edge of permanent ice and snow on mountaintops to seashores. They occur in brackish and freshwater marshes, ponds, streams, rainforests, deserts, tundra, and arid slopes. In other words, grasses are found wherever flowering plants have been successful. They are dominant in the vast expanses of North American prairies, of the Asian steppes, of the South American pampas and puna grasslands, and of the African veldt. A major part of our agricultural land is devoted to them. Grasses are with us in our cities, either as ornamentals or as **weeds** along sidewalks, in vacant lots, or in our lawns and gardens. Grasses are never far away. Throw a rock and it will probably land on a grass.

What Explains Their Success?

Several factors combine to make grasses so dominant. Their anatomical structure makes them tolerant to grazing animals and to fire. In most flowering plants, the youngest growth is at the tips of branches. But in grasses, these most vulnerable tissues are at the base of stems and relatively protected from the chewing action of herbivores, the blades of a lawnmower *(Agrostophagus horribilis)*, or the damage caused by prairie and forest fires.

Other critical features are found in their physiology and reproduction. Most higher plants have evolved a photosynthetic pathway that incorporates carbon dioxide into a three-carbon compound; others use a four-carbon intermediate. We refer to them as C-3 and C-4 plants. Grasses have evolved both, and it is possible to distinguish them by looking carefully at the internal structure of their leaves. The C-3 grasses are found typically in the cooler, temperate regions of the world. Most of the grasses found in Alaska, Canada, and Northern California have evolved this pathway. The C-4 plants are more efficient at taking up carbon dioxide and are better adapted to warmer, drier climates. This more specialized photosynthetic pathway has evolved independently in about 10 flowering plant families and is especially common in the grasses. Two of the larger subfamilies of grasses, the chloridoids and panicoids, are typically C-4. They are the common grasses of the subtropical and tropical regions. We find them more commonly in Southern California.

Grasses have been especially successful in evolving various methods of reproducing themselves. Most reproduce sexually. Their pollen- and egg-producing organs are in the same flower, and the flowers are wind pollinated. **Unisexual** flowers and even unisexual plants are not that uncommon. Although cross-pollination is the typical situation, many grasses are self-pollinated. The feathery stigmatic surface of these grass flowers is physiologically and genetically compatible with pollen from the same plant. Their seeds are the result of self-fertilization. In addition to cross- or self-fertilization, grasses have evolved a series of mechanisms, some of them obvious and others quite subtle, to produce offspring without the union of egg and sperm. These mechanisms are collectively referred to as "**asexual**" or "vegetative reproduction." A few grasses produce basal, swollen, bulb-like structures that are capable of generating fully functional mature plants. Grasses also produce both **aerial** and subterranean stems that, when fragmented, can grow into new plants. These stem segments have buds, which are regions of rapidly dividing cells, at regular intervals. A bud may be thought of as a condensed, immature side branch with the capability of producing leaves and flowers. We take advantage of this capability in propagating a number of our crops, such as sugar cane, pineapple, and the potato. We do not plant seeds of these crops; instead we plant stem tissue. The offspring of asexual or vegetative reproduction is genetically identical to the parent plant.

But there is another level of subtlety that is more difficult to detect. Some grasses have all of the trappings of sexual reproduction. They have flowers, they produce pollen, they may be cross- or self-pollinated, and they set viable seed. While it certainly looks like perfectly orthodox sexual reproduction, it is not. Grasses have evolved several mechanisms for producing fertile seeds without the fusion of egg and sperm—the essential feature of sexual reproduction. One of these mechanisms requires the transfer of pollen from one flower to another, even though the sperm nuclei in the pollen grains will never unite with the egg nuclei. Detailed anatomical and genetic studies are needed to reveal these pathways.

Another variable is introduced when we learn that some grasses may reproduce sexually for long periods of time, then switch to vegetative reproduction, and then revert back to sexual reproduction. This can be seen even within a single population. Environmental conditions may cause this change. This could allow grasses to have multiple options for reproducing themselves during droughts or in otherwise disturbed or stressed situations.

Hybridization, the production of offspring from the union of egg and sperm from closely related plants, is a well-known phenomenon. About 80 percent of the world's grass species are **hybrids**; this is probably a higher percentage than in any other plant family. These grasses combine the genetic heritage of two or more ancestral species, and with that combination comes the potential to invade and succeed in occupying new habitats. The downside to hybridization is that many hybrids are sterile. But a very high percentage of grasses have overcome this problem by means of multiplying some or all of complete chromosome sets, thereby restoring the complementary chromosomes required during nuclear division and yielding fertile egg and sperm. Such grasses are called **polyploids**.

Grasses have also evolved a complex system of highly reduced leaves, the bracts of a spikelet, which not only protects their flowers and fruits against desiccation but also assists in seed dispersal by wind or by tiny spines or barbs that attach them to animal hair, clothing, and so on.

Grasses have also been aided by the most successful animal species on our planet, *Homo sapiens*. As we humans spread from our ancestral home in Africa to occupy so much of the terrestrial landscape, we carried grasses with us, both on purpose and by accident. We have converted huge expanses of land to grow the cereal grasses. In building our cities, roads, farms, ranches, pastures, orchards, vineyards, and gardens we have disturbed the natural environment and opened it to invasion and occupation by weedy grasses. Or, as Nigel Calder (1983) put it so well, "The master of the planet Earth is now identifiable: it is grass."

Economic Importance

It is all but impossible to overestimate the economic importance of grasses. As the eminent American agrostologist Richard W. Pohl said, "The value of the grasses to the human race is incalculable; they affect and support virtually every facet of human existence" (1987). In our relatively short time on Earth as a recognizable species, we have developed intimate relationships with a number of plant families, exploiting them for a vast array of foods, fibers, building materials, medicines, toxins, and psychoactive products. No other plant family can approach the grasses in direct economic importance to us. Still more of the Earth's surface is used for pastures to feed our domesticated animals. Grasses are, of course, important food plants for many species of wild animals.

Sugar cane may have been the first plant that we domesticated. With one exception, all of the great civilizations, past and present, are based on the domestication of one of the cereal grains—wheat, rice, and millets in the Old World and maize in the New World. We now devote 70 percent of our farmland to growing cereals, and we derive 50 percent of

TABLE 2. How we use grasses

Use	Example
Food and flavorings	Cereals
	Edible shoots
	Culinary uses
	Sugar
	Fodder, forage, and silage
Industrial materials	Buildling supplies
	Flooring
	Fishing poles and canes
	Paper
	Thatching
	Basketry
	Brooms
	Twine and rope
	Packing and stuffing materials
	Aromatic and essential oils
	Alcohols
	Starch, plastics, and adhesives
Beverages	Fermented beverages
	Distilled beverages
Landscaping	Lawns
	Playing fields
	Golf courses
	Soil binders and stabilizers
	Ornamentals
Miscellaneous	Clothing
	Jewelry
	Reeds for wind instruments/organs
	Pipe bowls
	Insecticides
	Darts and blow guns
	Perfumes
	Medicines

our calories from them. Wheat is the single most widely grown crop plant in the world. Data from the Food and Agriculture Organization of the United Nations for 2009 reveal the magnitude of worldwide production of the major cereals in millions of metric tons (mmt): maize (corn) at 818 mmt, wheat at 686 mmt, and rice at 685 mmt. The only other food plant that comes close to cereals in annual production is the Irish or white potato, at 329 mmt.

Although one of the major achievements in our cultural evolution has been the domestication of a relatively small number of cereals and other plants and animals, many of us fail to realize just how dependent we have become on the small, seed-like fruits of the grass family. Should our global harvest of wheat, rice, and maize fail for a single year, billions of us would perish.

Grass Relatives

Grasses—along with lilies, orchids, sedges, and irises—belong to a major subgroup of flowering plants informally called "monocots," plants with a single seedling leaf, scattered bundles of conductive tissue in the stem, a circular pattern of vascular tissue in the roots, parallel **venation** in the leaf blade, and floral parts in threes or multiples of three. Botanists group closely related families into a category called an "order." The grass family and 17 others constitute the order *Poales*. Here we find the closest relatives of the grasses, little-known plants of the South Pacific that belong to families such as *Flagellariaceae, Joinvilleaceae, Centrolepidaceae*, and *Restionaceae*. You will never confuse any grasses in California or North America with plants of these families because they do not occur here, except in cultivation. Restiads, plants of the *Restionaceae* family, have become very popular ornamentals in California in recent years. Two other families of the order are more familiar to us: *Bromeliaceae*, which include the pineapple, Spanish-moss, and numerous brightly colored ornamentals; and *Typhaceae*, the cattails of our roadside ditches and lake margins. You are not likely to confuse plants of these families with grasses, even if you are as nearsighted as I am.

There are, however, two more distantly related families within the order whose plants resemble grasses, at least superficially. Rushes *(Juncaceae)* and sedges *(Cyperaceae)* are common in California. Rushes are easily distinguished from grasses by their small but evident greenish or brownish flowers with three sepals and three petals, and by their many-seeded fruit. Sedges require closer inspection. Their flowers are also borne in spikelets. Even the great Linnaeus once got them confused! Table 3 contrasts typical members of the three families.

Technical Descriptions of the Sedge and Rush Families

CYPERACEAE **(THE SEDGE FAMILY).** Perennial [annual] herbs of wet and marshy sites. Plants often with creeping rhizomes. Stems generally with solid internodes and often 3-sided (giving rise to the phrase "sedges have

TABLE 3. A comparison of grasses, sedges, and rushes

Feature	Grasses	Sedges	Rushes
Stems			
Shape in cross-section	round [flat]	triangular [round]	round
Internodes	hollow [solid]	solid	solid
Leaves			
Number of ranks	2	3 [2]	2–many
Sheaths	open [closed]	closed	open
Ligule	present [absent]	absent	absent
Spikelets			
Bract insertion	**distichous**	distichous, spiral	not applicable
Bracts per flower	2	1	not applicable
Flowers			
Perianth	2 [3] lodicules	0–6 bristles	3+3-parted
Stamen number	3 [6, 1, many]	1–3	6 [3]
Anther attachment	near middle	at base	at base
Stigmas	2 [3]	2–3	3
Carpels	2 [3]	3 [2]	3
Fruit and seed			
Fruit type	caryopsis	achene	**capsule**
Seeds	1-seeded	1-seeded	many-seeded

Note: Character states in brackets show the less typical situation.

edges"). Leaves from basal tufts or **cauline** and 3-ranked; sheaths usually closed; ligule generally absent. Flowers minute, bisexual or unisexual, spirally or 2-ranked in tiny spikes. Each flower is **subtended** by a small bract, often called a glume. The spike of reduced flowers and subtending bracts form the spikelet, which are themselves arranged in various inflorescences. Perianth of bristles, hairs, scales, or absent. Stamens 3 [1 or 6]. Carpels 2 or 3, united, 1-ovuled, with as many style-branches as carpels; ovary superior. Fruit an achene or nutlet, lens-shaped or 3-sided, sometimes enclosed in a membranous sac.

JUNCACEAE (THE RUSH FAMILY). Perennial or annual herbs, from erect or horizontal rhizomes. Leaves generally basal, **linear**, sheathing at base, sheaths generally open; blades sometimes absent. Flowers small, green, regular, bisexual or unisexual, in various inflorescences. Perianth 6-parted (in two sets of 3), sepal-like. Stamens 6 [3]. Carpels 3, united, 1-chambered; placentation axillary or parietal; style 1; stigmas 3, brush-like; ovary superior. Fruit a capsule.

Selected References

Calder, N. 1983. *Timescale: An Atlas of the Fourth Dimension*. New York: Viking Press.

Mabberley, D. J. 2008. *Mabberley's Plant-Book: A Portable Dictionary of Plants, Their Classification and Uses*. Third edition. Cambridge, UK: Cambridge Univ. Press

Pohl, R. W. 1987. "Man and the Grasses: A History." *In* Soderstrom, T. R. et al. (editors). *Grass Systematics and Evolution*. Washington, DC: Smithsonian Institution Press. Pp. 355–358.

THE NAMES OF GRASSES

It is a sad truth, but we have lost the faculty of giving lovely names to things. Names are everything.

Oscar Wilde, *The Picture of Dorian Gray,* 1891

Common Names of Grasses

Most of us refer to grasses by their common or vernacular names. They are often simple, easy to remember, descriptive, colorful, pleasing to the ear, and easy to pronounce. Given this impressive list of advantages, why not just use common names for grasses and be done with it? Here are some of the reasons:

- A grass may have more than one common name. *Sorghum bicolor* is variously named sorghum, sorgo, kafir, durra, milo, broom-corn, and chicken-corn. *Stipa hymenoides* is called Indian rice grass, Indian millet, silk grass, and sand bunch grass.
- The same common name may be used for more than one plant. We all know corn when we see it. You may be surprised to learn that in other English-speaking countries, their "corn" is what we call "wheat." "Oat grass" is applied to species of *Arrhenatherum, Danthonia,* and *Trisetum.* "Millet" is a common name for the several unrelated grasses that yield small edible grains.
- Common names may change from one region of the country to another and certainly from one language to another. Learning the French and Spanish common names used elsewhere in North America only makes the task more difficult.
- Many common names are confusing and inaccurate. For example, Kentucky blue grass is not blue, nor is it native to Kentucky. Broom-corn is not a kind of corn, but a variety of sorghum. Heavenly-bamboo is not a kind of bamboo, but a member of the barberry family.
- Common names do not provide an indication of close relationship among the plants that share the name. Sour-grass, arrow-grass, blue-eyed grass, grass (marijuana), and China-grass are not kinds of grasses, nor are they related to one another. Foxtail is a common name applied to plants in three different tribes of grasses.
- Some common names are certainly colorful and bring on a smile, but they tell us little about the plant. *Briza media* bears the whimsical names cow quakes, didder, dillies, and doddering dickies.

- Because there are no universally accepted rules for giving common names to grasses and no organization that reviews and approves them, we cannot say that a particular one is *the* correct common name.
- The most serious deficiency in the use of common names is that most grasses do not have "real" common names that are actually used by the general public. Only a small portion of the half million or so kinds of plants are important enough to us as crops, ornamentals, or weeds to have had common names applied. This is a problem for authors of floras and field guides, for consultants who write environmental impact statements, and for staff members in various state and federal agencies who must prepare material for general consumption. Authors have attempted to compensate for the lack of common names by inventing them, usually by translating the scientific name into English. The advantage of Orcutt's brome over *Bromus orcuttianus* or the spicate trisetum over *Trisetum spicatum* is not immediately apparent to me. I also doubt that anyone actually points to a plant and declares, "Oh, there's the one-and-a-half-flowered reed grass!"

A word or two about the spelling of the common names of grasses: You will notice inconsistencies from one text to another. For instance, *Stipa comata* is variously called needle and thread grass, needle-and-thread grass, and even needleandthread grass. Some authors capitalize common names, as in Giant Needle Grass. *Sorghum halepense* is Johnson grass, but *Tuctoria greenei* is Greene's tuctoria. Possessives come and go.

I have attempted to standardize the spelling of common names by following three simple rules:

- Common names are not capitalized unless they involve a proper noun, as in California fescue.
- The term "grass" stands alone as a separate word. It is pampas grass, not pampasgrass.
- When a common name is hyphenated, it is an indication that the grass is not what the common name suggests. Stiff-brome is not a type of brome, nor is mountain-rice a type of rice; but Japanese brome is a species of *Bromus*.

Scientific Names of Grasses

Advantages of Scientific Names

- Each kind of grass can have only one valid scientific name. Because these names are used all over the world, they facilitate the free transfer of ideas and information. Consider the difficulties that would arise if botanists in England, Germany, Iran, and the United States each had their own independent set of scientific names. The same scientific name may not be used for more than one kind of plant. Once it has been published, that name cannot be used again.

- Scientific names are published according to provisions of the *International Code of Nomenclature for Algae, Fungi, and Plants* (Barrie et al., 2012). It provides the basis for reviewing past scientific names (the rules are retroactive) and the rules for proposing names for newly discovered plants. Plants and animals can have the same scientific names because the rules for naming them are completely independent of one another. For example, *Tribolium* is the scientific name for the genus of a weedy grass **introduced** in Monterey County and also for a genus of flour beetles, which are major pests in wheat and other grains.

- Inherent in our system of scientific names is the concept of evolutionary or genetic relationship. We place einkorn wheat, emmer wheat, and bread wheat in the same genus *(Triticum).* We do so because we have concluded that the morphological, anatomical, genetic, and chemical traits that they share suggest that they are closely related.

Some Difficulties with Scientific Names

- Scientific names are largely the province of specialists and are not widely known or used by the general public. Everyone knows the common name crab grass. Few of us know *Digitaria ischaemum* var. *ischaemum.*

- They can be difficult to pronounce, especially if you did not learn to divide words into syllables early in your education. *Taeniatherum caput-medusae* can be intimidating. But sorghum is both a common name and a generic name, and the transition from fescue to *Festuca* and from brome to *Bromus* should not cause significant damage to the central nervous system. My own experience in introducing undergraduates to scientific names is that, once you get past the psychological barrier that these are terribly long words that only those who have had a strong background in Latin and Greek can master, you will become much more comfortable with them and begin using them rather easily.

- Although the concept that a plant can have only one legitimate scientific name is universally accepted, there can be considerable disagreement about what that name should be. No international organization or committee reviews and approves or rejects proposed new species names. Competent botanists examining the same evidence can come to different conclusions. Some of us are more conservative than others in recognizing and naming new species or varieties.

- Scientific names change as a result of new evidence. Just when you become comfortable with the scientific names of the grasses in your area, someone comes along and publishes a revision or a new monograph that changes some of them.
- They may also change for entirely legal reasons. When a scientific name was published it may have violated one or more provisions of the *International Code*. When these infractions are discovered by later researchers, the *Code* has provisions for determining a new name. Our **endemic** Eureka Valley dune grass was originally named *Ectosperma alexandrae*. But, unknown to the original publisher, the generic name *Ectosperma* had been published years before for a red alga, making its use as a grass name illegal. A new name was necessary, so this grass became *Swallenia alexandrae*, honoring Jason Swallen, a curator and grass expert at the Smithsonian Institution who was the first to recognize that this grass was a previously undescribed genus.

Components of Scientific Names

A new way of naming plants and animals was developed over two centuries ago. This system was popularized by Carolus Linnaeus (1707 to 1778), the leading botanist of his time. It was based on the principle that each organism is given a scientific name that consists of two components. The first element of the scientific name is the genus (or generic name), as in *Triticum*, the genus of wheat. The plural of genus is genera, not genuses. The second element is the **specific epithet**, as in *aestivum*, the particular kind of wheat called bread wheat. This second element of the scientific name is often incorrectly called the "species." It is the genus and specific epithet together that form the **species name**. *Triticum aestivum* is the species name of bread wheat. Because the name is the combination of two words, it is called a binomial and we call this scheme of giving scientific names to organisms the binomial system of nomenclature.

The binomial, for reasons of completeness and accuracy, is followed by the name (typically abbreviated) of the person or persons who first published that name for the plant. For example, in the scientific name *Zea mays* L., the "L." stands for Linnaeus. Because this book is not a technical flora, I will not use these initials or abbreviations.

It is often useful to recognize variation below the species level. The two most widely used categories are the subspecies (abbreviated "ssp." or "**subsp.**") and the variety (abbreviated "**var.**"). An additional explanation is needed for the term "variety." We have developed many different cultivated strains of crop plants and ornamentals. There are literally thousands of different kinds of rice. In general parlance, we often call these "varieties." However, for the purposes of formal nomenclature, these cultivated strains are considered too minor and often too short-lived to warrant giving them a scientific name. The variety of botanical nomenclature is not used in these instances. Instead, we employ the term **cultivar** (abbreviated "cv."), short for cultivated variety. For example, a kind of sorghum used to make molasses in the Southwest by Native Americans is *Sorghum bicolor* cv. "Apache Red Cane."

Many of our economic plants are of hybrid origin, the result of the accidental or purposeful crossing of two closely related plants. This can be reflected in its scientific name by inserting an "X." If the X occurs before the generic name, then the plant is considered the result of a cross between two plants in different genera. X *Agropogon* is an intergeneric hybrid between *Agrostis* and *Polypogon*. If the X occurs between the generic name and the specific epithet, then the plant is the product of a cross between two species in the same genus, as in *Tridens* x *oklahomensis*.

The Origin of Scientific Names

Most of the words that make up scientific names are derived from Latin or Greek, although there is no requirement that they must be. Modern names, anagrams, people's names, or even nonsensical ones have been used. The following examples may be helpful.

- Commemorative names (genera): *Ehrharta* (Jakob Ehrhart, a Swiss botanist and student of Linnaeus), *Lamarckia* (J. B. A. P. Monnet de Lamarck, the famous French naturalist), *Orcuttia* (Charles Russell Orcutt, a San Diego botanist), *Scribneria* (Frank Lamson Scribner, an American agrostologist).
- Commemorative names (specific epithets): *bolanderi* (Henry Bolander, author of the first California grass flora), *douglasii* (David Douglas, Scottish plant collector), *kelloggii* (Albert Kellogg, California physician and botanist), *stebbinsii* (G. Ledyard Stebbins, expert on plant evolution, especially of the grass family), *torreyana* (John Torrey, American botanist).
- Classical or aboriginal names (genera): *Agrostis, Bromus, Festuca*, and *Poa* are all ancient Greek or Latin names for grasses. Julius Caesar and Alexander the Great might have used them.
- Geographical names (specific epithets): *anglicus* (from England), *australis* (southern), *canadensis* (from Canada), *gallicus* (from France), *occidentalis* (west or western), *virginicus* (of Virginia). A word of caution: These epithets should not be taken too literally. "Virginia" was once used to indicate most of the southeastern United States.
- Habitat (specific epithets): *arenarius* (growing in sand), *arvensis* (of cultivated fields), *campestris* (of the fields), *fluviatilis* (of the rivers), *littoralis* (of the seashore), *palustris* (growing in swamps and marshes), *pratensis* (growing in meadows), *riparius* (of the river banks), *sativus* (cultivated).

- Growth form (specific epithets): *arboreus* (tree), *arundinaceus* (reed-like), *caespitosa* (growing in tufts or patches), *fasciculatus* (clumps or bundles), *pusillus* (insignificant), *repens* (creeping), *scandens* (climbing), *scoparius* (broom-like).
- Appearance (specific epithets): *alba* (white), *amabilis* (lovely in appearance), *barbata* (**bearded**), *bulbosum* (having a swollen part), *foliosa* (leafy), *glauca* (bluish-green), *gracilis* (slender), *hirsutus* (covered with coarse, stiff hairs), *inermis* (without spines or prickles), *mollis* (soft hairy), *racemosus* (full of clusters), *repens* (creeping), *rubra* (red), *tenuis* (thin, fine, slender).
- Use (specific epithets): *esculentus* (edible), *officinalis* (recognized as medicinally important), *sativa* (sown or planted),*textilis* (having useful fibers).
- Anagrams (genera): *Leymus* is a rearrangement of the letters in *Elymus,* and *Tuctoria* of *Orcuttia.*

Pronouncing Scientific Names

The *International Code* states that scientific names of plants are to be treated as Latin words, regardless of their origin. This has led some more scholastically inclined botanists to argue that we ought to pronounce scientific names as they were sounded in Latin and that great care should be taken in accenting the proper syllable. But there are traditional English, reformed academic, and Church Latin versions of Latin to choose from, each with its own set of rules for pronunciation.

Most American botanists pronounce the scientific names of plants as though they were English words. Some of us follow the rules in Latin for determining which syllable is accented; most of us do not. Many of us pronounce scientific names the way we were taught as undergraduates (if any formal discussion occurred) or, more commonly, we imitate the way our professors pronounced them when we took their classes. These become the familiar and "correct" way to pronounce scientific names.

You will find possibly mind-numbing explanations of the rules of pronunciation in some of the sources at the end of this chapter, especially in William T. Stearn's authoritative *Botanical Latin.* Here is a considerably less scholarly approach that you might find useful.

- Pronounce all of the syllables. The epithet *occidentale* is pronounced oc-ci-den-**tal**-e, not oc-ci-**den**-tal. We do this in daily life. Think of Nike, finale, diabetes, and so on.
- Words of two syllables are always accented on the first syllable. If there are three or more, the last is never accented. The accent will fall on the next to the last syllable, as in ar-**ven**-sis, or the one to its left, as in **an**-gli-cus. Deciding which to accent requires some knowledge of long and short vowels, diphthongs, and whether the

word is of Greek or Latin origin. Individuals with this knowledge are increasingly rare.

- Commemorative names or eponyms present a problem because following the strict rules of accenting can render the person's name unrecognizable. The epithet *jamesii* should be pronounced ja-**mes**-e-i, not **james**-e-i. Most American botanists ignore this.
- Try to be consistent.

Writing Scientific Names

There are a few simple rules that must be followed in writing scientific names. The genus is always capitalized; the specific epithet should not be. The rules of nomenclature allow them to be if they are commemorative, as in *Elymus Smithii* (a relative, no doubt) or if the epithet was once itself a generic name, as in *Arundo Donax*, the giant reed grass. Even in such instances, however, the rules discourage capitalization. The generic name and specific epithet are underlined when they appear in handwritten or typed material. They are put in italics or bold-face in printed text.

The Correct Name of the Grass Family

Before closing this chapter, let me address a point of confusion regarding the correct scientific name of the family. In older references, the grass family was routinely called *Gramineae*, although in more recent publications the family name is almost always *Poaceae*. This would suggest that the older name is now considered incorrect for some reason and that it has been replaced by a newer, correct one. Regardless of what some textbooks may state, this is not the case.

One of the basic principles of botanical nomenclature is that we are to use the first properly published name for a plant or group of plants (genus, family, order, etc.). The name *Gramineae* was published by Antoine Laurent de Jussieu in 1789; John Hendley Barnhart published the family name *Poaceae* in 1895. *Gramineae* is clearly the older name. The problem arises because another section of the *International Code* requires that all family names must end in the suffix -aceae. *Gramineae* was the first properly published name for the family, but has the wrong ending; *Poaceae* has the right ending, but came along a century later. The same problem is found in seven other plant families, all of them well known and economically important. All were named long before the rules of nomenclature were adopted. The solution that is permitted under the rules is a compromise. These eight families have two equally correct family names. The *Code* accepts *Gramineae* and allows *Poaceae* as an alternative family name. I use *Gramineae*. It was the first name to be published, and it is the form used in the text of the *Code* itself.

Selected References

Barrie, F. R. et al. (editors). 2012. *International Code of Nomenclature for Algae, Fungi, and Plants (Melbourne Code),* adopted by the Eighteenth International Botanical Congress, Melbourne, Australia, July 2011. Konigstein, Germany: Koeltz Scientific Books.

Clifford, H. T. & P. D. Bostock. 2007. *Etymological Dictionary of Grasses.* Berlin: Springer.

Coombes, A. J. 1985. *Dictionary of Plant Names: The Pronunciation, Derivation and Meaning of Botanical Names, and Their Common-Name Equivalents.* Portland, OR: Timber Press.

Gledhill, D. 2008. *The Names of Plants.* Fourth edition. Cambridge UK: Cambridge Univ. Press.

Hyam, R. & R. Pankhurst. 1995. *Plants and Their Names: A Concise Dictionary.* Oxford: Oxford Univ. Press.

Neal, B. 1992. *Gardener's Latin.* Chapel Hill, NC: Algonquin Books.

Quattrocchi, U. 2006. *CRC Dictionary of Grasses: Common Names, Scientific Names, Eponyms, Synonyms, and Etymology.* Boca Raton, FL: CRC Press. Three volumes.

Stearn, W. T. 1992. *Botanical Latin: History, Grammar, Syntax, Terminology and Vocabulary.* Fourth edition. Devon: David & Charles.

GRASS CLASSIFICATION
An Overview

Order is heaven's first law.

Alexander Pope, 1734

There has never been any significant disagreement about the limits of the family itself. Grasses are grasses. However, there has been considerable controversy about the major groupings within the family—its subfamilies and tribes. These are formal categories in the taxonomic hierarchy. Their names are governed by the rules in the *International Code.* Subfamily names end in the suffix -oideae, as in *Bambusoideae.* Tribe names end in the suffix -eae, as in *Paniceae.*

The great British botanists Robert Brown in 1814 and George Bentham in 1881 both theorized that there were two great groups of grasses, one of them centered in the tropics and the other in the temperate parts of the world. Today we call them the subfamilies *Panicoideae* and *Poöideae.* Their systems, based largely on easily observed features, would dominate grass systematics for many decades. Bentham's system was used by Albert Spear Hitchcock of the Smithsonian Institution, the most influential expert on American grasses for much of the 20th century. His *Manual of the Grasses of the United States* was the essential reference for almost 70 years. For students of my generation, it was the Bible. I still consult it frequently and I keep a copy in my vehicle in case of an emergency. Hitchcock's influence on the names of grasses and their position in subfamilies and tribes is evident in California's floras from 1912 to 1959. This is not true of *The Jepson Manual,* because there plants are arranged alphabetically by genus.

In this book, I use a system that combines elements of the publication of the Grass Phylogeny Working Group (2001), the *Flora of North America North of Mexico* (Barkworth et al. 2003, 2007), and Soreng et al. (2000, ongoing). When compared with earlier California floras, we see significant increase in the number of subfamilies, tribes, genera, species and taxa (singular **taxon**). By "taxa" I mean the number of species, subspecies, and varieties. This change is the result of: (1) finding previously described grasses that had been unreported for California; (2) discovering new, undescribed grasses, many of them found only in California; and (3) new investigations that resulted in dividing a genus or species into two or more genera, species, subspecies, or varieties. A comparison of the first comprehensive treatment of California grasses with my own shows the dramatic changes.

These changing concepts are based on new information, using equipment, technology, and computer-aided analysis not available to earlier

TABLE 4. California grass flora: Then and now

Source	Tribes	Genera	Species	Taxa
Bolander, 1866	10	49	110	110
Smith, 2013	18	117	547	603

workers. Linnaeus had a plant press and a primitive microscope at his disposal, and A. S. Hitchcock relied mainly on a dissecting microscope. New sources and techniques provide very useful, but at times conflicting, information that is used to support a modern system of grass systematics. They include:

- the anatomy of the leaf in cross-section;
- the nature of **silica bodies** deposited in leaf cells;
- the anatomy of the leaf epidermis;
- the anatomy of the embryo within the grass seed;
- the chemical composition of starch grains;
- the number of chromosomes and their behavior during nuclear division;
- differences in photosynthetic pathways;
- antigen-antibody reactions; and
- molecular data derived from DNA and RNA analysis, especially in the chloroplasts.

The older systems had fewer subfamilies, tribes, and genera. These were defined on the basis of more or less easily observed features, especially those of the inflorescence type and the features of the bract system associated with the flowers. It was relatively easy to learn to recognize the two subfamilies and 14 tribes of California grasses using only a hand lens or dissecting microscope. But as new anatomical, chemical, cytological, and genetic information became available, the integrity of these subgroupings came into question and they came to be seen as artificial assemblages of unrelated grasses. All of the grasses with much-branched, **diffuse** inflorescences and a single floret per spikelet should not be grouped with one another into a single tribe. They were not all related to one another according to this more complete spectrum of macro- and micro-characters. The newer systems—and there is much agreement among them—show us a much more accurate picture of relationships and evolutionary trends. Unfortunately, the days of being able to define subfamilies and tribes on the basis of a few easily observed characteristics are over. I should also point out that there are also several instances where subfamilies, tribes, and genera have been merged.

To provide some context, there are nine subfamilies and 24 tribes of grasses in the conterminous United States, of which eight subfamilies and 18 tribes are found in California.

Selected References

Barkworth, M. E., K. M. Kapels, S. Long, & M. P. Piep (editors). 2003. *Flora of North America North of Mexico.* Vol. 25. *Magnoliophyta: Commelinidae* (in part): *Poaceae,* part 2. New York: Oxford Univ. Press.

Barkworth, M. E., K. M. Kapels, S. Long, L. K. Anderton, & M. B. Piep (editors). 2007. *Flora of North America North of Mexico.* Vol. 24. *Magnoliophyta: Commelinidae* (in part): *Poaceae,* part 1. New York: Oxford Univ. Press.

Bolander, H. N. 1866. *Grasses of the State: Transactions of the California State Agricultural Society, during the Years 1864 and 1865.* Sacramento: State Printer.

Grass Phylogeny Working Group. 2001. "Phylogeny and Subfamilial Classification of the Grasses (Poaceae)." *Annals Missouri Botanical Garden* 88 (3): 373–457.

Hitchcock, A. S. 1951. *Manual of the Grasses of the United States.* Second edition, revised by Agnes Chase. Misc. Publ. No. 200. Washington, DC: United States Department of Agriculture.

Soreng, R. J., G. Davidse, P. M. Peterson, F. O. Zuloaga, E. J. Judziewicz, T. S. Figueiras, O. Morrone, & K. Romaschenko. 2000, ongoing. *A World-Wide Phylogenetic Classification of Poaceae (Gramineae).* Available at www.tropicos.org.

THE STRUCTURE OF GRASSES

VEGETATIVE STRUCTURE

The Root System

Most mature grass plants have a fibrous root system that is finely divided and lacks a clearly dominant root. This system is also termed **adventitious**, in that the primary root system is short-lived and is quickly replaced by roots that arise from plant parts other than the primary root and its branches. Typically these roots are found at the base of the stems. **Prop roots** are aerial roots that arise from stem nodes, penetrate the soil, and serve to support the grass plant. Maize often produces very conspicuous prop roots. The extent and penetration of the grass root system is variable. In one often-quoted study (Dittmer, 1937), a single rye plant growing in one cubic foot of soil grew a root system with a total length of 387 miles and with a combined root and root hair surface of 6,876 square feet. By comparison, the total leaf blade surface area of that plant was 15 square feet.

Roots of are little direct economic importance to us, although they do retard erosion by structuring the soil. Some roots contain aromatic principles, such as oil of vetiver. Root hair anatomy has yielded some features of taxonomic importance.

The Stem System

The aerial stem of a grass plant is technically called a culm. I use the term "stem," which is just as precise. Stems are typically round in cross-section, soft, and herbaceous in our temperate grasses. Some reeds and canes have much tougher stems. They certainly appear woody in the giant reed *(Arundo donax)*. Some other grasses, such as typical bamboos, appear to be woody; after all, we build things with bamboo. However, plant anatomists assure us that we are not seeing true woody tissue in these stems. A grass stem may be only a centimeter or so to as much as 40 m tall in some of the tropical bamboos. The stem is divided into nodes and internodes. The nodes are regions where leaves are attached, and are typically easy to locate because they are swollen. The region between two successive nodes is the internode. It is typically hollow, but several exceptions occur in some commonly encountered grasses, particularly in the bluestem tribe. Some studies suggest that about half of the grasses may have solid internodes. These plants also tend to have a specialized spikelet structure and to inhabit arid regions.

Grasses also produce horizontal stems. The rhizome is a horizontal stem at or below the surface of the ground that bears reduced, scale-like leaves. Stolons, on the other hand, are horizontal stems running along the surface of the ground and they often bear ordinary foliage leaves. Both types of stems have buds at their nodes that can serve as a means of vegetative reproduction. Although these definitions sound precise, the distinction between the two is sometimes subtle. Bermuda grass *(Cynodon dactylon)*, for example, produces both rhizomes and stolons, depending upon environmental conditions. Some grasses, such as onion grass, produce small onion-like bulbs (but without the odor); others, such as bulbous oat grass, have **corms**—swollen hard stems surrounded by dry, papery, scale-like leaves, similar to the "bulb" of the gladiola. Collect underground plant parts. They are often essential for identification and scientific specimens are incomplete without them.

Grass leaves are both alternate and two-ranked. They are alternate because only one leaf arises at a node. They are two-ranked because if the leaf borne at the first node comes off one side of the stem (as you look down from above), then the leaf at the second node will arise from the other side. Looking down on the stem and leaf system, the points of insertion or attachment are 180 degrees opposite one another. Grass leaves that are noticeably two-ranked, especially if the blades are stiffened, are termed distichous, as in salt grass *(Distichlis spicata).*

Grass leaves are typically composed of a blade or lamina, a sheath, and a ligule. The blade is usually linear—most grass leaves do look like grass leaves!—but it may be thread-like, needle-like, or even oval. The venation is typically parallel, with all of the veins being more or less the same size or with one of them forming a more prominent **midrib**. Some bamboos and a few herbaceous grasses appear to have **petioles**, but these are actually nothing more than constrictions of the blade or sheath. Such leaves are said to be pseudopetiolate.

The grass sheath is usually interpreted as a flattened petiole. It is most often rounded in cross-section, but in some grasses the sheath may be conspicuously flattened. Typically the sheath is "open"—the condition in which its edges come together and touch one another or overlap slightly, but are not fused into a cylinder around the nodes. This is a useful character for separating most grasses from most sedges. But beware! Some very common grasses—such as orchard grass, onion grasses, and bromes—have closed sheaths. In these instances, the two edges are fused for much or all of their length. Wind action and careless use of a dissecting needle can convert closed sheaths to open ones.

The ligule is a membranous flap of tissue or a series of hairs (or both) at the junction of the blade and sheath. Its function may be to prevent water from entering the sheath or to hold the leaf tightly to the stem. Not all grasses have ligules. Their absence or presence and structure are

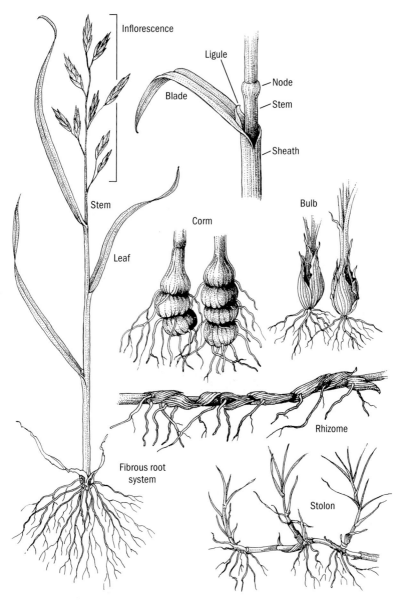

Figure 1. Vegetative structure (stems)

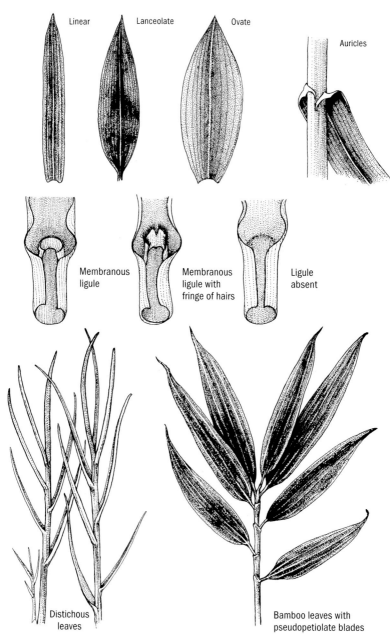

Leaf blades

Linear   Lanceolate   Ovate

Auricles

Membranous ligule

Membranous ligule with fringe of hairs

Ligule absent

Distichous leaves

Bamboo leaves with pseudopetiolate blades

Figure 2. Vegetative structure (leaves)

of taxonomic importance and are used in identification. Grass leaves, especially those of the barley tribe, have ear- or claw-shaped appendages called **auricles**. These paired structures arise at the base of the blade in some grasses, but laterally at the sheath apex in others.

Selected Reference

Dittmer, H. J. 1937. "A Quantitative Study of the Roots and Root Hairs of Winter Rye Plant." *Amer. J. Bot.* 24: 417–419.

REPRODUCTIVE STRUCTURE

Flowers

Most of us have never seen grass flowers; in fact, we are perhaps not even aware that grasses are flowering plants. This is understandable. Grass flowers are small and hidden away from easy view by a system of reduced leaves (bracts). This is another way of saying that grasses do not strike most people as being terribly pretty. But, come closer!

The brightly colored sepals and petals that make the somewhat distantly related lilies and orchids so attractive have been lost through the gradual processes of evolutionary reduction. All that remains for most grasses are two, or rarely three, almost microscopic structures called lodicules. Their shape, texture, venation, and surface features are of taxonomic significance. They swell in the early morning, thereby forcing apart the bracts that enclose the flower and promoting wind pollination. Not all grasses have lodicules.

The reproductive structures that have been retained are modified for wind pollination. The male component is the stamen, which consists of a delicate, thread-like supporting stalk called a **filament** and a sac-like region of pollen-producing tissue, the anther. Most grasses have three stamens; some have two or one, a few have six, and bamboo flowers may have hundreds of them. Any deviation from three stamens is almost always an important feature in identification. The female portion of the grass flower is the **gynoecium** or **pistil**. It consists of a one-chambered, one-seeded ovary. At the apex of the ovary are two **styles** (rarely one or three) that are separate to their bases and a **terminal** pair of feathery stigmas that trap airborne pollen. These same terms are used in all other flowering plant families.

Grass flowers vary in the presence or absence of reproductive parts. A bisexual flower is one that has both stamens and a pistil. A **pistillate** flower has only the pistil, while the **staminate** flower has only the complement of stamens. A **neuter** or sterile flower has no reproductive structures. All grass keys will ask you to distinguish among bisexual or perfect, staminate, pistillate, or neuter flowers or spikelets. A friendly warning: What is so easily defined on paper is often very difficult to interpret under the dissecting microscope or hand lens. Look at several flowers before reaching your decision. A common error arises when anthers develop early, shed their pollen, shrivel up, and fall from the plant. A quick glance can lead to the mistaken notion that the flower is pistillate. Look carefully for filaments as a clue to the presence of fallen anthers.

Fruit and Seed

When seen in cross-section, the ovary of the grass flower has a single chamber (locule) with one seed inside. In the vast majority of grasses, this seed will mature into the grain or caryopsis, in which the seed coat is all but completely fused to the ovary wall. This fruit type is unique to the family. Because they are small and one-seeded, grains are often confused with seeds. Most of us never think of kernels of corn or grains of wheat or rice as fruits, but they are.

In a few grasses, the seed is more or less separate from the ovary wall, producing a fruit type called an achene. A well-known example of an achene is the sunflower seed. You have probably cracked open the fruit wall to extract the single seed inside. Try doing that to corn or wheat. The seed contains **endosperm** and the embryo. Endosperm, which literally means "within the seed," provides nourishment for the developing embryo and later for the young seedling. The endosperm is typically solid and starchy in most grasses; in a few, such as June grass and false oat, it is a liquid composed of oil, starch, and protein.

SPIKELET STRUCTURE

COMPONENTS. The word itself literally means a small spike; that is an accurate description. A spikelet consists of a central stalk, one or more grass flowers, the minute side branches to which they are attached, and a series of bracts that enclose them. Some spikelets, especially those containing a single flower, may be quite small. Others are a few centimeters long and easily seen without magnification. The spikelet, although characteristic of *Gramineae*, is not its exclusive property; sedges also have spikelets. Because their spikelets are superficially similar, it is easy to confuse the two families. Refer back to Table 3 for a comparison.

All grass spikelets are put together according to the same basic plan. The tiny grass flower and its associated bracts are attached to an unbranched central axis called a rachilla. In many spikelets, especially those with more than one flower, the rachilla breaks apart at maturity. It may be extended beyond the flower(s) as a slender bristle.

At the base of the rachilla are two bracts that are empty or sterile, in that they do not have flowers in their axils. Each of the two basal bracts is a glume. Careful inspection will show that one bract is **inserted** slightly below the other. The lower bract is the first or lower glume; the one attached slightly above it is the second or upper glume. They may be similar in length, width, shape, and texture, or they may be significantly different from one another. The lower glume is typically shorter than the upper one. While most grass spikelets have two glumes, a few have only one, and in even fewer they are completely suppressed. In some grasses, the glumes are very narrow, bristle-like, and easily misinterpreted.

In addition to glumes, a spikelet contains one or more florets, each inserted at its own point of attachment on the rachilla. The term floret means "a small flower," which is a source of error and confusion. A floret is a single flower, along with two (rarely one) bracts that enclose it. The number of florets in a spikelet is of great diagnostic importance. A spikelet with a single floret is said to be one-flowered, one with two florets is two-flowered, and so on.

The two bracts that enclose the flower are the lemma and the palea. The lemma is typically the more conspicuous bract. It is usually larger and of firmer texture, its edges often partially enclosing the palea. The lemma may resemble the subtending glumes in texture and color. In one of the great subfamilies of grasses *(Panicoideae)*, an obvious difference in texture exists between the two bracts. The lemma typically has an odd number of veins of vascular tissue running its length. These were usually called "nerves" in older references. Occasionally the lemma will appear veinless.

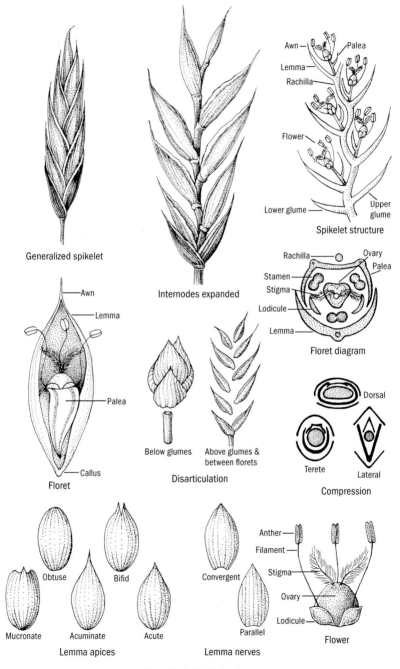

Generalized spikelet

Internodes expanded

Spikelet structure

Awn — Palea

Lemma — Rachilla

Flower — Lower glume — Upper glume

Floret

Awn

Lemma

Palea

Callus

Disarticulation

Below glumes

Above glumes & between florets

Floret diagram

Rachilla — Ovary — Palea

Stamen — Stigma

Lodicule

Lemma

Compression

Dorsal

Terete — Lateral

Lemma apices

Mucronate — Obtuse — Bifid — Acuminate — Acute

Lemma nerves

Convergent — Parallel

Flower

Anther — Filament — Stigma — Ovary — Lodicule

Figure 3. Spikelet structure

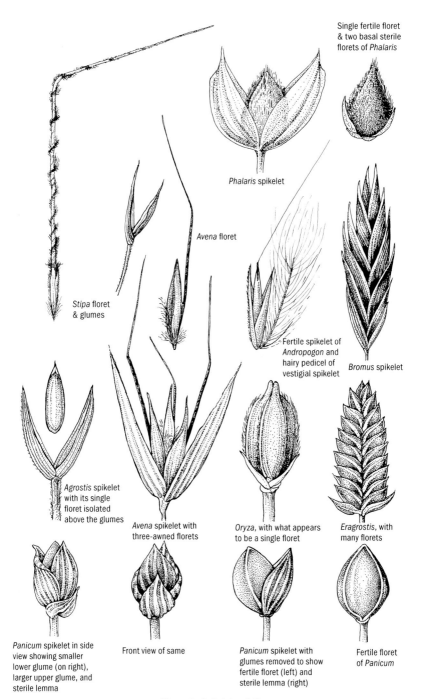

Single fertile floret & two basal sterile florets of *Phalaris*

Phalaris spikelet

Avena floret

Stipa floret & glumes

Fertile spikelet of *Andropogon* and hairy pedicel of vestigial spikelet

Bromus spikelet

Agrostis spikelet with its single floret isolated above the glumes

Avena spikelet with three-awned florets

Oryza, with what appears to be a single floret

Eragrostis, with many florets

Panicum spikelet in side view showing smaller lower glume (on right), larger upper glume, and sterile lemma

Front view of same

Panicum spikelet with glumes removed to show fertile floret (left) and sterile lemma (right)

Fertile floret of *Panicum*

Figure 4. Spikelet variation

Vein number is of great importance in identifying an unknown grass. Counting their number can be a challenge. It is very easy to overlook those that lie close to the edge of the lemma. In most instances, the veins of the lemma will converge with one another toward its apex, but in some grasses, they are parallel to one another. When viewed in cross-section, a lemma often appears to be a rounded bract; sometimes it is conspicuously flattened or even V-shaped. It may also have a prominent rib (keel) running down its center, the term being derived from the structure found on the bottom of a ship or boat. The lemma is attached directly to the rachilla. Usually it has a flower in its axil, in which case it is a **fertile lemma**. If the flower is absent, it is called a **sterile lemma**.

Unlike the glume or lemma, the palea is not the source of many taxonomic features. It tends to be delicate, membranous, two-veined, and two-keeled. The two veins may be very close to one another or close to the margins. The palea may be as long as the lemma, but it is usually somewhat shorter. It is reduced or absent in the bent grasses *(Agrostis)* and a few other grasses. The keels may be hairy or even **winged**. The palea is not attached directly to the rachilla. The palea subtends the flower itself and it is attached to the tiny flower stalk. You will have to take my word for it, because it is all but impossible to see this level of detail with a hand lens or even under the dissecting microscope. The palea typically breaks away with its lemma, but in the love grasses *(Eragrostis)* they remain attached to the rachilla after the lemmas have fallen.

The apex of a glume or lemma may bear a short, sharp point called a **mucro**. These bracts may also have a more elongate, substantial, hair- or bristle-like projection known as an awn, which may be a few millimeters to several centimeters long. Awns may be straight, bent, or twisted. Some are terminal, while others arise from the back of a glume or lemma at about their midpoints. Others come from or near the base of the bract. While glumes and/or lemmas are commonly awned, it is unusual in temperate grasses to find an awned palea.

The hardened base of a lemma or of a floret is its callus. In some instances, the callus is a combination of lemma and rachilla tissue. It may be rounded or sharp-pointed, as in the needle grasses *(Stipa)*. The callus may lack hairs or it may be clothed in a conspicuous tuft of them.

COMPRESSION. Spikelets are either round in cross-section (cylindrical) or they are flattened (**compressed**). **Terete** spikelets are relatively uncommon. Compressed spikelets are very common and they come in two models. If the bracts are flattened as though pressure were brought to bear from the sides of the bracts, then the spikelet is **laterally compressed**. If the spikelet is flattened as though pressure were brought to bear from the backs of the bracts, then it is **dorsally** or **dorsiventrally compressed.** This distinction may be made clearer by drawing on two familiar animals: Turtles are dorsally compressed; fish are laterally compressed.

DISARTICULATION. At maturity, most spikelets will break apart at prede-termined points of separation. The process is called **disarticulation** and it occurs in various ways. This breaking apart may occur:

- below the lower glume, so that the entire spikelet falls from the plant;
- above the glumes and between the florets so that empty glumes are all that remain;
- with the florets falling separately or in clusters, sometimes with a prominent segment of the rachilla remaining attached;
- between the first and second glume (an unusual situation); or
- above glumes, but with lemmas persisting (an unusual situation).

Most of our grasses exhibit option one or two. It takes some practice to determine disarticulation. You can force it to occur with a dissection needle, but not necessarily where it would under natural conditions. I recommend that you always observe older spikelets to find bare pedi-cels or empty glumes. There is a tendency, and it is nothing more than that, for spikelets that are laterally compressed to break apart above the glumes and for those that are dorsally compressed to disarticulate below the glumes.

SEXUALITY. An individual floret, a spikelet, or a grass plant is bisexual (perfect or hermaphroditic) if it has both stamens and carpels; staminate (male) if it has only male florets; pistillate (female) if it has only female florets; or sterile (neuter or barren) if it lacks either functional carpels or stamens (or, especially in older literature, if a floret were staminate).

There is another level of complexity to determining the sexuality of a grass plant. In many grasses, the lower florets of a spikelet are typically bisexual, with the upper florets progressively smaller and sterile. Another common situation is seen in the spikelet of panicoid grasses, in which the upper floret is bisexual and the lower is sterile. A less common possibility is the several-flowered spikelet that has both upper and lower florets that are sterile, while those in the middle are fertile.

Some grasses with unisexual spikelets are **monoecious**, a condition that occurs when an individual plant produces both staminate and pistil-late spikelets. Or they are **dioecious**, which happens if an individual plant produces either staminate or pistillate spikelets. And the plot thickens. Some grasses bear various combinations of bisexual and unisexual spike-lets on the same or different plants of a species.

VARIATIONS ON A THEME. To summarize, a typical grass spikelet consists of two glumes and one or more florets. It is laterally or dorsally com-pressed, or less often terete. The spikelet disarticulates above or below the glumes. The lemmas and/or the glumes may be awned. While this is the basic plan, the spikelet is subject to a fascinating series of modifications. One of the most important of these is the reduction and loss of spikelet parts. One or both glumes may be missing. In spikelets with more than one floret, the upper one(s) are often smaller than the lower one(s) and they may be sterile. Sometimes the uppermost floret is well developed and fertile while the one or two florets below it are reduced. In a few grasses, the middle florets are the best developed, while those above and below are reduced or sterile. The palea may be reduced or absent.

In most grasses, all of the spikelets on a plant are very similar to one another, differing perhaps in size as a function of their age. A few grasses, on the other hand, bear spikelets that are strikingly different from one another. We are talking about fundamentally different architecture. Such spikelets are said to be dissimilar or **dimorphic**. What you are often seeing is the difference between fertile and sterile spikelets of a species.

Variation in spikelet structure can be frustrating at first, but proper interpretation can be more easily assured if you take the time now to learn the basic positional relationships of the spikelet parts. Table 5 presents some spikelet configurations that you will encounter in the California grass flora. I have named each of them after a well-known genus where they are found.

TABLE 5. Eight spikelet models

Grass	Model
Festuca, fescue	2 glumes + 2–several fertile florets
Avena, oat	2 large glumes + 2 or 3 fertile florets
Phalaris, canary grass	2 glumes + 2 small sterile lemmas + 1 fertile floret
Agrostis, bent grass	2 glumes + 1 fertile floret
Oryza, rice	0 glumes + 1 fertile floret
Andropogon, bluestem	2 glumes + 1 sterile lemma + 1 fertile floret
Panicum, panic grass	2 dissimilar glumes + 1 sterile lemma + 1 fertile floret
Paspalum, paspalum	1 glume + 1 sterile lemma + 1 fertile floret

INFLORESCENCES
The Arrangement of Spikelets

A grass stem, whether it is the main stem or a lateral branch, may bear one to several hundred spikelets. This flowering portion of the grass plant is its inflorescence. A stem may bear only one inflorescence or it may have several of them. If it emerges from the uppermost sheath of a primary stem, it is a terminal inflorescence. If it arises from the node of a lower sheath, it is an axillary or lateral inflorescence.

At first, it may be difficult to determine just how much of what you are seeing is a single inflorescence. A good rule of thumb is that there are never well-developed foliage leaves within an inflorescence. Whether terminal or axillary, the uppermost or outermost spikelet marks the top of an inflorescence. The lowest spikelet on a stalk emerging from the uppermost foliage leaf marks its base.

We use the same terms to describe grass inflorescences that we use in other plant families, but with an important difference. In almost all other plant families, the basic unit of the inflorescence is the flower. In the daisy or sunflower family *(Compositae)*, the terms apply to heads of tiny flowers; in grasses and sedges, they apply to the arrangements of spikelets.

COMPONENTS. The stem that supports an entire inflorescence is the **peduncle**, while the stalk that supports an individual spikelet is its **pedicel**. The true pedicel of a grass flower is, of course, within the spikelet. This error in terminology goes back over two hundred years to a time when Carolus Linnaeus and others erroneously interpreted the spikelet as a flower.

If there is a clearly defined axis within the inflorescence, it is called a **rachis**. Note that the rachis is the axis of an entire inflorescence of spikelets, while the rachilla is the central axis of an individual spikelet. The rachis may be delicate, wiry, or even thickened with spikelets partially embedded in its tissue. It may break apart at maturity or remain intact.

INFLORESCENCE TYPES. The exact arrangement of spikelets determines the inflorescence type. This terminology can be frustrating because it has not been standardized, and authors of keys and descriptions vary shamefully in its usage. No scheme is without its problems, but I have found the following one useful.

In the spike, the spikelets are attached directly to an unbranched rachis. Pedicels are, for all practical purposes, absent. The number of spikelets attached at a single site on the rachis (node) is variable. One, two, three, or a cluster of several spikelets per node are common. Many grasses—especially those in the barley tribe—have this inflorescence type.

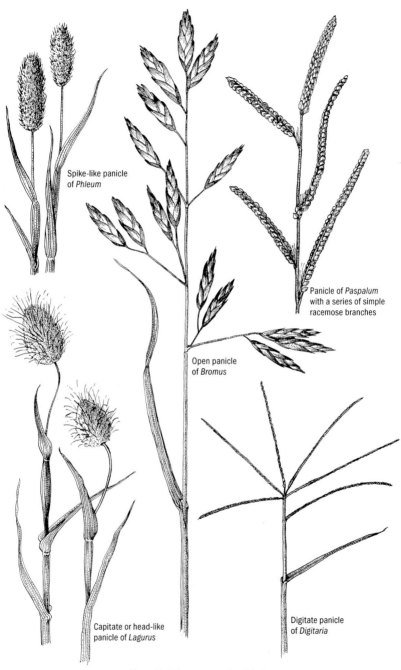

Spike-like panicle of *Phleum*

Panicle of *Paspalum* with a series of simple racemose branches

Open panicle of *Bromus*

Capitate or head-like panicle of *Lagurus*

Digitate panicle of *Digitaria*

Figure 5. Inflorescences (panicles)

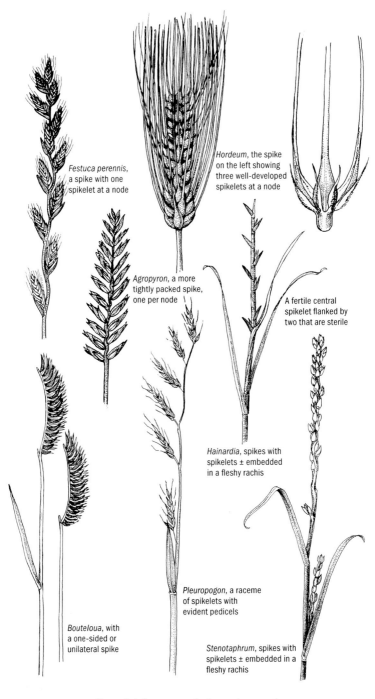

Festuca perennis, a spike with one spikelet at a node

Hordeum, the spike on the left showing three well-developed spikelets at a node

Agropyron, a more tightly packed spike, one per node

A fertile central spikelet flanked by two that are sterile

Hainardia, spikes with spikelets ± embedded in a fleshy rachis

Pleuropogon, a raceme of spikelets with evident pedicels

Bouteloua, with a one-sided or unilateral spike

Stenotaphrum, spikes with spikelets ± embedded in a fleshy rachis

Figure 6. Inflorescences (spikes and racemes)

In the **raceme**, spikelets are borne on well-developed pedicels arising from an unbranched rachis. Typically spikelets occur in pairs or trios at a given node, or less frequently as only one spikelet per node, as in the semaphore grasses *(Pleuropogon)*. The raceme is much less common than the spike. The distinction between the two is arbitrary, the degree of pedicel development being the difference. I try to use 1 mm as the dividing line in distinguishing the spike (less than 1 mm long) and the raceme (more than 1 mm long).

The **rame** is a specialized modification of the raceme in which stalked (**pedicellate**) and **sessile** spikelets occur together in pairs or trios. The pedicels may be of equal or unequal length. The rame is typical of the barley and bluestem tribes. Many authors do not use this term, but I have found it useful.

In the spike, raceme, or rame, the spikelets may be more or less evenly attached on either side of the rachis so that the inflorescence is **balanced**, or they may be attached on just one side of the rachis, so that the inflorescence is one-sided.

The **panicle** is the most common inflorescence type in the family. Here the spikelets are borne on secondary or tertiary branches of a much-branched system. This means that the spikelets are not attached directly to a central axis in the way that they are in the spike, raceme, or rame. Panicles may be large, open, diffuse, and conspicuously branched or they may be so **contracted** and dense that they appear to be some sort of spike. Teasing and dissection may be necessary to reveal this cryptic branching. I encourage you to take the time for a closer inspection.

Sometimes, under unfavorable environmental conditions, a panicle may exhibit much-reduced branching. An extreme form of the panicle is the solitary spikelet, in which the inflorescence consists of a single spikelet, as in the poverty oat *(Danthonia unispicata)*. We believe that the solitary spikelet is the result of evolutionary reduction of a more typical much-branched panicle with multiple spikelets.

In many grasses, inflorescences are composed of unbranched or sparingly branched arms. If we look at any particular branch, it bears a spike, a raceme, or a rame of spikelets. The branches may be **digitate**—clustered at the apex of a peduncle, as in windmill grass *(Chloris)*, Bermuda grass *(Cynodon dactylon)*, and crab grasses *(Digitaria)*. They may also be **racemose**—attached at various points along the central axis, as in barnyard grass *(Echinochloa)* and salt marsh grass *(Spartina)*.

In a few grasses, individual plants may bear two distinctly different inflorescences. In maize or corn *(Zea mays)*, the familiar tassel is an open, branched inflorescence of male spikelets, while the ear is a compact arrangement of female spikelets surrounded by layers of leaves. Several other California grasses also have these dissimilar spikelets, but they are much smaller and require a more intimate inspection.

CALIFORNIA GRASS FLORA
A Numerical Overview

California's grasses are mostly native perennials:

- There are 8 subfamilies, 18 tribes, 117 genera, 547 species, and 603 taxa (species, subspecies, and varieties) of grasses in California.
- 39% of the grasses known from the conterminous U.S.A. occur in California.
- Our grass flora is larger than that of Canada (434 taxa) and any other state, except Texas (681).
- 181 taxa (30.0%) are annuals
- 422 taxa (70.0%) are perennials
- 328 taxa (54.4%) are native
- 275 taxa (45.6%) are naturalized grasses native to other states or countries
- 54 taxa (8.9%) are endemic (found only in California)
- 274 taxa (45.4%) are native, but also found in other states
- 15 taxa (2.5%) are listed as endangered, rare, or threatened by state or federal agencies
- On average, there are 50 genera of grasses per county, ranging from the fewest in Kings County (22) to the most in Riverside County (77).
- On average, there are 197 grasses per county, ranging from the fewest in Kings County (37) to the most in San Bernardino County (351).

Henry Bolander published the first attempt at a comprehensive summary of California's grasses in 1866. There have been several others since. A comparison of 11 of them is presented in Table 6. Notice how often the name Hitchcock appears. Albert Spear Hitchcock (1865 to 1935) was, at the time of his death, our country's leading expert on the grass family. He was the author of the *Manual of the Grasses of the United States*, the holy writ for grass students of my generation. The grass treatment in *A California Flora* by Philip Munz was also based on Hitchcock's *Manual*.

How does the richness of the California grass flora rank with other states? In Table 7, I compare it with Florida, Texas, and the conterminous United States; and in Table 8 with other Pacific Coast and southwestern states.

The number of taxa makes for a useful comparison, but it is only part of the story. What about the grass flora in terms of its subfamilies? Notice that the grass flora of Alaska is almost entirely made up of fescue grasses and their relatives, while that of Florida is mostly panic grasses and their

TABLE 6. A comparison of comprehensive surveys of the California grass flora

Survey	Subfamilies	Tribes	Genera	Species	Taxa
Bolander, 1866	—	10	49	110	110
Thurber in Watson, 1880	—	3	61	172	182
Hitchcock in Jepson, 1912	2	9	76	337	364
Hitchcock in Jepson, 1925	2	9	77	341	370
Hitchcock & Chase, 1951	2	9	95	446	483
Munz, 1959 & 1968	2	9	103	496	537
Hickman, 1993	—	—	117	436	470
Barkworth et al., 2003; 2007	8	17	136	487	548
Peterson & Soreng, 2007	8	18	145	524	—
USDA Plants Database, 2008	—	—	146	542	607
Baldwin et al., 2012	—	—	100	446	492

— = Not indicated.

TABLE 7. A comparison of California grass flora with those of two other grass-rich states and the conterminous United States

	California	Florida*	Texas*	United States*
Genera	117	137	149	205
Taxa	603	440	681	1,545

*Genera and taxa for Florida from Wunderlin & Hansen, 2008; for Texas from Hatch & Haile, 2012; for the United States from Smith, 2012.

TABLE 8. A comparison of the grass flora of California with those of neighboring states

Category	California	Washington*	Oregon*	Nevada*	Arizona*
Subfamilies	8	7	8	7	7
Tribes	18	15	18	15	16
Genera	117	75	86	73	98
Taxa	603	337	411	312	461

*Data for genera and taxa from USDA Plants Database.

relatives. We may have eight subfamilies represented in the California flora, but 93 percent of our grasses belong to just three of them (Table 9).

How does a list of our five largest genera of California grasses (in terms of taxa) compare with that of the five largest genera in the conterminous United States and in the world (Table 10)?

TABLE 9. A percent comparison of grass floras by subfamily composition

Grass Subfamily	California	Florida	Texas	Alaska	United States
Needle grasses	2.0	3.6	3.8	0.0	2.8
Reed grasses	0.6	0.4	0.3	0.0	0.4
Bamboos	0.6	1.3	0.3	0.0	1.4
Windmill grasses	16.6	21.4	31.2	0.5	22.4
Poverty grasses	2.2	0.4	0.7	1.4	1.1
Rices	1.2	2.3	1.6	0.0	1.2
Panic grasses	15.1	56.9	38.7	0.5	27.1
Fescues	61.5	13.6	23.3	97.6	43.4

TABLE 10. The five largest genera in California, the United States, and the world

California		United States*		World*	
Genus	No. of species	Genus	No. of species	Genus	No. of species
Blue grass (Poa)	37	Panic grass (Panicum)	77	Blue grass (Poa)	500+
Needle grass (Stipa)	35	Muhly (Muhlenbergia)	76	Fescue grass (Festuca)	c. 500
Brome, chess (Bromus)	33	Wild rye (Elymus)	68	Panic grass (Panicum)	c. 400
Wild rye (Elymus)	31	Blue grass (Poa)	66	Love grass (Eragrostis)	350
Muhly (Muhlenbergia)	22	Needle grass (Stipa)	62	Crown grass (Paspalum)	330
Fescue (Festuca)	22				
Bent grass (Agrostis)	22				

*Data for the United States from Smith, 2012; data for the world from Mabberley, 2008.

While this book is intended to introduce you to the more commonly encountered grasses in California, I thought you might find a comprehensive numerical conspectus of interest. Tables 11 and 12 provide those data.

TABLE 11. A comprehensive numerical summary of California grasses

Genus, Common Name	Species	Taxa	Annual, Perennial		
			Endemic	Native	Introduced
Acrachne, monsoon grass†	1	1			1, 0
Aegilops, goat grass	5	5			5, 0
X *Agropogon*, beard grass	1	1			0, 1
Agropyron, wheat grass	1	1			0, 1
Agrostis, bent grass	22	24	0, 5	3, 9	3, 4
Aira, hair grass	2	4			4, 0
Alopecurus, foxtail grass	6	7	0, 1	2, 2	1, 1
Ammophila, beach grass	2	2			0, 2
Amphibromus, Australian wallaby grass†	1	1			0, 1
Andropogon, bluestem	2	3		0, 2	0, 1
Anthoxanthum, sweet vernal grass	5	5		0, 1	1, 3
Apera, bent grass	2	2			2, 0
Aristida, three-awn grass	8	13		1, 10	1, 1
Arrhenatherum, tall oat grass	1	1			0, 1
Arundo, giant reed grass	1	1			0, 1
Avena, oat	5	5			5, 0
Axonopus, carpet grass†	2	2			0, 2
Bambusa, hedge bamboo†	1	1			0, 1
Beckmannia, slough grass	1	1		1, 0	
Blepharidachne, eyelash grass	1	1		0, 1	
Bothriochloa, bluestem	4	4		0, 1	0, 3
Bouteloua, grama grass	6	6		2, 4	
Brachypodium, false or stiff brome	5	5			1, 4
Briza, quaking grass	3	3			2, 1
Bromus, brome, chess, ripgut	33	38	0, 2	1, 11	21, 3
Calamagrostis, reed grass	11	13	0, 4	0, 9	
Catapodium, fern grass	1	1			1, 0
Cenchrus, sandbur, feather grass	12	12			3, 9
Chloris, windmill grass	4	4			1, 3
Cinna, reed grass	2	2	0, 1	0, 1	
Cortaderia, pampas grass	2	2			0, 2
Crypsis, prickle grass	3	3			3, 0
Cynodon, Bermuda grass	3	3			0, 3
Cynosurus, dogtail grass	2	2			1, 1
Dactylis, orchard grass	1	1			0, 1
Dactyloctenium, crowfoot grass	1	1			0, 1
Danthonia, oat grass	4	4		0, 3	0, 1

Continued ▶

TABLE 11. *(continued)*

Genus, Common Name	Species	Taxa	Annual, Perennial Endemic	Native	Introduced
Dasyochloa, fluff grass	1	1		0, 1	
Deschampsia, hair grass	4	6		1, 5	
Digitaria, crab grass	6	6		0, 1	3, 2
Dinebra, viper grass	1	1			1, 0
Distichlis, salt grass, shore grass	2	2		0, 2	
Echinochloa, barnyard grass	7	8			8, 0
Ehrharta, veldt grass	3	3			1, 2
Eleusine, goose grass	3	3			3, 0
X *Elyhordeum*, wild rye x barley	3	3		0, 3	
Elymus, wild-rye	31	35	0, 5	0, 23	1, 6
Enneapogon, pappus grass	1	1		0, 1	
Eragrostis, love grass	13	15		6, 1	5, 3
Eremochloa, centipede grass[†]	1	1			0, 1
Eriochloa, cup grass	4	4		1, 0	3, 0
Erioneuron, hairy wooly grass	2	2		0, 2	
Eustachys, finger grass[†]	1	1			0, 1
Festuca, fescue	22	25	0, 3	2, 12	3, 5
Gastridium, nit grass	1	1			1, 0
Gaudinia, fragile oat grass[†]	1	1			1, 0
Glyceria, manna grass	9	9	0, 1	0, 6	0, 2
Hainardia, one-glumed hard grass	1	1			1, 0
Heteropogon, tanglehead	1	1			0, 1
Hilaria, galleta	2	2		0, 2	
Holcus, velvet grass	2	2			0, 2
Hordeum, barley	10	14	0, 1	3, 3	6, 1
Hyparrhenia, thatching grass	1	1			0, 1
Imperata, satintail	1	1		0, 1	
Kikuyuochloa, Kikuyu grass	1	1			0, 1
Koeleria, June grass	1	1		0, 1	
Lagurus, hare's tail	1	1			1, 0
Lamarckia, goldentop	1	1			1, 0
Leersia, rice cut grass	2	2		0, 1	0, 1
Leptochloa, sprangletop	4	6		4, 1	1, 0
Lolium, stiff rye grass	1	1			1, 0
Melica, onion grass, melic	12	14	0, 3	0, 11	
Melinis, ruby grass	1	1			0, 1
Miscanthus, silver grass	1	1			0, 1
Muhlenbergia, muhly, deer grass	22	22	0, 1	3, 17	0, 1
Munroa, false buffalo grass	1	1		1, 0	
Neostapfia, Colusa grass	1	1	1, 0		

Genus, Common Name	Species	Taxa	Annual, Perennial		
			Endemic	Native	Introduced
Orcuttia, Orcutt grass	5	5	4, 0	1, 0	
Oryza, rice	2	2			2, 0
Panicum, panic grass, **rosette** grass	14	16	0, 1	2, 5	2, 6
Parapholis, hard grass	2	2			0, 2
Paspalum, paspalum, knot grass	9	9		0, 1	1, 7
Phalaris, canary grass	11	11	1, 0	1, 2	5, 2
Phleum, timothy	2	2		0, 1	0, 1
Phragmites, common reed	1	3		0, 2	0, 1
Phyllostachys, bamboo	2	2			0, 2
Pleuropogon, semaphore grass	3	4	0, 3	0, 1	
Poa, blue grass	37	43	0, 9	4, 23	1, 6
Polypogon, beard grass	8	8			3, 5
Pseudosasa, arrow bamboo[†]	1	1			0, 1
Puccinellia, alkali grass	8	8	0, 1	2, 4	0, 1
Rostraria, Mediterranean hair grass	1	1			1, 0
Rytidosperma, wallaby grass	4	4			0, 4
Saccharum, Ravenna grass	1	1			0, 1
Schismus, Mediterranean grass	1	2			2, 0
Schizachyrium, bluestem	1	1		0, 1	
Sclerochloa, hard grass	1	1			1, 0
Scleropogon, burro grass	1	1		0, 1	
Scribneria, Scribner's grass	1	1		1, 0	
Secale, rye	1	1			1, 0
Setaria, foxtail	10	10		0, 1	7, 2
Sorghum, sorghum, broomcorn	2	4			3, 1
Spartina, cord grass	6	6		0, 2	0, 4
Sphenopholis, wedge-scale	1	1		0, 1	
Sporobolus, dropseed	8	8		0, 5	1, 2
Stenotaphrum, St. Augustine grass	1	1			0, 1
Stipa, needle or spear grass	35	39	0, 4	0, 26	1, 8
Swallenia, Eureka Valley dune grass	1	1	0, 1		
Torreyochloa, false manna grass	2	2		0, 2	
Tribolium, Capetown grass	1	1			0, 1
Tridens, slim tridens	1	1		0, 1	
Trisetum, trisetum, oat grass	5	5		0, 4	0, 1
Triticum, wheat	1	1			1, 0

Continued ▶

TABLE 11. *(continued)*

Genus, Common Name	Species	Taxa	Annual, Perennial		
			Endemic	Native	Introduced
Tuctoria, spiral grass	2	2	2, 0		
Urochloa, signal grass	2	2		1, 0	1, 0
Ventenata, North Africa grass	1	1			1, 0
Zoysia, Japanese or Korean lawn grass	1	1			0, 1

† = presumed extinct or extirpated or doubtfully naturalized in California.

TABLE 12. Numerical conspectus of the California grass flora

Number of genera = 117
Number of species = 547
Number of taxa = 603

Nativity and duration	No. of taxa	% of flora
Native grasses	328	54.4
Naturalized grasses	275	45.6
Annual grasses	181	30.0
Perennial grasses	422	70.0
Endemic annuals	8	1.3
Endemic perennials	46	7.6
Native annuals	43	7.1
Native perennials	231	38.3
Naturalized annuals	130	21.6
Naturalized perennials	145	24.0

Selected References

Baldwin, B. G., D. H. Goldman, D. J. Keil, R. Patterson, T. J. Rosatti, & D. H. Wilken. 2012. *The Jepson Manual: Vascular Plants of California.* Second edition. Berkeley: University of California Press.

Barkworth, M. E., K. M. Capels, S. Long, L. K. Anderton, & M. P. Piep (editors). 2007. *Flora of North America North of Mexico.* Vol. 24. *Magnoliophyta: Commelinidae* (in part): *Poaceae,* part 1. New York: Oxford Univ. Press.

Barkworth, M. E., K. M. Capels, S. Long, & M. P. Piep (editors). 2003. *Flora of North America North of Mexico.* Vol. 25. *Magnoliophyta: Commelinidae* (in part): *Poaceae,* part 2. New York: Oxford Univ. Press.

Bolander, H. N. 1866. *Grasses of the State: Transactions of the California State Agricultural Society during the Years 1864 and 1865.* Sacramento: State Printer.

Hatch, S. L. & K. C. Haile. 2012. "Checklist of Texas Grass Species and a Key to the Genera." *Phytoneuron* 2012–2057: 1–60.

Hickman, J. C. (editor). 1993. *The Jepson Manual: Higher Plants of California.* Berkeley: University of California Press.

Hitchcock, A. S. 1912. "Gramineae." *In* W. L. Jepson, *A Flora of California.* San Francisco: Cunningham, Curtiss & Welch. Pp. 82–189.

Hitchcock, A. S. 1925. "Gramineae." *In* W. L. Jepson, *Manual of the Flowering Plants of California.* Berkeley: University of California Press. Pp. 72–144.

Hitchcock, A. S. 1951. *Manual of the Grasses of the United States.* Second edition, revised by Agnes Chase. Misc. Publ. No. 200. Washington, DC: U.S. Dept. of Agriculture.

Mabberley, D. J. 2008. *Mabberley's Plant Book: A Portable Dictionary of Plants, Their Classification and Uses.* Cambridge, UK: Cambridge Univ. Press.

Munz, P. A. 1959. *A California Flora.* In collaboration with D. D. Keck. Berkeley: University of California Press. Pp. 1462–1550.

Munz, P. A. 1968. *Supplement to* A California Flora. Berkeley: University of California Press. Pp. 186–198.

Peterson, P. M. & R. J. Soreng. 2007. "Systematics of California Grasses." *In* M. R. Stromber, J. D. Corbin, & C. M. D'Antonio (editors). *California Grasslands: Ecology and Management.* Berkeley: University of California Press. Pp. 7–20.

Smith, J. P. 2013. *A Catalogue of the Grasses of the Conterminous United States.* Misc. Publ. No. 4 (18th edition). Arcata, CA: Humboldt State Univ. Herbarium.

Thurber, G. 1880. "Gramineae." *In* S. Watson. *Botany of California.* Boston, MA: Little, Brown, and Co. Pp. 253–328.

United States Department of Agriculture, Natural Resources Conservation Service. *The Plants Database.* Available at http://plants.usda.gov.

Wunderlin, R. P. & B. F. Hansen. 2008. *Atlas of Florida Vascular Plants.* Available at www.plantatlas.usf.edu.

WHERE DO GRASSES GROW IN CALIFORNIA?

I am the grass. I cover all.

Carl Sandburg, 1918

Grasses are everywhere in California! They are commonly encountered as natives in almost every habitat and as introductions and weeds where we live, travel, and grow our crops. They reach their greatest expression in California's grasslands—areas where grasses and grass-like plants (mostly sedges) are the dominant life form. We do not say they are dominant because of their diversity: typically only three or four grass species are common and collectively they account for only about 20 percent of the flora at any particular site. Most of the plants in a grassland area are broad-leaved herbs. Grasses are dominant by virtue of the sheer number of individual plants, which means that they constitute the largest component of the biomass. Grasslands typically occur in subhumid to semi-arid regions where there is a marked periodicity of rainfall. This wet/dry regime is a feature of the Mediterranean climate in California. The amount of rain, typically 10 to 20 inches per year, is intermediate between the typical rainfall in the forest and the desert. Rainfall, along with other environmental factors—especially the damaging effect of fires on woody plants—also explains the relative scarcity of trees and shrubs in grasslands.

Plant ecologists speak of different types of grasslands. **Prairies** are more or less level, rolling grasslands of temperate areas, typically treeless, and with characteristically rich soils. **Savannas** are grasslands with scattered shrubs and trees, and are often seen as transitional between the grassland and forest vegetation. They are typically associated with an alternating wet and dry season climate. **Steppes** are semi-arid grasslands dominated by short, perennial bunch grasses.

Meadows are open fields dominated by grasses and other non-woody plants; many are moist year around. They may be natural or artificially cleared. In the original sense, meadows were areas where hay was cut to feed domesticated animals. **Pastures** are tracts of grasslands that are maintained or modified for grazing of domesticated animals or to yield forage. **Rangeland** is the term applied to a vegetation type dominated by grasses and grass-like plants that is actively managed for livestock.

Grasslands cover about 24 percent to 43 percent of the Earth's surface, depending on the criteria used. The largest of North America's plant formations, they originally covered almost 3 million square miles,

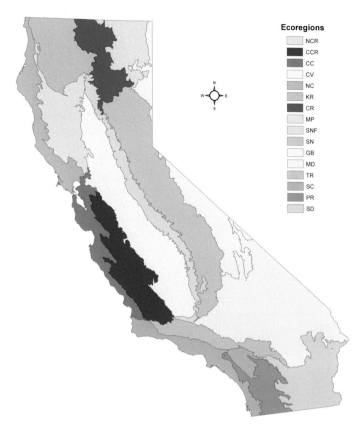

Ecoregions

- NCR
- CCR
- CC
- CV
- NC
- KR
- CR
- MP
- SNF
- SN
- GB
- MD
- TR
- SC
- PR
- SD

Map 1. California ecoregions. NCR = North Coast Range. CCR = Central Coast Range. CC = Central Coast. CV = Central Valley. NC = North Coast. KR = Klamath Region. CR = Cascade Range. MP = Modoc Plateau. SNF = Sierra Nevada foothills. SN = Sierra Nevada. GB = Great Basin. MD = Mojave Desert. TR = Transverse Range. SC = South Coast. PR = Peninsular Range. SD = Sonoran Desert.

Map by Lloyd Simpson, based on "Ecological Subregions of California," R5-EM-TP-005, of the Pacific Southwest Region, U.S. Forest Service.

or about 39 percent of the United States. Most of California's grasslands occur primarily in the Central Valley and in low elevations to the South Coast. The top five counties in terms of grassland coverage are Kern, San Luis Obispo, Fresno, Siskiyou, and Santa Barbara. Another 5 percent to 6 percent of woodlands and savannas incorporate an extensive grass component. Perennials dominate in only about 1 percent; 80 percent are privately owned; only 4 percent are in reserves and enjoy some level of protection. Almost all of California's grasslands have been significantly degraded by introduced grasses and other flowering plants, and by our activities.

In the description of selected genera and species, I will provide distribution information based on the geographic subdivisions of California that appeared in the *Jepson Manual* (Hickman 1993) and as shown in Map 1.

In the text that follows, I will recognize the Valley Grassland and the Coastal Prairie. Then I will present a series of other habitats and the grasses that you would expect to find there. These lists are not meant to be inclusive. This section begins with those that are strongly associated with particular habitats, such as the coastal strand or vernal pools, and ends with grasses, native and naturalized, that are especially adapted to disturbed areas.

Coastal Prairie

The coastal prairie extends from Del Norte to Santa Barbara County, from inside the coastal strand and salt marshes to about 20 to 30 miles inland. It occurs mostly below 3,000 ft on coastal bluffs, uplifted marine terraces, and hills, commonly on south-facing slopes; and inland on bald hills, treeless hilltops, and ridges. It coexists with the coastal scrub over large areas in a continuum from grasses and other herbaceous plants to dense woody shrubs and trees. Grazing, agriculture, changing fire regimes, and urbanization have eliminated or degraded the coastal prairie so that

Figure 7. North Coast grassland in Humboldt County

Figure 8. *Danthonia* grassland in Del Norte County

TABLE 13. Grasses of the Coastal Prairie

Scientific Name	Common Name
Native Perennials	
Agrostis blasdalei	Blasdale's bent grass
Agrostis clivicola	coast bent grass
Agrostis densiflora	California bent grass
Agrostis hallii	Hall's bent grass
Agrostis pallens	seashore bent grass
Anthoxanthum occidentale	vanilla grass
Bromus carinatus	California brome
Calamagrostis nutkaensis*	Pacific reed grass
Danthonia californica*	California oat grass
Deschampsia caespitosa*	tufted hair grass
Elymus californicus	California bottlebrush
Elymus condensatus	giant wild-rye
Elymus glaucus	blue wild-rye
Festuca idahoensis*	Idaho fescue
Festuca occidentalis*	western fescue
Festuca rubra, in part*	red fescue
Hordeum brachyantherum	meadow barley
Koeleria macrantha	June grass
Melica geyeri	Geyer's onion grass
Melica imperfecta	Coast Range melic
Poa secunda	Nevada blue grass
Poa unilateralis	sea bluff blue grass
Stipa cernua	nodding needle grass
Stipa coronata	giant needle grass
Stipa lepida	small-flowered needle grass
Stipa pulchra	purple needle grass
Naturalized Annuals	
Agrostis capillaris	colonial bent grass
Aira caryophyllea	silver hair grass
Avena barbata	slender wild oat
Avena fatua	wild oat
Briza maxima	rattlesnake grass
Briza minor	small quaking grass
Bromus diandrus	ripgut brome
Bromus hordeaceus	soft brome
Bromus madritensis subsp. *rubens*	foxtail brome
Festuca myuros	rat-tail fescue
Festuca perennis, in part	rye grass
Festuca rubra	red fescue

Scientific Name	Common Name
Naturalized Perennials	
Agrostis stolonifera	red top
Anthoxanthum odoratum	sweet vernal grass
Dactylis glomerata	orchard grass
Festuca arundinacea	tall fescue
Festuca perennis	rye grass
Festuca rubra, in part	red fescue
Holcus lanatus	velvet grass
Poa pratensis	Kentucky blue grass
Rytidosperma penicellatum	hairy poverty grass

*Pre-European contact dominants.

today this perennial grassland component is one of the most threatened in the United States. It has a rich flora, replete with many rare and endangered plants. Almost 80 plant species are endemic to the coastal prairie.

Rainfall varies from about 80 in. to 15 in. from north to south. Temperature changes are relatively small, with cool summers and mild winters. Along the coast, there is extensive fog during summer and winter months. Soils are similar to those of the prairies of the Midwest. Inland grasslands and those more to the south can resemble the Central Valley, with Nevada blue grass *(Poa secunda)* and purple needle grass *(Stipa pulchra)* present in both areas. The region is especially suitable for sheep and cattle grazing, which is largely responsible for the transformation from native bunch grasses to annual introduced weedy species.

Valley Grassland

The annual grassland component of our flora occupies most of the floor of the Central Valley, the low valleys of the Coast Ranges, extending southward to the Transverse and Peninsular ranges, and the valleys of Southern California into Baja California, Mexico. This grassland evolved under a Mediterranean-style climate. Rainfall is generally about 6 in. to 20 in. annually, 90 percent of it falling between October and April. Summer temperatures in excess of 100 degrees F are common, as are winter frosts.

TABLE 14. Grasses of the Valley Grassland

Scientific Name	Common Name
Native Annuals	
Agrostis hendersonii	Henderson's bent grass
Agrostis microphylla	small-leaved bent grass
Alopecurus saccatus	Pacific foxtail
Beckmannia syzigachne	American slough grass
Bromus arizonicus	Arizona brome
Bromus carinatus	California brome
Festuca microstachys	Pacific fescue
Festuca octoflora	six-weeks fescue
Hordeum depressum	alkali barley
Leptochloa fusca subsp. *fascicularis*	sprangletop
Neostapfia colusana	Colusa grass
Orcuttia inaequalis	San Joaquin Valley Orcutt grass
Orcuttia pilosa	hairy Orcutt grass
Orcuttia viscida	Sacramento Orcutt grass
Puccinellia simplex	little alkali grass
Scribneria bolanderi	Scribner's grass
Tuctoria greenei	awnless spiral grass
Tuctoria mucronata	Crampton's spiral grass
Native Perennials	
Agrostis exarata	spike bent grass
Aristida divaricata*	poverty three-awn
Aristida ternipes*	spider grass
Bromus laevipes	Chinook brome
Danthonia californica	California oat grass
Deschampsia caespitosa	**tufted** hair grass
Deschampsia elongata	slender hair grass
Distichlis spicata	salt grass
Elymus elymoides	squirreltail
Elymus glaucus*	blue wild-rye
Elymus multisetus	big squirreltail
Elymus triticoides*	beardless wild-rye
Hordeum brachyantherum	meadow barley
Hordeum jubatum	foxtail barley
Hordeum pusillum	little barley
Koeleria macrantha*	June grass
Leersia oryzoides	rice cut grass

Scientific Name	Common Name
*Melica californica**	California melic
*Melica imperfecta**	small-flowered melic
Muhlenbergia asperifolia	scratch grass
*Muhlenbergia rigens**	deer grass
Panicum acuminatum	Pacific panic grass
Paspalum distichum	knot grass
Phalaris arundinacea	reed canary grass
Phragmites australis	common reed
*Poa secunda**	Nevada blue grass
Puccinellia nuttalliana	Nuttall's alkali grass
*Sporobolus airoides**	alkali sacaton
*Stipa cernua**	nodding needle grass
*Stipa pulchra**	purple needle grass

Naturalized Annuals

Aegilops spp.	goat grasses
Aristida oligantha	prairie three-awn
Avena barbata	slender wild oat
Avena fatua	wild oat
Brachypodium distachyon	stiff-brome
Bromus diandrus	ripgut brome
Bromus hordeaceus	soft brome
Bromus madritensis subsp. *rubens*	foxtail brome
Elymus caput-medusae	medusa head grass
Festuca myuros	rat-tail fescue
Festuca perennis	annual rye grass
Hordeum murinum	mouse barley
Phalaris paradoxa	hood canary grass

Naturalized Perennials

Anthoxanthum odoratum	sweet vernal grass
Festuca perennis	perennial rye grass
Holcus lanatus	velvet grass
Phalaris aquatica	Harding grass
Phragmites australis	common reed
Poa compressa	Canada blue grass
Poa pratensis	Kentucky blue grass

*Pre-European contact dominants.

Today the Central Valley is dominated by highly productive agriculture and by a flora of annual weeds native to other regions of the world, especially to the Mediterranean. During the dry season, these exotic annuals constitute the famous "golden hills" of our travel brochures. In other words, the largest grassland in California is not a more or less pristine region of native grasses, but a giant weed patch. Human activities associated with European settlement of California began this transformation. They include ranching, begun by the Spanish in 1769; the year-long grazing of cattle and sheep; farming; fire suppression; urban and industrial development; road building; and water transport and flood control projects. These activities, compounded by periods of significant drought, have virtually eliminated the native grasses of the Central Valley. Some ecologists call the grasses that now occupy this region the "new natives" in recognition of what appears to be their permanent status.

If we could stroll through the Central Valley in the early 1700s, before European contact, what would we see? One of the first to address this question was the noted plant ecologist Frederick Clements. In 1920, he saw purple needle grass *(Stipa pulchra)* growing along railroad rights-of-way. This was the basis for his hypothesis that the Central Valley was originally occupied by various cool-season, perennial, highly palatable bunch grasses. This concept enjoyed an aura of metaphysical certitude for several decades, largely because of the reputation and influence of Clements himself.

Although Clements's model has remained widely accepted, challenges to it began almost immediately and have become increasingly strong. As early as 1922, other scientists began suggesting that the Central Valley was once dominated by low shrubs with leathery, evergreen leaves; or by **rhizomatous-stoloniferous** grasses, such as *Elymus triticoides,* and sedges (*Carex* spp.); or by annual native grasses; or by a rich flora of nongrass herbaceous plants.

Today plant ecologists present a new paradigm. While the "non–bunch grass dominance theory" is still being refined, it does appear to have a robust core concept—the Central Valley of California was never a homogeneous grassland dominated by perennial grasses, but instead it existed as a much more complex mosaic of grasses and herbs whose presence was related to specific ecological conditions. After all, the Central Valley contains rich loams, relatively infertile soils, marshes, vernal pools, and alkali flats. *Stipa pulchra* and other perennial bunch grasses were there in the foothills and sometimes also on the valley floors, but only on soils with certain characteristics.

Figure 9. Central Valley grassland.

Where Else Do Grasses Occur?

Of course, grasses are also associated with other habitats. Some are restricted to one type, such as seashore blue grass (*Poa douglasii*) to the coastal strand, rice cut grass (*Leersia oryzoides*) to freshwater sites, or Eureka Valley dune grass (*Swallenia alexandrae*) to interior dunes in Inyo County. Many others can be found in several habitats. Some weedy European annuals are essentially ubiquitous.

Coastal Strand

Beaches and adjacent dunes occupy a narrow, discontinuous band along the coastline. Together they account for less than 1 percent of the state's land area. Sand is typically unstable, a characteristic we have attempted to overcome by introducing European beach grass *(Ammophila arenaria)*.

TABLE 15. Grasses of the coastal strand

Scientific Name	Common Name
Native Annuals	
Festuca microstachys	Pacific fescue
Native Perennials	
Agrostis pallens	seashore bent grass
Elymus mollis	sea lyme grass
Elymus x vancouverensis	Vancouver wild-rye
Festuca rubra	red fescue
Poa confinis	dune blue grass
Poa douglasii	seashore blue grass
Poa macrantha	seashore blue grass
Naturalized Annuals	
Aira caryophyllea	silver hair grass
Avena fatua	wild oat
Briza maxima	rattlesnake grass
Briza minor	small quaking grass
Bromus diandrus	ripgut brome
Festuca bromoides	brome six-weeks grass
Festuca perennis	rye grass
Hordeum murinum subsp. *murinum*	mouse barley
Poa annua	annual blue grass
Polypogon maritimus	maritime beard grass
Polypogon monspeliensis	rabbit's-foot grass
Naturalized Perennials	
Ammophila arenaria	European beach grass
Anthoxanthum odoratum	sweet vernal grass
Cortaderia jubata	pampas grass
Dactylis glomerata	orchard grass
Festuca arundinacea	tall fescue
Poa pratensis	Kentucky blue grass

Coastal Salt Marshes

Coastal salt marshes are scattered along the entire coastline, from sea level to about 10 ft. Most are now found in the San Francisco Bay region.

Figure 10. Coastal marsh in San Diego County

TABLE 16. Grasses of the coastal salt marshes

Scientific Name	Common Name
Native Perennials	
Distichlis littoralis	shore grass
Distichlis spicata	salt grass
Spartina foliosa	California cord grass
Naturalized Annuals	
Hainardia cylindrica	thintail
Parapholis incurva	curved sickle grass
Naturalized Perennials	
Polypogon elongatus	beard grass
Spartina densiflora	Chilean cord grass
Spartina patens	salt meadow cord grass

Freshwater Sites

Some grasses grow typically or exclusively in ephemeral or permanent moist to aquatic sites, including lakes, ponds, reservoirs, irrigation canals, rivers, and streams, and their margins; marshes, wet meadows, fens, swales, seeps, and roadside ditches at low elevations.

TABLE 17. Grasses of freshwater sites

Scientific Name	Common Name
Native Annuals	
Alopecurus spp.	meadow foxtails
Beckmannia syzigachne	American slough grass
Eragrostis hypnoides	creeping love grass
Eriochloa spp.	cup grasses
Hordeum depressum	alkali barley
Leptochloa viscida	sticky sprangletop
Muhlenbergia filiformis	pull-up muhly
Phalaris spp.	canary grasses
Native Perennials	
Alopecurus spp.	meadow foxtails
Calamagrostis bolanderi	Bolander's reed grass
Calamagrostis canadensis	bluejoint
Calamagrostis nutkaensis	Pacific reed grass
Cinna bolanderi	Bolander's wood reed
Cinna latifolia	wood reed grass
Deschampsia atropurpurea	mountain hair grass
Deschampsia caespitosa	Pacific hair grass
Deschampsia elongata	slender hair grass
Eriochloa spp.	cup grasses
Glyceria spp.	manna grasses
Hordeum arizonicum	Arizona barley
Imperata brevifolia	California satintail

Scientific Name	Common Name
Leersia oryzoides	rice cut grass
Leptochloa spp.	sprangletops
Melica subulata	Alaska onion grass
Muhlenbergia californica	California muhly
Muhlenbergia filiformis	pull-up muhly
Muhlenbergia utilis	Aparejo grass
Panicum acuminatum	panic grass
Paspalum distichum	knot grass
Phalaris spp.	canary grasses
Phragmites australis	common reed
Pleuropogon spp.	semaphore grasses
Poa leptocoma	bog blue grass
Poa napensis	Napa blue grass
Polypogon spp.	beard grasses
Puccinellia spp.	alkali grasses
Spartina gracilis	alkali cord grass
Sphenopholis obtusata	prairie wedge-scale
Torreyochloa spp.	false manna grasses

Naturalized Annuals

Alopecurus spp.	meadow foxtails
Crypsis spp.	prickle grasses
Echinochloa spp.	barnyard grass, cockspur
Eriochloa spp.	cup grass
Oryza sativa	rice
Phalaris spp.	canary grasses

Naturalized Perennials

Alopecurus spp.	meadow foxtails
Arundo donax	giant reed
Echinochloa spp.	barnyard grass, cockspur
Phalaris spp.	canary grasses
Poa palustris	fowl blue grass

Vernal Pools

Vernal pools are seasonal wetlands. Water collects in depressions from late winter to early spring because of an impermeable layer, and then the shallow pools dry up as the drier weather comes in the later spring and summer. These pools are scattered across the state and are especially common in the Central Valley grassland. Most of our federally listed grasses are found here. Spring wildflower displays are often spectacular.

Figure 11. Vernal pool: Hog Lake in Tehama County

Serpentine Outcrops

California's **serpentines** cover more than 1,200 square miles, more or less forming a ring around the Central Valley. What sets them apart is the low ratio of calcium to magnesium in their soil, whose chemistry thereby excludes many plants. Serpentines are the home of many rare plants and some of our most spectacular wildflower displays.

TABLE 18. Grasses of vernal pools

Scientific Name	Common Name
Native Annuals	
Agrostis elliottiana	Elliott's bent grass
Agrostis microphylla	small-leaved bent grass
Alopecurus saccatus	Pacific meadow foxtail
Deschampsia danthonioides	annual hair grass
Festuca microstachys	Pacific fescue
Neostapfia colusana*	Colusa grass
Orcuttia californica*	California Orcutt grass
Orcuttia inaequalis*	San Joaquin Valley Orcutt grass
Orcuttia pilosa*	hairy Orcutt grass
Orcuttia tenuis*	slender Orcutt grass
Orcuttia viscida*	Sacramento Orcutt grass
Phalaris lemmonii	Lemmon's canary grass
Pleuropogon californicus	California semaphore grass
Tuctoria greenei*	awnless spiral grass
Tuctoria mucronata*	prickly spiral grass
Naturalized Annuals	
Aira caryophyllea	hair grass
Briza minor	small quaking grass
Bromus hordeaceus	soft brome
Crypsis schoenoides	prickle grass
Elymus caput-medusae	medusa head grass
Festuca bromoides	brome six-weeks fescue
Poa annua	annual blue grass
Polypogon monspeliensis	rabbit's-foot grass

*State- and federally listed endemics.

TABLE 19. Grasses of serpentine outcrops

Scientific Name	Common Name
Native Annuals	
Agrostis elliottiana	Elliot's bent grass
Agrostis hendersonii	Henderson's bent grass
Agrostis microphylla	small-leaved bent grass
Alopecurus saccatus	Pacific meadow foxtail
Deschampsia danthonioides	annual hair grass

Continued ▶

TABLE 19. *(continued)*

Scientific Name	Common Name
Festuca microstachys	Pacific fescue
Hordeum depressum	alkali barley
Hordeum intercedens	bobtail barley
Scribneria bolanderi	Scribner's grass
Native Perennials	
Calamagrostis ophitidis	serpentine reed grass
Danthonia californica	California oat grass
Deschampsia elongata	slender hair grass
Elymus elymoides	squirreltail
Elymus glaucus	blue wild-rye
Festuca californica	California fescue
Festuca idahoensis	Idaho fescue
Hordeum brachyantherum	meadow barley
Koeleria macrantha	June grass
Melica californica	California melic
Melica imperfecta	Coast Range melic
Melica subulata	Alaska onion grass
Melica torreyana	Torrey's melic
Phalaris californica	California canary grass
Poa piperi	Piper's blue grass
Poa secunda	Nevada blue grass
Poa tenerrima	delicate blue grass
Stipa lemmonii var. *pubescens*	Crampton's needle grass
Stipa lepida	foothill needle grass
Stipa pulchra	purple needle grass
Naturalized Annuals	
Aegilops triuncialis	barbed goat grass
Avena barbata	slender wild oat
Bromus diandrus	ripgut grass
Bromus hordeaceus	soft brome
Bromus madritensis subsp. *rubens*	foxtail brome
Elymus caput-medusae	medusa head
Festuca perennis	annual rye grass
Naturalized Perennial	
Festuca perennis	perennial rye grass

Chaparral

Chaparral is one of the most characteristic vegetation types of our state. The dominants are leathery-leaved, evergreen shrubs or dwarf trees. This vegetation often occurs on shallow, rocky soils at low elevations throughout the state. Grasses are often found in early successional stages.

TABLE 20. Grasses of the chaparral

Scientific Name	Common Name
Native Annuals	
Festuca octoflora	six-weeks fescue
Poa howellii	Howell's blue grass
Native Perennials	
Agrostis hooveri	Hoover's bent grass
Aristida purpurea var. *parishii*	Parish's three-awn
Elymus glaucus	blue wild-rye
Elymus stebbinsii	Stebbins' wild-rye
Festuca californica	California fescue
Melica frutescens	woody melic
Melica imperfecta	Coast Range melic
Melica torreyana	Torrey's melic grass
Poa piperi	Piper's blue grass
Stipa cernua	nodding needle grass
Stipa coronata	giant needle grass
Stipa diegoensis	San Diego needle grass
Stipa lepida	foothill needle grass
Stipa pulchra	purple needle grass
Naturalized Annuals	
Festuca bromoides	brome six-weeks fescue
Festuca myuros	rat-tail fescue

Conifer Forests

Grasses are found as understory plants in a variety of coniferous forest settings. They cover about 20 percent of California's land area. The construction of logging roads has opened these forests and created disturbed areas where weeds and some natives now thrive.

TABLE 21. Grasses of the conifer forests

Scientific Name	Common Name
Native Annuals	
Agrostis scabra	tickle grass
Bromus carinatus	California brome
Poa bolanderi	Bolander's blue grass
Native Perennials	
Agrostis exarata	spike bent grass
Agrostis hallii	Hall's bent grass
Agrostis x idahoensis	Idaho bent grass
Agrostis scabra	tickle grass
Anthoxanthum occidentale	vanilla grass
Bromus carinatus	California brome
Bromus ciliatus	fringed brome
Bromus grandis	tall brome
Bromus laevipes	woodland brome
Bromus orcuttianus	Orcutt's brome
Bromus suksdorfii	Suksdorf's brome
Bromus vulgaris	Columbia brome
Calamagrostis stricta	northern reed grass
Cinna bolanderi	Bolander's reed grass
Cinna latifolia	wood reed grass
Danthonia unispicata	one-spike oat grass
Deschampsia atropurpurea	mountain hair grass
Elymus californicus	California bottlebrush grass
Elymus lanceolatus	thick spike wild-rye
Elymus sierrae	Sierra wild-rye
Festuca occidentalis	western fescue
Glyceria borealis	northern manna grass
Glyceria elata	tall manna grass
Melica bulbosa	western melic, onion grass
Melica californica	California melic
Melica fugax	little onion grass
Melica geyeri	Geyer's onion grass
Melica harfordii	Harford's melic

Scientific Name	Common Name
Melica spectabilis	purple onion grass
Melica stricta	nodding onion grass
Melica subulata	Alaska onion grass
Melica torreyana	Torrey's melic
Poa kelloggii	Kellogg's blue grass
Torreyochloa erecta	spike false manna grass
Trisetum canescens	tall false oat
Trisetum cernuum	nodding oat grass
Trisetum wolfii	Wolf's false oat
Naturalized Perennials	
Cortaderia jubata	jubata grass

Woodlands and Savannas

The boundaries between forests, woodlands, and savannas are not sharp. Forests have more or less continuous canopies; woodlands have fewer individual trees and are more open. In a savanna, trees and shrubs are smaller, even more widely spaced, with understories dominated by various grasses and other herbaceous plants.

TABLE 22. Grasses of woodlands and savannas

Scientific Name	Common Name
Native Annuals	
Bouteloua spp.	grama grass
Bromus carinatus	California brome
Festuca octoflora	six-weeks fescue
Poa howellii	Howell's blue grass
Native Perennials	
Agrostis exarata	spike bent grass
Agrostis hallii	Hall's bent grass
Agrostis hooveri	Hoover's bent grass
Agrostis pallens	thin grass
Bouteloua spp.	grama grasses
Bromus carinatus	California brome
Bromus grandis	tall brome
Calamagrostis bolanderi	Bolander's reed grass
Calamagrostis canadensis	bluejoint

Continued ▶

TABLE 22. *(continued)*

Scientific Name	Common Name
Elymus cinereus	ashy wild-rye
Elymus condensatus	giant wild-rye
Elymus glaucus	blue wild-rye
Elymus lanceolatus	thick spike wild-rye
Elymus spicatus	blue bunch wheat grass
Elymus trachycaulus	slender wheat grass
Festuca californica	California fescue
Festuca idahoensis	Idaho fescue
Festuca occidentalis	western fescue
Koeleria macrantha	June grass
Melica californica	California melic
Melica frutescens	woody melic
Melica geyeri	Geyer's onion grass
Melica imperfecta	Coast Range melic
Poa howellii	Howell's blue grass
Sporobolus contractus	spike dropseed
Sporobolus cryptandrus	sand dropseed
Stipa cernua	nodding needle grass
Stipa lemmonii	Lemmon's needle grass
Stipa nevadensis	Sierra needle grass
Stipa parishii	Parish's needle grass
Stipa pinetorum	pine needle grass
Stipa pulchra	purple needle grass
Tridens muticus	slim tridens

Naturalized Annuals

Aristida oligantha	old field three-awn
Bromus diandrus	ripgut
Bromus hordeaceus	soft brome
Festuca myuros	rat-tail fescue
Festuca perennis	rye grass
Hordeum murinum subsp. *leporinum*	hare barley

Naturalized Perennials

Festuca perennis	perennial rye grass

Montane Meadows

The presence of montane meadows is almost always correlated with a shallow water table that provides moisture to the plants for all or most of the year. The dominant plants are typically grasses and sedges. They are found often at elevations of 2,000 ft to 8,000 ft.

TABLE 23. Grasses of montane meadows

Scientific Name	Common Name
Native Perennials	
Agrostis spp.	bent grasses
Bromus carinatus	California brome
Calamagrostis breweri	Brewer's reed grass
Deschampsia spp.	hair grasses
Elymus glaucus	blue wild-rye
Elymus trachycaulus	slender wheat grass
Elymus triticoides	beardless wild-rye
Festuca brachyphylla subsp. *breviculmis*	alpine fescue
Glyceria elata	tall manna grass
Muhlenbergia richardsonis	mat muhly
Poa secunda	pine blue grass
Stipa lemmonii	Lemmon's needle grass
Stipa occidentalis	California needle grass
Trisetum spicatum	narrow false oat
Naturalized Perennials	
Arrhenatherum elatius	tall oat grass
Bromus inermis	smooth brome
Dactylis glomerata	orchard grass
Festuca arundinacea	alta fescue
Phleum pratense	timothy
Poa pratensis	Kentucky blue grass

Subalpine and Alpine Meadows

We find extensive subalpine and alpine meadows in California's mountains. The meadows in the subalpine areas mix with forests and patches of woodlands with increased elevation. In the alpine region, above the tree line, vegetation is dominated by wet and dry meadows and turfs of perennial grasses and sedges, and by fell fields—vegetation similar to that of the arctic tundra. Unfortunately, the distinction between subalpine and alpine is clearer in print than it is in the field.

TABLE 24. Grasses of the subalpine and alpine meadows

Scientific Name	Common Name
Native Perennials	
Agrostis humilis	mountain bent grass
Agrostis pallens	leafy bent grass
Calamagrostis breweri	Brewer's reed grass
Calamagrostis canadensis	bluejoint
Calamagrostis muiriana	Muir's reed grass
Calamagrostis purpurascens	purple reed grass
Deschampsia spp.	hair grasses
Elymus elymoides	squirreltail
Elymus scribneri	Scribner's wild-rye
Festuca brachyphylla subsp. *breviculmis*	alpine fescue
Festuca saximontana var. *purpusiana*	Rocky Mountain fescue
Festuca viridula	green-leaved fescue
Muhlenbergia richardsonis	mat muhly
Phleum alpinum	mountain timothy
Poa abbreviata subsp. *pattersonii*	Patterson's blue grass
Poa cusickii subsp. *epilis*	mountain blue grass
Poa glauca subsp. *rupicola*	timberline blue grass
Poa keckii	Keck's blue grass
Poa leptocoma subsp. *leptocoma*	bog blue grass
Poa lettermanii	Letterman's blue grass
Poa pringlei	Pringle's blue grass
Poa secunda	Nevada blue grass
Poa stebbinsii	Stebbins' blue grass
Stipa kingii	King's mountain-rice
Trisetum spicatum	spike trisetum
Trisetum wolfii	Wolf's false oat

Cool Deserts

A cool desert region occurs above about 4,100 ft east of the Cascades and Sierra Nevada, and includes the Modoc Plateau and the eastern border of California. The climate is cold and dry. The vegetation is composed of the Great Basin flora and many of the grasses are associated with the sagebrush (*Artemisia* spp.) steppe.

Warm Deserts

This province occupies much of southeastern California. It is subdivided into the Mojave and Sonoran deserts. The dominant plant is creosote bush *(Larrea tridentata)*, forming extensive shrub lands interspersed with grasslands and desert woodlands.

TABLE 25. Grasses of the cool deserts

Scientific Name	Common Name
Native Perennials	
Elymus cinereus	Great Basin wild-rye
Elymus elymoides	squirreltail
Elymus hispidus	intermediate wheat grass
Elymus smithii	western wheat grass
Elymus spicatus	blue bunch wheat grass
Festuca idahoensis	Idaho fescue
Koeleria macrantha	June grass
Poa secunda	Nevada blue grass
Stipa comata	needle-and-thread grass
Stipa thurberiana	Thurber's needle grass
Naturalized Annuals	
Bromus japonicus*	Japanese brome
Bromus tectorum*	cheat grass
Elymus caput-medusae*	medusa head
Ventenata dubia*	North Africa grass
Naturalized Perennials	
Agropyron cristatum*	crested wheat grass

*Transformative species according to Keeler-Wolf et al. 2007: 31.

Figure 12. Desert grassland in San Bernardino County

TABLE 26. Grasses of the warm deserts

Scientific Name	Common Name
Native Perennials	
Aristida californica var. *californica*	California three-awn
Aristida purpurea var. *nealleyi*	Nealley's three-awn
Aristida purpurea var. *wrightii*	Wright's three-awn
Bouteloua gracilis	blue grama
Dasyochloa pulchella	fluff grass
Distichlis spicata	salt grass
Hilaria rigida	big galleta
Sporobolus airoides	alkali sacaton
Stipa comata	needle-and-thread grass
Stipa hymenoides	Indian rice grass
Stipa speciosa	desert needle grass
Naturalized Annuals	
Bromus madritensis subsp. *rubens**	red brome
*Bromus tectorum**	cheat grass
*Schismus barbatus**	Mediterranean or Arabian schismus

*Noteworthy invasive/transformative species.

Interior Alkali Sinks, Marshes, and Meadows

These are areas, mostly below 4,000 ft, on the floor of the Central Valley, on sites east of the Sierra Nevada, and in such well-known places as Panamint Valley and Death Valley. There is little or no water drainage. The dominant vegetation is composed of fleshy, salt-tolerant plants.

Interior Dunes

Dunes are not just a coastal phenomenon. Active and partially stabilized dunes and sand fields occur in the warm deserts, in the southern Central Valley, and in the interior coast ranges.

TABLE 27. Grasses of interior alkali sinks, marshes, and meadows

Scientific Name	Common Name
Native Annuals	
Deschampsia danthonioides	annual hair grass
Hordeum depressum	alkali barley
Leptochloa fusca subsp. fascicularis	clustered salt grass
Native Perennials	
Distichlis spicata	salt grass
Elymus smithii	western wheat grass
Muhlenbergia asperifolia	scratch grass
Pleuropogon californicus	California semaphore grass
Puccinellia spp.	alkali grasses
Sporobolus airoides	alkali sacaton
Naturalized Annuals	
Bromus hordeaceus	soft brome
Festuca perennis	rye grass
Hainardia cylindrica	thintail
Hordeum murinum	wall or hare barley
Polypogon maritimus	Mediterranean beard grass

TABLE 28. Grasses of the interior dunes

Scientific Name	Common Name
Native Perennials	
Bouteloua gracilis	blue grama
Hilaria rigida	big galleta
Panicum urvilleanum	desert panic grass
Spartina gracilis	alkali cord grass
Stipa hymenoides	Indian rice grass
Stipa speciosa	desert needle grass
*Swallenia alexandrae**	Eureka Valley dune grass
Naturalized Annuals	
Bromus madritensis subsp. *rubens***	foxtail brome
*Bromus tectorum***	cheat grass
*Schismus barbatus***	schismus

* State- and federally listed species.
** Invasive/transformative species.

Grasses of Widespread Occurrence

The title says it all. The list in Table 29 is based primarily on those grasses shown as occurring throughout the state (CA) or the California Floristic Province (CA-FP) in Hickman (1993).

TABLE 29. Grasses of widespread occurrence

Scientific Name	Common Name
Native Annuals	
Eragrostis pectinacea	tufted love grass
Festuca microstachys	Pacific fescue
Panicum capillare	witch grass
Phalaris angusta	timothy canary grass
Native Perennials	
Agrostis exarata	spike bent grass
Agrostis pallens	dune bent grass
Distichlis spicata	salt grass
Elymus glaucus	blue wild-rye

Scientific Name	Common Name
Elymus multisetus	big squirreltail
Hordeum jubatum	foxtail barley
Phalaris arundinacea	reed canary grass
Phragmites australis	common reed
Poa secunda	Nevada blue grass
Puccinellia nuttalliana	Nuttall's alkali grass

Naturalized Annuals

Avena barbata	slender wild oat
Avena fatua	wild oat
Bromus arenarius	Australian chess
Bromus catharticus	rescue grass
Bromus diandrus	ripgut
Bromus hordeaceus	soft brome
Bromus japonicus	Japanese brome
Bromus madritensis	Spanish or red brome
Bromus tectorum	downy brome
Echinochloa crus-galli	barnyard grass
Eragrostis cilianensis	stink grass
Festuca bromoides	brome six-weeks fescue
Festuca myuros	rat-tail fescue
Festuca perennis	rye grass
Hordeum murinum	mouse barley
Poa annua	annual blue grass
Polypogon monspeliensis	rabbit's-foot grass
Setaria viridis	green bristle grass

Naturalized Perennials

Agrostis stolonifera	red top
Bromus catharticus	rescue grass
Cynodon dactylon	Bermuda grass
Dactylis glomerata	orchard grass
Festuca arundinacea	tall fescue
Festuca perennis	rye grass
Paspalum dilatatum	Dallis grass
Phalaris aquatica	Harding grass
Phleum pratense	timothy
Poa bulbosa	bulbous blue grass
Poa compressa	Canada blue grass
Poa pratensis	Kentucky blue grass

Acknowledgments

This chapter benefitted greatly from the information and advice offered by my colleague, John O. Sawyer. On the other hand, without his kind assistance it would have been much shorter and completed much earlier.

Selected References

Baldwin, B. G., D. H. Goldman, D. J. Keil, R. Patterson, T. J. Rosatti, & D. H. Wilken. 2012. *The Jepson Manual: Vascular Plants of California.* Berkeley: University of California Press. Pp. 1412–1498.

Barbour, M. G., T. Keeler-Wolf, & A. A. Schoenherr (editors). 2007. *Terrestrial Vegetation of California.* Third edition. Berkeley: University of California Press.

Barbour, M. & V. Whitworth. 1992. "California's Grassroots: Native or European?" *Pacific Discovery* 45: 8–15.

Barry, W. J. 1972. *Central Valley Prairie:* Vol. 1. *California Prairie Ecosystem.* Sacramento: California State Dept. Parks and Recreation.

Bartolome, J. W., W. J. Barry, T. Griggs, & P. Hopkinson. 2007. "Valley Grassland." *In* M. G. Barbour, T. Keeler-Wolf, & A. A. Schoenherr. *Terrestrial Vegetation of California.* Third edition. Berkeley: University of California Press. Pp. 367–393.

Beetle, A. A. 1947. "Distribution of the Native Grasses of California." *Hilgardia* 17 (9): 309–357.

Crampton, B. 1974. "Distribution of Grasses in California." *In Grasses in California.* Berkeley: University of California Press. Pp. 29–38.

Ford, L. D. & G. F. Hayes. 2007. "Northern Coastal Scrub and Coastal Prairie." *In* M. G. Barbour, T. Keeler-Wolf, & A. A. Schoenherr. *Terrestrial Vegetation of California.* Third edition. Berkeley: University of California Press. Pp. 180–207.

Hamilton, J. G. 1997. "Changing Perceptions of Pre-European Grasslands in California." *Madroño* 44(4): 311–333.

Hickman, J. C. (editor). 1993. "Poaceae." *In The Jepson Manual: Higher Plants of California.* Berkeley: University of California Press. Pp. 1225–1303.

Holland, V. L. & D. J. Keil. 1995. *California Vegetation.* Dubuque, IA: Kendall/Hunt Publ.

Holstein, G. 2001. "Pre-Agricultural Grassland in Central California." *Madroño* 48(4): 253–264.

Huenneke, L. F. & H. A. Mooney (editors). 1989. *Grassland Structure and Function: California Annual Grassland.* Dordrecht, The Netherlands: Kluwer Acad. Publ.

Keeler-Wolf, T., J. M. Evens, A. I. Solomeshch, V. L. Holland, & M. G. Barbour. 2007. "Community Classification and Nomenclature." *In* M. R. Stromberg, J. D. Corbin, & C. M. D'Antonio. *California Grasslands: Ecology and Management.* Berkeley: University of California Press. Pp. 21–34.

Kraemer, M. B. 2010. "An Overview of North Coast Grasses: Diversity and Distribution across the Landscape." *Grasslands* 20(3): 4–6, 15–18.

Minnich, R. A. 2008. *California's Fading Wildflowers: Lost Legacy and Biological Invasions.* Berkeley: University of California Press.

Munz, P. A. 1959. "California Plant Communities." *In A California Flora.* In collaboration with D. D. Keck. Berkeley: University of California Press. Pp. 10–18.

Sawyer, J. O., T. Keeler-Wolf, & J. M. Evens. 2008. *A Manual of California Vegetation.* Second edition. Sacramento: California Native Plant Society.

Stebbins, G. L. & C. Dremann. 2000. "One Hundred and Forty of California's Native Grasses." *Grasslands* 9(1): 3–6.

Stromberg, M. R., J. D. Corbin, & C. M. D'Antonio (editors). 2007. *California Grasslands: Ecology and Management.* Berkeley: University of California Press.

Stromberg, M. R., P. Kephart, & V. Yadon. 2001. "Composition, Invasibility, and Diversity in Coastal California Grasslands." *Madroño* 48(4): 236–252.

Wester, L. 1981. "Composition of Native Grasslands in the San Joaquin Valley, California." *Madroño* 28(4): 231–241.

ENDEMIC GRASSES

One of the defining features of the California flora is its high number of endemics. For a plant to be considered endemic, it must be native to a region and confined to it. The size of the area or some other feature that describes an area becomes the defining criterion. A grass may be endemic to North America, or to California, or to the San Francisco Bay Area, or to serpentine soils or to coastal dunes. There are 348 grasses endemic to the conterminous United States; 92 of them occur in only one state (Smith 2010b). Of those, 54 occur only in California. That number is higher than all of the other states combined. Three grass genera (*Neostapfia, Swallenia,* and *Tuctoria*) are endemic to California; again this is unmatched by any other state. A fourth genus, *Orcuttia,* is all but endemic; one of its species also occurs in Baja California, Mexico.

Some of our endemic grasses are much more widespread than others. Nine of them are restricted to a single county. Of those, six appear to be known from one to a few locations in that county.

Agrostis blasdalei var. *marinensis*: two collections along Dillon Beach Road
Agrostis clivicola var. *punta-reyesensis*: one or two collections from near Abbott's Lagoon
Poa napensis: almost all (all?) from 2 miles north of Calistoga
Puccinellia howellii: junction of S. R. 299 and Crystal Creek Road
Swallenia alexandrae: Eureka Dunes, south end of Eureka Valley

At the other end of the spectrum, Torrey's melic grass (*Melica torreyana*) is known from 36 counties. Marin, Mendocino, and Sonoma counties tie for first place in the number of endemic grasses (11). Only Imperial and King counties appear to have no endemic grasses.

What follows is an inventory in three parts: (1) grasses endemic to California as it is defined politically; (2) those found in California and adjacent Oregon; and (3) those found in California and adjacent Baja California, Mexico. The second and third lists accept the biogeographical proposition that the flora that is best developed here and most characteristic of California extends slightly beyond our northern and southern political borders, and that it would be appropriate to include those regions when discussing endemism in the California floristic province. County-level distribution is shown.

TABLE 30. California's endemic grasses

Scientific Name, Common Name	Distribution by County
Endemic to California	
Agrostis blasdalei var. *blasdalei*, Blasdale's bent grass	Mendocino to Santa Cruz
Agrostis blasdalei var. *marinensis*, Marin bent grass	Marin
Agrostis clivicola var. *clivicola*, coastal bent grass	Mendocino, Yolo, & Sonoma
Agrostis clivicola var. *punta-reyesensis*, Point Reyes bent grass	Marin
Agrostis hooveri, Hoover's bent grass	San Luis Obispo & Santa Barbara
Alopecurus aequalis var. *sonomensis*, Sonoma foxtail	Sonoma & Marin
Bromus hallii, Hall's brome	Tulare, Kern, Los Angeles, San Bernardino, & Riverside
Bromus pseudolaevipes, Coast Range brome	Tehama to San Bernardino & San Diego
Calamagrostis bolanderi, Bolander's reed grass	Del Norte, Humboldt, Mendocino, & Yolo
Calamagrostis foliosa, leafy reed grass	Del Norte, Humboldt, & Mendocino
Calamagrostis muiriana, Muir's reed grass	Tuolumne & Mono to Tulare & Inyo
Calamagrostis ophitidis, serpentine reed grass	Humboldt, Mendocino, Sonoma, Lake, Napa, & Marin
Cinna bolanderi, Bolander's reed grass	Mariposa, Madera, & Tulare
Elymus californicus, California bottlebrush grass	Sonoma to Santa Cruz; Mono
Elymus x *gouldii*, Gould's wild-rye	San Francisco Bay Area to San Diego & Riverside
Elymus pacificus, Pacific wild-rye	Mendocino to San Luis Obispo
Elymus stebbinsii, Stebbins' wild-rye	Butte; Mariposa to San Diego
Festuca brachyphylla var. *breviculmis*, alpine fescue	Alpine to Riverside
Festuca californica subsp. *hitchcockiana*, Hitchcock's California fescue	San Luis Obispo
Festuca californica var. *parishii*, Parish's California fescue	Santa Barbara, Los Angeles, San Bernardino
Hordeum brachyantherum subsp. *californicum*, California barley	Widespread
Melica geyeri var. *aristulata*, Geyer's onion grass	Tehama, Napa, Marin, San Luis Obispo

Continued ▶

TABLE 30. *(continued)*

Scientific Name, Common Name	Distribution by County
Melica stricta var. *albicaulis*, nodding onion grass	Ventura & San Bernardino
Melica torreyana, Torrey's melic grass	Humboldt to Plumas south to Los Angeles
Muhlenbergia jonesii, Modoc muhly	Siskiyou & Modoc to Mono
Neostapfia colusana, Colusa grass	Colusa, Yolo, Napa, Stanislaus, & Merced
Orcuttia inaequalis, San Joaquin orcutt grass	Stanislaus, Merced, Madera, Fresno, & Tulare
Orcuttia pilosa, hairy Orcutt grass	Tehama, Glenn, Stanislaus, Merced, & Madera
Orcuttia tenuis, slender Orcutt grass	Siskiyou & Modoc to Sacramento
Orcuttia viscida, Sacramento Orcutt grass	Sacramento
Panicum acuminatum var. *thermale*, Geyser's panic grass	Shasta, Plumas, Nevada, Sonoma, & El Dorado
Phalaris lemmonii, Lemmon's canary grass	Humboldt, Glenn, & Butte to San Diego
Pleuropogon californicus var. *californicus*, California semaphore grass	Mendocino to Amador & Stanislaus
Pleuropogon californicus var. *davyi*, Davy's semaphore grass	Mendocino, Lake, & Sonoma
Pleuropogon hooverianus, North Coast semaphore grass	Mendocino, Sonoma, & Marin
Poa atropurpurea, San Bernardino blue grass	San Bernardino & San Diego
Poa diaboli, San Luis Obispo blue grass	San Luis Obispo
Poa douglasii, seashore blue grass	Del Norte to Santa Barbara
Poa keckii, Keck's blue grass	Alpine, Tuolumne, Mono, Fresno, Tulare, & Inyo
Poa kelloggii, Kellogg's blue grass	Humboldt to Santa Cruz
Poa napensis, Napa blue grass	Napa
Poa sierrae, Sierra blue grass	Butte, Plumas, Placer, & Madera
Poa stebbinsii, subalpine blue grass	El Dorado to Tulare & Inyo
Poa tenerrima, delicate blue grass	Tehama, Butte, Sierra, El Dorado, Amador, Tuolumne; San Luis Obispo
Puccinellia howellii, Howell's alkali grass	Shasta
Stipa kingii, King's mountain-rice	Tuolumne, Mono, Mariposa, Madera, Fresno, Tulare, & Inyo
Stipa latiglumis, Yosemite needle grass	Siskiyou, Butte, Alpine, Mariposa, San Bernardino, & Riverside
Stipa lemmonii var. *pubescens*, Crampton's needle grass	Tehama & Lake

Scientific Name, Common Name	Distribution by County
Stipa stillmanii, Stillman's needle grass	Trinity & Shasta to El Dorado
Swallenia alexandrae, Eureka Valley dune grass	Inyo
Tuctoria greenei, awnless spiral grass	Shasta to Tulare
Tuctoria mucronata, prickly spiral grass	Solano

Endemic to California and adjacent southwestern Oregon

Agrostis hendersonii, Henderson's bent grass	Shasta to Merced
Calamagrostis breweri, Brewer's reed grass	Humboldt, Trinity, & Siskyou; Nevada to Tulare
Melica californica, California melic	Humboldt to San Luis Obispo, Kern, & San Bernardino
Phalaris californica, California canary grass	Humboldt to San Luis Obispo
Poa piperi, Piper's blue grass	Del Norte
Poa rhizomata, timber blue grass	Siskiyou & Trinity

Endemic to California and adjacent Baja California Norte, Mexico

Bromus grandis, tall brome	Napa & Placer to San Diego
X *Elyhordeum californicum*, California wild rye	Insufficient data
Elymus condensatus, giant wild-rye	Siskiyou & Modoc to San Diego
Elymus x *gouldii*, Gould's wild-rye	Mendocino to San Diego
Hordeum intercedens, bobtail barley	Nevada; Merced to San Diego
Melica californica, California melic	Humboldt to San Luis Obispo, Kern, & San Bernardino
Muhlenbergia californica, California muhly	Los Angeles, San Bernardino, & Riverside
Orcuttia californica, California Orcutt grass	Sacramento; Ventura, Los Angeles, Riverside, & San Diego
Poa thomasii, Catalina grass	Los Angeles, Catalina & San Clemente islands
Stipa cernua, nodding needle grass	Sutter to San Diego
Stipa coronata, crested needle grass	Mendocino; Monterey & San Benito to San Diego
Stipa diegoensis, San Diego needle grass	Santa Barbara to San Diego
Stipa lepida, small-flowered needle grass	Sonoma & Sacramento to San Diego
Stipa pulchra, purple needle grass	Humboldt & Shasta to San Diego

Selected References

Beetle, A. A. 1947. "Distribution of the Native Grasses of California." *Hilgardia* 17(9): 309–357.

Consortium of California Herbaria. Available at http://ucjeps.berkeley.edu/consortium/. Used as the primary source of county occurrences.

Crampton, B. 1961. "The Endemic Grasses of the California Floral Province." *Leaflts. West. Bot.* 9(9/10): 154–158.

Hoover, R. F. 1937. Endemism in the Flora of the Great Valley of California. PhD dissertation, University of California, Berkeley. 76 pp.

Howell, J. R. 1955. "A Tabulation of California Endemics." *Leaflts. West. Bot.* 7(11): 257–264.

Howell, J. T. 1957. "The California Floral Province and Its Endemic Genera." *Leaflts. West. Bot.* 8(5): 138–141.

Noldeke, A. M. & J. T. Howell. 1960. "Endemism and a California Flora." *Leaflts. West. Bot.* 9(8): 124–127.

Smith, J. P., Jr. 2010a. *An Annotated Checklist of the Endemic and Presumed Extinct Vascular Plants of California.* Misc. Publ. No. 9. Fifth edition. Arcata, CA: Humboldt State Univ. Herbarium.

Smith, J. P., Jr. 2010b. *Grasses of the Conterminous United States: An Annotated Checklist.* Misc. Publ. No. 4. Seventeenth edition. Arcata, CA: Humboldt State Univ. Herbarium.

Stebbins, G. L. & J. Major. 1965. "Endemism and Speciation in the California Flora." *Ecol. Monogr.* 35: 1–35.

RARE, ENDANGERED, AND THREATENED GRASSES

Some grasses have been declared rare, endangered, or threatened by virtue of official action taken by the United States Fish and Wildlife Service (USFWS) or by the California Department of Fish and Game (CDFG), the federal and state entities legally empowered to make such declarations. The California Native Plant Society has also been monitoring the state's rare and endangered plants for several decades and publishes an inventory of its findings, now in its eighth edition. Although its rating scheme has no independent legal standing, it is seen as scientifically authoritative.

TABLE 31. Rare, endangered, and threatened grasses of California
(See Note for Rating and Listing Definitions)

Scientific Name	Rating, Listing
Agrostis blasdalei var. blasdalei	1B.2
Agrostis hendersonii	3.2
Agrostis hooveri	1B.2
Agrostis humilis	2.3
Alopecurus aequalis var. sonomensis	1B.1, FE
Anthoxanthum nitens*	2.3
Blepharidachne kingii	2.3
Bouteloua trifida	2.3
Calamagrostis stricta ssp. inexpansa	2.1
Calamagrostis foliosa	4.2, SR
Calamagrostis ophitidis	4.3
Cinna bolanderi	1B.2
Deschampsia atropurpurea	4.3
Digitaria californica	2.3
Elymus californicus	4.3
Elymus salinus	2.3
Elymus scribneri	2.3
Enneapogon desvauxii	2.2
Erioneuron pilosum	2.3
Festuca minutiflora	2.3
Glyceria grandis	2.3
Hordeum intercedens	3.2

Continued ▶

TABLE 31. *(continued)*

(See Note for Rating and Listing Definitions)

Scientific Name	Rating, Listing
Imperata brevifolia	2.1
Muhlenbergia appressa	2.2
Muhlenbergia arsenei	2.3
Muhlenbergia fragilis	2.3
Muhlenbergia pauciflora	2.3
Munroa squarrosa	2.2
Neostapfia colusana	1B.1, FT, SE
Orcuttia californica	1B.1, FE, SE
Orcuttia inaequalis	1B.1, FT, SE
Orcuttia pilosa	1B.1, FE, SE
Orcuttia tenuis	1B.1, FT, SE
Orcuttia viscida	1B.1, FE, SE
Panicum acuminatum var. *thermale**	1B.1, SE
Pleuropogon hooverianus	1B.1, ST
Poa abbreviata subsp. *marshii*	2.3
Poa abbreviata subsp. *pattersonii*	2.3
Poa atropurpurea	1B.2, FE
Poa diaboli	1B.2
Poa lettermanii	2.3
Poa napensis	1B1, FE, SE
*Poa thomasii**	1B.2
Puccinellia howellii	1B.1
Puccinellia parishii	1B.1
Puccinellia pumila	2.2
Scleropogon brevifolius	2.3
Sphenopholis obtusata	2.2
*Stipa arida**	2.3
*Stipa divaricata**	2.3
*Stipa exigua**	2.3
Stipa lemmonii var. *pubescens*	3.2
Swallenia alexandrae	1B.2, FE, SR
Tuctoria greenei	1B.1, FE, SR
Tuctoria mucronata	1B.1, FE, SE

*Names conforming to use in this book.

Abbreviations and Definitions

For federally listed plants, **FE** = federally listed as endangered; **FT** = federally listed as threatened. Under the provisions of the Endangered Species Act, a plant is endangered if it is "in danger of extinction throughout all or a significant portion of its range." A species is threatened if it is "likely to become an endangered species within the foreseeable future throughout all or a significant portion of its range."

For state-listed plants, **SE** = state-listed as endangered; **SR** = state-listed as rare; **ST** = state-listed as threatened. The California Department of Fish & Game Code declares a plant endangered when "its prospects of survival and reproduction are in immediate jeopardy from one or more causes." A plant is threatened when "although not presently threatened with extinction, it is likely to become an endangered species in the foreseeable future in the absence of . . . special protection and management efforts." A plant is rare when "although not presently threatened with extinction, it is in such small numbers throughout its range that it may become endangered if its present environment worsens."

For California Native Plant Society Lists, **1A** = plants presumed extinct in California; **1B** = plants rare, threatened, or endangered in California and elsewhere; **2** = plants rare, threatened, or endangered in California, but more common elsewhere. Threat ranks: **0.1** = seriously threatened in California; **0.2** = fairly threatened in California; **0.3** = not very threatened in California.

Selected References

California Native Plant Society. 2011. The CNPS inventory of rare and endangered plants. Available at www.cnps.org/cnps/rareplants/inventory.

California Natural Diversity Database. 2011. *Special Vascular Plants, Bryophytes, and Lichens List.* Sacramento: California Department of Fish and Game. Natural Diversity Database. Available at www.dfg.ca.gov.

United States Department of Agriculture. Natural Resources Conservation Service. 2011. Federal Threatened & Endangered Plants Database. Available at http://plants.usda.gov/threat.html.

WEEDY GRASSES

Weeds are of great economic importance, but mostly in a negative sense. They cost the American farmer several billion dollars each year by reducing both the quantity and quality of our crops. Their damage causes a loss as large as insect injury and disease combined. Another aspect of weeds is their intimate association with our own species. Many of them are essentially our wards and they would not have their present day distribution without our encouragement. As the noted American botanist Edgar Anderson once observed, ". . . the history of weeds is the history of man."

What Is a Weed?

There are many definitions, in addition to the somewhat literary one offered by Emerson. In reviewing them, a plant is typically considered a weed if it:

- appears without being planted or cultivated;
- grows out of place, where we do not want it to grow;
- grows spontaneously in areas that we have disturbed;
- is useless, unwanted, or undesirable;
- interferes with human activity, such as agriculture or horticulture;
- impacts natural ecosystems;
- is persistent and not easily controlled or eradicated; or
- we think it is ugly.

Inherent in most definitions is the idea that a plant is a weed if it is growing where we do not wish it to be and that it interferes with our desire to raise crops or have an attractive lawn or garden by competing with plants that we favor for that location. Most weeds are not native. They have either been accidentally introduced, or they may be crops or ornamental plants that have escaped from our fields and gardens, invaded natural or disturbed areas, and then persist without our assistance. Not all weeds are rank and unsightly, which can make them even more of a threat. We stop along roadsides and gather them up and take them home. You can actually purchase pampas grass at nurseries and national discount chains.

Although some weeds have become quite comfortable in our lawns, vacant lots, and roadsides, other introduced plants invade natural vegetation types and can cause considerable damage. The worst of them may be thought of as transformative species. They are so successful at outcompeting the native species that they replace them, and in so doing they transform the appearance of the landscape. Cheat grass, medusa head, and Mediterranean grass come quickly to mind.

Weeds are such a problem in the agricultural states that there is legislation against them. Many states have weed laws that require the farmer to use varying degrees of control against them. The "primary noxious weeds" are considered so bad that the land owner is required to destroy them if he discovers them on his property. I will list them for you later.

The Biological Features of Weeds

Many grasses are excellent weeds because they:

- can persist in an area from year to year, some by means of seed banks in the soil;
- reproduce sexually and vegetatively, by means of rhizomes and stolons, or self-pollinate;
- have seeds that can germinate and set seed under diverse environmental conditions;
- produce a large number of seeds;
- have seedlings that grow rapidly;
- have a "general purpose" set of genes that will enable plants to compete very effectively against native plants on disturbed sites;
- may be unpalatable or even toxic to livestock or herbivores by virtue of chemical and physical defense mechanisms (awns, spines, barbs, etc.);
- produce toxic substances that allow them to out-compete other plants in the immediate vicinity; and
- are physically attractive, which means we may bring them into our homes and gardens and thereby aid in their dispersal.

What Is Positive about Weeds?

- In ruined and abandoned areas, weeds make up much of the flora.
- Many of the more attractive plants that flourish in our cities and along our roadsides these days are weeds.
- Weeds prevent or retard erosion. The California Department of Transportation plants them on our roadsides.

The Weedy Grasses of California

The next two tables present compilations of our weedy grasses. In Table 32 are the commonly encountered weeds of our roadsides. Several of them have also been successful in invading both natural and disturbed areas.

Table 33 provides a list of those grasses that are so egregious that they have been singled out by experts as being of special concern. The California Department of Food and Agriculture (CDFA) and the United States Department of Agriculture (USDA) are legally charged with declaring certain plants to be noxious weeds at the state and federal levels. Table 33 also includes grasses cited by three non-governmental organizations: the California Invasive Plant Council (Cal-IPC), the Invasive Species Council of California (ISCC), and the Weed Science Society of America (WSSA). The D&H entry is a book by DiTomaso and Healy on the weeds of California and the western states that I consider especially authoritative.

TABLE 32. Weedy roadside grasses of California

Scientific Name	Common Name
Native Annuals	
Bouteloua barbata	six-week's grama
Panicum capillare	witch grass
Naturalized Annuals	
Aegilops spp.	goat grasses
Agropyron cristatum	crested wheat grass
Agrostis capillaris	colonial bent grass
Agrostis scabra	tickle grass
Aira caryophyllea	hair grass
Avena barbata	slender wild oat
Avena fatua	wild oat
Brachypodium distachyon	false brome
Briza maxima	rattlesnake grass
Briza minor	small quaking grass
Bromus catharticus	rescue grass

Scientific Name	Common Name
Bromus diandrus	ripgut grass
Bromus tectorum	downy brome
Chloris virgata	feather finger grass
Cynosurus echinatus	dogtail grass
Digitaria ischaemum	smooth crab grass
Digitaria sanguinalis	hairy crab grass
Echinochloa crus-galli	barnyard grass
Elymus caput-medusae	medusa head
Eragrostis cilianensis	stink grass
Festuca myuros	rat-tail grass
Gastridium phleoides	nit grass
Poa annua	annual blue grass
Schismus barbatus	schismus
Secale cereale	rye grass
Setaria viridis	green bristle grass
Sorghum bicolor	sorghum

Naturalized Perennials

Agrostis stolonifera	red top
Anthoxanthum odoratum	sweet vernal grass
Arrhenatherum elatius	tall oat grass
Cenchrus setaceus	crimson fountain grass
Cenchrus villosus	feathertop
Cortaderia jubata	pampas grass
Cynodon dactylon	Bermuda grass
Dactylis glomerata	orchard grass
Ehrharta calycina	perennial veldt grass
Eragrostis curvula	weeping love grass
Festuca arundinacea	tall fescue
Festuca perennis	rye grass
Holcus lanatus	velvet grass
Paspalum dilatatum	Dallis grass
Phleum pratense	timothy
Poa bulbosa	bulbous blue grass
Sorghum halepense	Johnson grass

TABLE 33. California's Weedy Grasses
(See Note for Definitions)

Scientific Name	Organizations with Criteria Met
Aegilops cylindrica	CDFA, ISC, WSS, D&H
Aegilops geniculata	CDFA, ISS, WSS, D&H
Aegilops triuncialis	CDFA, ISS, WSS, D&H
Agrostis avenacea	IPC, ISC, WSS, D&H
Agrostis stolonifera	IPC, ISC, WSS, D&H
Aira caryophyllea	IPC, WSS
Aira praecox	IPC
Alopecurus pratensis	IPC, WSS, D&H
Alopecurus myosuroides	ISC, WSS
Ammophila arenaria	IPC, ISC, WSS, D&H
Anthoxanthum odoratum	IPC, ISC, WSS, D&H
Arundo donax	CDFA, IPC, ISC, WSS, D&H
Avena barbata	IPC, ISC, WSS, D&H
Avena fatua	IPC, ISC, WSS, D&H
Avena sterilis	USDA, ISC, WSS
Brachypodium distachyon	ISC, WSS, D&H
Brachypodium sylvaticum	CDFA, IPC, ISC, WSS
Briza maxima	IPC, ISC, WSS, D&H
Briza minor	WSS, D&H
Bromus catharticus	WSS, D&H
Bromus diandrus	IPC. ISC, WSS, D&H
Bromus hordeaceus	IPC, ISC, WSS, D&H
Bromus japonicus	ISC, WSS, D&H
Bromus madritensis subsp. *rubens*	IPC, ISC, WSS, D&H
Bromus tectorum	IPC, ISC, WSS, D&H
Cenchrus ciliaris	ISC, WSS
Cenchrus echinatus	CDFA, ISC, WSS, D&H
Cenchrus incertus	CDFA, ISC, WSS, D&H
Cenchrus longispinus	CDFA, ISC, WSS, D&H
Cenchrus macrourus	USDA, WSS
Cenchrus setaceus	IPC, ISC, WSS, D&H
Cenchrus villosus	IPC, ISC, WSS, D&H
Chloris virgata	WSS, D&H
Cortaderia jubata	CDFA, IPC, ISC, WSS, D&H
Cortaderia selloana	IPC, ISC, WSS, D&H
Crypsis schoenoides	WSS, D&H
Cynodon dactylon	IPC, ISC, WSS, D&H
Cynosurus echinatus	IPC, ISC, WSS, D&H
Dactylis glomerata	IPC, ISC, WSS, D&H

Scientific Name	Organizations with Criteria Met
Digitaria ischaemum	WSS, D&H
Digitaria sanguinalis	ISC, WSS, D&H
Echinochloa colona	ISC, WSS, D&H
Echinochloa crus-galli	WSS, D&H
Echinochloa oryzicola	ISC, WSS
Echinochloa phyllopogon	ISC, D&H
Ehrharta calycina	IPC, ISC, WSS, D&H
Ehrharta erecta	IPC, ISC, WSS
Ehrharta longiflora	IPC, ISC, WSS
Eleusine indica	WSS, D&H
Elymus caput-medusae	CDFA, IPC, ISC, WSS, D&H
Elymus hispidus	IPC
Elymus ponticus	IPC
Elymus repens	CDFA, ISC, WSS, D&H
Eragrostis cilianensis	WSS, D&H
Eragrostis minor	WSS, D&H
Eragrostis pectinacea	WSS, D&H
Eriochloa acuminata	WSS, D&H
Festuca arundinacea	IPC, ISC, WSS, D&H
Festuca bromoides	IPC, ISC, WSS
Festuca myuros	ISC, WSS, D&H
Festuca perennis	IPC, ISC, WSS, D&H
Festuca pratensis	IPC, WSS
Gastridium phleoides	WSS, D&H
Glyceria declinata	ISC
Heteropogon contortus	WSS, D&H
Holcus lanatus	IPC, ISC, WSS, D&H
Hordeum marinum	IPC, ISC, WSS, D&H
Hordeum murinum	IPC, ISC, WSS, D&H
Hyparrhenia hirta	IPC, WSS
Kikuyuochloa clandestina	USDA, CDFA, IPC, ISC, WSS, D&H
Leptochloa fuscas subsp. *fascicularis*	WSS, D&H
Leptochloa fusca subsp. *uninervia*	WSS, D&H
Muhlenbergia schreberi	ISC, WSS, D&H
Oryza rufipogon	USDA, CDFA, ISC, WSS, D&H
Panicum antidotale	CDFA, ISC, WSS, D&H
Panicum capillare	WSS, D&H
Panicum miliaceum	ISC, D&H
Panicum repens	ISC, D&H

Continued ▶

TABLE 33. *(continued)*
(See Note for Definitions)

Scientific Name	Organizations with Criteria Met
Paspalum dilatatum	WSS, D&H
Paspalum distichum	WSS, D&H
Paspalum vaginatum	IPC, WSS
Phalaris aquatica	IPC, ISC, WSS, D&H
Phalaris arundinacea	IPC, ISC, WSS
Phalaris minor	WSS, D&H
Phalaris paradoxa	WSS, D&H
Phleum pratense	IPC
Phragmites australis	ISC, D&H
Poa annua	IPC, WSS, D&H
Poa bulbosa	WSS, D&H
Poa pratensis	IPC, ISC, WSS, D&H
Polypogon interruptus	IPC, WSS
Polypogon monspeliensis	ISC, WSS, D&H
Rostraria cristata	D&H
Rottboellia cochinchinensis	USDA, WSS, D&H
Rytidosperma penicellatum	IPC
Saccharum ravennae	ISC, WSS
Schismus barbatus var. *arabicus*	IPC, ISC, WSS, D&H
Schismus barbatus var. *barbatus*	IPC, ISC, WSS, D&H
Secale cereale	ISC, WSS
Setaria faberi	CDFA, ISC, WSS, D&H
Setaria pumila	USDA, IPC, ISC, WSS, D&H
Setaria viridis	IPC, ISC, WSS, D&H
Sorghum bicolor	ISC, WSS, D&H
Sorghum halepense	USDA, CDFG, IPC, ISC, WSS, D&H
Spartina alterniflora	IPC, ISC, WSS, D&H
Spartina alterniflora x *foliosa*	ISC
Spartina x *anglica*	IPC, ISC, WSS
Spartina densiflora	IPC, ISC, WSS
Spartina patens	IPC, ISC, WSS
Sporobolus indicus	IPC, WSS, D&H
Stipa brachychaeta	CDFA, IPC, ISC, WSS, D&H
Stipa capensis	IPC, ISC, WSS
Stipa manicata	IPC
Stipa miliacea	IPC, ISC
Stipa tenuissima	CDFA, IPC
Zoysia spp.	IPC

Abbreviations and Criteria

CDFA = California Department of Food & Agriculture. The CDFA developed and maintains the state list of noxious weeds, ". . . any species of plant that is or is liable to be troublesome aggressive intrusive detrimental or destructive to agriculture silviculture or important native species and difficult to control or eradicate which the director by regulation designates to be a noxious weed." A = plants of limited distribution where eradication or containment are possible; entry into state prohibited. B = plants of limited distribution; eligible to enter state, but subject to regulation. C = plants usually widespread; eligible to enter state, but subject to regulation.

IPC = California Invasive Plant Council. "Plants were evaluated only if they invade California wildlands with native habitat values. The Inventory does not include plants found solely in areas of human-caused disturbance such as roadsides and cultivated agricultural fields." L = limited; ecological impacts minor on a statewide level. M = moderate; substantial, but not severe ecological impacts. H = high; severe ecological impacts. WL = watch list.

ISC = Invasive Species Council of California. "Develop and maintain a list of invasive species that have a reasonable likelihood of entering or have entered California for which an exclusion detection eradication control or management action by the state might be taken."

USDA = United States Department of Agriculture. A weed is "any plant that poses a major threat to agriculture and/or natural ecosystems within the United States." A noxious weed is "any plant or plant product that can directly or indirectly injure or cause damage to crops, including nursery stock or plant products livestock poultry or other interests of agriculture irrigation navigation the natural resources of the United States the public health or the environment." NW = noxious weed.

WSS = Weed Science Society of America. A weed is "any plant that is objectionable or interferes with the activities or welfare of man." The WSAA column should not be interpreted to mean that the society has determined that these grasses are weedy in California. I included it to show how often grasses that have been classed as weedy here exhibit that same life style elsewhere in the country.

And a Few More

In my wanderings around the state, I have encountered a few more weedy grasses that I think we should worry about:

AEGILOPS NEGLECTA. Three-awned goat grass. Its occurrence in California has been only recently confirmed. It has been misidentified as *Ae. triuncialis,* which also occurs in the state. I have seen major infestations in Shasta and Butte counties.

ARRHENATHERUM ELATIUS. Tall oat grass. Common along roadsides and in fields, especially in the northern half of the state.

DISTICHLIS SPICATA. Salt grass. We tend to think of this plant in terms of salt marshes, but it occurs in disturbed situations in all but nine counties, most of them in the Sierra Nevada.

ECHINOCHLOA ORYZOIDES. Early water grass. At first, this was a problem plant for rice growers in the Sacramento Valley. Now we find it in wet places from Modoc County south to Kern, Santa Barbara, and Imperial counties. And it is attractive.

ELYMUS ELYMOIDES. Squirreltail. Jepson (1923 to 1925) reported it from Southern California through the deserts to the Sierra Nevada and north to Siskiyou County. Now it is present in almost every county.

HORDEUM VULGARE. Barley. This escapes from cultivated fields and is planted for erosion control. It is an ephemeral roadside weed in most counties this side of the Cascade-Sierra Nevada axis.

LAMARCKIA AUREA. Goldentop. This distinctive and attractive weed ranges from Butte County south to San Diego County. Most of the several hundred collections in our herbaria are from Southern California.

MELINIS REPENS. Natal grass, ruby grass. This grass is known from only four counties in Southern California. I think that it is becoming more common. Of the 62 specimens in the Consortium of California Herbaria (ranging back to 1914), 46 have been collected since 2000.

PARAPHOLIS INCURVA. Curved sickle grass. As with salt grass, we tend to think of sickle grass as a creature of the coastal salt marshes. But it is also in the interior along roadsides, and it has invaded the Sacramento National Wildlife Refuge as well as other sites in the Central Valley, and it can also be found in the San Bernardino Mountains.

TRIBOLIUM OBLITERUM. Capetown grass. As its common name suggests, this grass is native to South Africa. It is well established in an area 4 miles in diameter at Fort Ord. It has been spreading and attempts to eradicate it have not been successful.

TRITICUM AESTIVUM. Bread wheat. Like barley, this crop escapes from cultivation and persists for a short time as a roadside weed. It occurs from Humboldt and Modoc counties in the north to San Diego and Imperial counties.

VENTENATA DUBIA. North Africa grass. We have very few collections of this grass in our herbaria, which does not provide an accurate reflection of its commonness. I have become obsessed with North Africa grass in recent years, but also very frustrated because when I find it in the field—and I have found it in many places—I am either too early or, more likely, too late in the season. In other words, it comes and goes rather quickly, which explains in part why we have so few specimens.

Selected References

California Department of Food and Agriculture. 2011. Encycloweedia: Data sheets. Available at www.cdfa.ca.gov.

California Invasive Plant Council. 2006. California Invasive Plant Inventory. 20 pp. Available at www.cal-ipc.org.

California Invasive Plant Council. 2007. "New Weeds Added to Cal-IPC Inventory." *Cal-IPC News* Spring 2007: 10.

California Invasive Plant Council. 2010. Watchlist. 7 pp.

DiTomaso, J. M. & E. A. Healy. 2007. *Weeds of California and Other Western States.* Vol. 2. *Geraniaceae–Zygophyllac*eae. Publ. No. 3488. Oakland: University of California, Agriculture & Natural Resources. Pp. 1004–1318.

United States Department of Agriculture. *Invasive and Noxious Weeds.* Available at http://plants.usda.gov.

Weed Science Society of America. 2010. *Composite List of Weeds.* Available at www.wssa.net.

TOXIC GRASSES

Because the grass family is the source of so many important food plants, it may come as a surprise to learn that it is also the home of a number of poisonous plants—those that can disrupt the normal state of health of the victim. Symptoms range from relatively mild skin irritations to death. In other words, toxic or poisonous plants are not just those that kill the victim. The victims of grass toxicity can be wild and domesticated animals, humans, and even other plants. Mechanisms of grass poisoning include plant parts (especially awns and sharp-pointed calluses) that cause mechanical injury, absorption of toxins from the soils that render the grass poisonous, and ingestion of one or more toxins synthesized by the grass itself or by a fungus that has infected the plant.

GRASS POLLEN ALLERGY. Millions of us are sensitive to grass pollen. Our immune system recognizes the protein in pollen as something foreign. This stimulates B cells in the body to reproduce and to form specific antibodies, which in turn attach themselves to the surface of tissues of the eyes, nose, and mouth. When grass pollen is next encountered, its protein is flagged for destruction by these antibodies. Specialized

TABLE 34. Grasses that cause pollen allergies

Scientific Name	Common Name
Alopecurus pratensis	meadow foxtail
Anthoxanthum odoratum*	sweet vernal grass
Arrhenatherum elatius	tall oat grass
Bromus hordeaceus	soft brome
Cynodon dactylon*	Bermuda grass
Cynosurus cristatus	crested dogtail
Dactylis glomerata*	orchard grass
Elymus repens	quack grass
Festuca perennis	rye grass
Holcus lanatus	velvet grass
Phleum pratense*	timothy
Poa annua	annual blue grass
Poa pratensis*	Kentucky blue grass
Secale cereale	rye
Sorghum halepense*	Johnson grass

* Major culprits.

cells rupture and release various inflammatory chemicals to fight the intruder, which cause the symptoms we experience. I discovered many years ago that I am allergic to some grasses, but not others, and that my immune system distinguishes subfamilies! Many of us would be able to verify the following list of symptoms from our own experiences: nasal congestion or running nose, coughing and wheezing, difficulty in breathing, sneezing, itchy, watery, swollen eyes, inflammation of sinuses, and sore throat.

MECHANICALLY INJURIOUS GRASSES. Some grasses are toxic only in the broadest sense because they are armed with structures, especially stout awns, that can cause mechanical injury. The sites of penetration, often around or in the eyes, snout, or soft parts of the mouth cavity, can become infected, which may cause further complications.

NITRATE-NITRITE INTOXICATION. Some grasses, especially cereal crops and agricultural weeds, are toxic because they absorb nitrates or nitrites or both from fertilizer-rich soils and then sequester it in the plant **body**. Symptoms appear abruptly and include weakness, incoordination, rapid respiration, and collapse. Death may occur within minutes.

CYANOGENIC GLYCOSIDES. Hundreds of plants in unrelated families make compounds called cyanogenic glycosides. As long as they remain intact in plant tissues, they are not of concern. However, chewing action, freezing and thawing cycles, wilting, and drought can all bring about enzymatic action that splits these glycosides into a sugar component and HCN (hydrogen cyanide or prussic acid). HCN is readily absorbed through the skin and is dangerous when inhaled. HCN poisons at the cellular level by blocking the release of oxygen from red blood cells. Symptoms of cyanide poisoning include instantaneous collapse (in large doses), weakness,

TABLE 35. Mechanically injurious grasses

Genus	Common Names
Awns	
Aristida spp.	three-awns
Avena fatua	wild oat
Bromus spp.	bromes
Hordeum spp.	barleys
Setaria spp.	foxtails, bristle grasses
Stipa spp.	needle grasses
Leaf margins	
Leersia spp.	cut grasses
Spartina spp.	cord grasses
Spines	
Cenchrus spp.	sandburs

giddiness, headache, nausea, vomiting, coma, and death from cellular asphyxiation.

PHOTOSENSITIZATION. Sensitive animals are poisoned when they eat grasses that contain certain pigments that react with sunlight to form toxins that can cause damage to their skin and underlying tissues. Liver damage may also be involved. The best-known non-grass example of this phenomenon in California is the Klamath weed or St. John's wort (*Hypericum perforatum*), a member of *Hypericaceae*.

GRASS TETANY. Also known as "grass staggers," this syndrome appears to be associated with ionic imbalances in the blood serum after animals have eaten large amounts of lush growth. Low magnesium levels are typical. Animals first show signs of excitement (tremors, nervousness, twitching), poor coordination, and refusal to eat. This is followed by cardiovascular involvement, convulsions, labored respiration, coma, and death within minutes to hours.

PHALARIS STAGGERS. This syndrome, named after the canary grasses *(Phalaris)* can cause a progressive neurological disorder in sheep and cattle. Afflicted animals exhibit hypersensitivity, rapid pulse, and a stiff-legged walk; they appear blind, cannot find water, do not feed properly, and eventually die from starvation, dehydration, or both. Tryptamine alkaloids are the toxic principles. A second sudden death syndrome has recently been described. *Phalaris* plants contain a compound that inhibits a ruminant's ability to metabolize nitrogen. This results in higher levels of ammonia in the blood, which can cause brain damage. Symptoms include wandering, uncoordinated gait, convulsions, coma, and death.

FUNGAL INFECTION OF GRASSES. Some of the best-known cases of poisoning from grasses in cattle and livestock are not caused by the grass

TABLE 36. Grasses that absorb nitrates and nitrites

Scientific Names	Common Names
Avena sativa	oat
Cenchrus americanus	pearl millet
Cenchrus purpureus	Napier grass
Cynodon spp.	Bermuda grasses
Echinochloa frumentacea	billion dollar grass
Festuca spp.	fescue, rye grasses
Hordeum jubatum	foxtail barley
Hordeum vulgare	barley
Sorghum spp.	sorghums
Triticum aestivum	bread wheat
Zea mays	maize, corn

itself, but by parasitic fungi that live on and in the plants. It is the fungus that makes the toxin. These fungi are the subject of much recent research, particularly those that infect fescue grasses. Perhaps 90 percent of the tall fescue *(Festuca arundinacea)* plants in the United States are affected.

The symptoms of "fescue foot" are those associated with gangrene. Ergot-like alkaloids cause constrictions in blood vessels that may lead to tissue death. Symptoms include loss of feet and the sloughing off of the tips of tails and ears. This is followed by weight loss, reduced milk production, and abortions.

TABLE 37. Grasses that produce HCN, hydrogen cyanide

Scientific Names	Common Names
Agrostis stolonifera	creeping bent grass
Andropogon spp.	bluestems
Avena sativa	oat
Bothriochloa spp.	Old World bluestems
Bouteloua gracilis	blue grama
Briza spp.	quaking grasses
Cortaderia spp.	pampas grasses
Cynodon spp.	Bermuda grass
Dactyloctenium aegyptium	Egyptian crowfoot
Eleusine coracana	African millet
Eleusine indica	goose grass
Elymus spp.	wild-ryes
Festuca perennis	perennial rye grass
Festuca spp.	fescues
Glyceria spp.	manna grasses
Holcus lanatus	velvet grass
Hordeum vulgare	barley
Lagurus ovatus	hare's tail
Lamarckia aurea	goldentop
Leptochloa dubia	green sprangletop
Oryza sativa	rice
Poa pratensis	Kentucky blue grass
Secale cereale	rye
Sorghum bicolor	sorghum
Sorghum halepense	Johnson grass
Triticum aestivum	bread wheat
Zea mays	maize, corn

ERGOTISM. I suspect that the most widely known example of fungal poisoning in grasses involves the ergot fungus, *Claviceps purpurea*. It infects rye *(Secale cereale),* one of the minor cereals. As part of its life cycle, the fungus makes a toxic beaked structure that replaces the grain. Notorious cases of poisoning in humans have been recorded through the centuries.

Ergot poisoning takes two distinct forms. In chronic or gangrenous

TABLE 38. Grasses that cause photosensitization

Scientific Names	Common Names
Avena sativa	oat
Cenchrus incertus	southern sandbur
Cynodon spp.	Bermuda grass
Echinochloa crus-galli	barnyard grass
Eriochloa contracta	prairie cup grass
Hordeum murinum	wall barley
Hordeum vulgare	barley
Secale cereale	rye
Setaria italica	foxtail millet
Sorghum spp.	sorghum
Triticum aestivum	bread wheat

TABLE 39. Grasses that cause tetany

Scientific Names	Common Names
Agropyron spp.	wheat grasses
Avena sativa	oat
Bromus spp.	bromes
Dactylis glomerata	orchard grass
Ehrharta longiflora	annual veldt grass
Elymus spp.	wild-ryes
Festuca perennis	perennial rye grass
Festuca spp.	fescues
Hordeum spp.	barleys
Lolium rigidum	annual rye grass
Phalaris spp.	Canary grasses
Phleum pratense	timothy
Polypogon monspeliensis	rabbit's foot grass
Secale cereale	annual rye
Triticum aestivum	bread wheat

ergotism, small amounts of contaminated grains are consumed over a long period of time. The ergot alkaloids cause constriction of blood vessels, death of tissues, and loss of extremities. In **acute** or convulsive ergotism, larger amounts are consumed more quickly and act on the central nervous system to produce a crawling sensation on the skin, tingling in the fingers, ringing in the ears, headache, vertigo, vomiting, diarrhea, hallucinations, painful muscular contractions (seizures similar to those in the severe form of epilepsy), and death. Not a pleasant sight.

Ergot-like alkaloids produced by related fungal species are the cause of "paspalum staggers" and "rye grass staggers." These have similar effects: increased nervousness, tremors, lack of coordinated movement, convulsions, which can lead to starvation, dehydration, and death.

TABLE 40. Grasses commonly infected by toxic fungi

Scientific Names	Common Names
Agropyron spp.	wheat grasses
Agrostis spp.	bent grasses
Andropogon spp.	bluestems
Cynodon spp.	Bermuda grass, star grasses
Elymus spp.	wild-ryes
Festuca spp.	fescues, rye grasses
Glyceria spp.	manna grasses
Hilaria spp.	tobosa, galleta
Holcus spp.	velvet grasses
Paspalum spp.	water grasses
Poa spp.	blue grasses
Sphenopholis spp.	wedge-scales

TABLE 41. Grasses commonly infected by the ergot fungus

Scientific Names	Common Names
Agrostis spp.	bent grasses
Bromus spp.	bomes
Dactylis glomerata	orchard grass
Elymus spp.	wild-ryes
Koeleria spp.	June grasses
Phalaris spp.	Canary grasses
Poa spp.	blue grasses
Secale cereale	rye
Sorghum spp.	sorghum

Selected References

Burrows, G. E. & R. J. Tyrl. 2001. "Poaceae." *In Toxic Plants of North America*. Ames, IA: Iowa State Univ. Press. Pp. 870–977. [The primary source of grasses listed in this section.]

Fuller, T. C. & E. McClintock. 1986. "Poaceae." *In Poisonous Plants of California*. Berkeley: University of California Press. Pp. 292–304.

Kingsbury, J. M. 1964. "Gramineae." *In Poisonous Plants of the United States and Canada*. Englewood Cliffs, NJ: Prentice-Hall. Pp. 475–500.

Wagstaff, D. J. 2008. *International Poisonous Plants Checklist: An Evidence-Based Reference*. Boca Raton, FL: CRC Press.

ETHNOBOTANICAL USES

"Ethnobotany" may be defined as the study of the interactions of people and plants, especially the use of plants by people **indigenous** to a particular area. The purpose of this section is to catalogue the grasses that were used by Native Americans, the part of the plant used, and for what purpose from the time they migrated into what we now call California about 12,000 to 15,000 years ago. These people built their villages, worked, and camped in the grasslands. It was there and in adjacent woodlands that Native Americans gathered seeds, fruits, and bulbs; domesticated plants and animals; and by the judicious use of fire managed and modified the landscape. This story is repeated many times around the world.

In studying this subject, I was not surprised to learn that Native Americans ate the seed-like grains of a number of California grasses. Their use of grass fibers in basketry and thatching is also well known. But I was certainly impressed by how many different species were utilized and in how many different ways.

TABLE 42. Grasses used by California's indigenous peoples

Scientific Name, Common Name	Grass Part Used	Ethnobotanical Use
Agropyron spp., crested wheat grass	grains	food
Agrostis spp., bent grass	grains	food
Alopecurus aequalis, meadow foxtail	grains	food
Anthoxanthum occidentale, vanilla grass	infusion of entire plant	medicine
Aristida spp., three-awn grass	grains	food
Arundo donax, giant reed grass	stems	construction, arrow shafts, flutes, clappers
Arundo donax, giant reed grass	young shoots	food
Avena barbata, slender wild oat	grains	food
Avena fatua, wild oat	grains	food
Avena sativa, cultivated oat	grains	food
Beckmannia syzigachne, American slough grass	grains	food
Briza minor, small quaking grass	grains	food
Briza minor, small quaking grass	spikelets	ornamentation
Bromus carinatus, California brome	grains	food

Continued ▶

TABLE 42. *(continued)*

Scientific Name, Common Name	Grass Part Used	Ethnobotanical Use
Bromus diandrus, ripgut grass	grains	food
Bromus hordeaceus, soft brome	grains	food
Bromus tectorum, downy brome	grains	food
Bromus spp., brome	grains	food
Calamagrostis nutkaensis, Pacific reed grass	grains	food
Cinna latifolia, wood reed grass	stems	baskets
Deschampsia danthonioides, annual hair grass	grains	food
Deschampsia elongata, slender hair grass	grains	food
Distichlis spicata, salt grass	leaves and stems	salt extracted by beating plants
Distichlis spicata, salt grass	leaves and stems	burned and ash used for flavoring
Distichlis spicata, salt grass	plant	brushing material and removing cactus spines
Echinochloa crus-galli, barnyard grass	grains	food
Elymus cinereus, Great Basin wild-rye	grains	food
Elymus condensatus, giant wild-rye	stems	arrow shafts
Elymus condensatus, giant wild-rye	stems	thatching, brush handles, knives, tobacco pipes
Elymus condensatus, giant wild-rye	grains	food
Elymus glaucus, blue wild-rye	grains	food
Elymus glaucus, blue wild-rye	plant	medicine to settle arguments
Elymus multisetus, big squirreltail	grains	food
Elymus trachycaulus, slender wheat grass	grains	food
Elymus triticoides, beardless wild-rye	grains	food
Elymus spp., wild-rye	stems	arrow shafts
Elymus spp., wild-rye	entire plants	thatching for houses
Elymus spp., wild-rye	grains	food, medicine
Eragrostis mexicana subsp. *virescens*, Chilean love grass	grains	food
Eragrostis secundiflora var. *oxylepis*, sand love grass	grains	food
Festuca temulenta, darnel	grains	food
Festuca spp., fescue	grains	food
Glyceria borealis, northern manna grass	grains	food
Glyceria spp., manna grass	grains	food

Scientific Name, Common Name	Grass Part Used	Ethnobotanical Use
Hilaria spp., galleta	stems	basketry
Holcus lanatus, velvet grass	spikelets	insect entrapment
Hordeum brachyantherum, meadow barley	grains	food
Hordeum murinum subsp. *glaucum,* blue foxtail	grains	food
Hordeum murinum subsp. *leporinum,* hare barley	grains	food
Hordeum vulgare, cultivated barley	grains	food
Hordeum spp., barley	grains	food
Hordeum spp., barley	entire plant	poultice for medicine
Melica bulbosa, onion grass	bulbs	food
Melica imperfecta, Coast Range melic	grains	food, ritual
Muhlenbergia rigens, deer grass	roots	food
Muhlenbergia rigens, deer grass	stems of flowering stalks	basketry
Muhlenbergia rigens, deer grass	leaves	cordage, women's skirts, cosmetic piercings
Panicum urvilleanum, desert panic grass	grains	food
Panicum spp., panic grass	grains	food
Phalaris spp., canary grass	grains	food
Phragmites australis, common reed	stems	arrow shafts
Phragmites australis, common reed	stems	pulverized for food
Phragmites australis, common reed	stems	warp, woof, and white patterns in basketry
Phragmites australis, common reed	stems	flutes, whistles, clappers, other instruments
Phragmites australis, common reed	stems and leaves	carrying nets, cordage, and snares
Phragmites australis, common reed	stems	tobacco pipes
Phragmites australis, common reed	stems	gambling sticks
Phragmites australis, common reed	stems	cut umbilical cord
Phragmites australis, common reed	stems	making hammocks for babies
Phragmites australis, common reed	stems	splints for broken limbs
Phragmites australis, common reed	stems	ground into flour, cooked into taffy-like food
Phragmites australis, common reed	leaves	baskets, mats, screens, thatching
Phragmites australis, common reed	leaves	carry tobacco

Continued ▶

TABLE 42. *(continued)*

Scientific Name, Common Name	Grass Part Used	Ethnobotanical Use
Phragmites australis, common reed	young shoots and leaves	boiled as potherb
Phragmites australis, common reed	honeydew, insect excreta	made into a sweet drink
Phragmites australis, common reed	entire plant	thatching for houses
Poa spp., blue grass	grains	food
Poa spp., blue grass	plant	blue-green dye used to color tattoos
Sporobolus airoides, alkali sacaton	grains	food
Sporobolus airoides, alkali sacaton	stems	foundation in basket weaving
Sporobolus spp., dropseed	stems	foundation material for coiled baskets
Stipa hymenoides, sand grass	grains	food
Stipa speciosa, desert needle grass	grains	food

Selected References

Anderson, M. K. 2007. "Native American Uses and Management of California's Grasslands." *In* M. R. Stromberg, J. D. Corbin, & C. M. D'Antonio (editors). *California Grasslands: Ecology and Management.* Berkeley: University of California Press. Pp. 57–66.

Baker, M. A. 1981. The Ethnobotany of the Yurok, Tolowa, and Karok Indians of Northwest California. Master of Arts thesis. Humboldt State University, Arcata, CA. 141 pp.

Bean, L. J. & K. S. Saubel. 1972. *Temalpakh (from the Earth): Cahuilla Indian Knowledge and Usage of Plants.* Banning, CA: Malki Museum.

Ebeling, W. 1986. *Handbook of Indian Foods and Fibers of Arid America.* Berkeley: University of California Press.

Hammett, J. E. & E. J. Lawlor. 2004. "Paleoethnobotany in California." *In* P. E. Minnis (editor). *People and Plants in Ancient Western North America.* Washington, DC: Smithsonian Books. Pp. 278–366.

Heizer, R. F. & A. B. Elasser. 1980. *The Natural World of the California Indians.* Berkeley: University of California Press.

Hendryx, M. 1991. *Plants and the People: The Ethnobotany of the Karuk Tribe.* Yreka, CA: Siskiyou County Museum.

Lightfoot, K. G. & O. Parrish. 2009. *California Indians and Their Environment.* Berkeley: University of California Press.

Mead, G. R. 1972. "The Ethnobotany of California Indians: A Compendium of the Plants, Their Users, and Their Uses." *Occ. Publ. Anthrop.* No. 30. Mus. Anthrop. Univ. Northern Colorado, Greeley.

Moerman, D. E. 1998. *Native American Ethnobotany.* Portland, OR: Timber Press.

Strike, S. S. 1994. *Ethnobotany of the California Indians.* Vol. 2. "Aboriginal uses of California's indigenous plants." Champaign, IL. Koeltz Scientific Books

Timbrook, J. 2007. *Chumash Ethnobotany: Plant Knowledge among the Chumash People of Southern California.* Santa Barbara and Berkeley: Santa Barbara Mus. Nat. Hist. & Heyday Books.

The Collection and Preparation of Grass Specimens

The principal reason for plant collecting is to provide permanent, representative specimens for identification, documentation, and further study. Many of these specimens will eventually become housed in an herbarium, a permanent collection of pressed and dried plant specimens. Here they will be examined by botanists and others interested in such matters as identification, distribution, blooming and fruiting times, general morphological features, anatomical details, chemical constituents, and even DNA analysis. Herbarium specimens are frequently loaned to experts doing monographic work and duplicates are often exchanged among herbaria.

Collecting Specimens

The goal is to collect and prepare a specimen that is as much like the living plant as possible, given the constraints of the pressing and drying techniques. Color may fade or change and three-dimensional forms are flattened, but a wealth of scientific information and even a certain aesthetic quality remain intact. Grasses make splendid specimens. Traditionally, grass keys and technical descriptions were based on pressed specimens.

Always keep in mind that the specimen you collect must be identified or confirmed. At some point, every grass key will ask you to determine whether a plant is an annual or a perennial, whether rhizomes are present or absent, the position of inflorescence branches, whether mature spikelets break apart above or below the glumes, and so on. Make it a standard practice to gather underground parts. Top-snatching is a dreadful habit. Roots and other underground plant parts should be cleaned carefully to remove soil or mud. I recommend that you collect specimens not only of grasses that appear to be at their peak of maturity, but also of those that are past that point. These older specimens will be useful in settling matters regarding disarticulation and caryopsis features.

A major problem facing the inexperienced collector is determining what constitutes enough plant material to make an acceptable specimen. In the case of small annual grasses, a specimen may not be a single plant, but a few to many, depending upon their size. A single larger annual plant or smaller perennial is usually sufficient. With experience comes the almost unconscious habit of deciding that a particular plant will make a suitable specimen because it will fit on an herbarium sheet of 12 in. × 18 in. Robust perennials, such as pampas grass and bamboos, must be sampled. Complete specimens are not practical.

EQUIPMENT. When collecting, I have the following items with me: a field press, plant press, plastic bags, digger, clippers, pocket knife, camera, notebook, and a GPS device. While none of them is essential, having the proper collecting gear close at hand can result in greater efficiency and better specimens. By a "digger," I mean a geologist's pick, a dandelion digger, a gardener's trowel, or even a large screwdriver.

Grasses will maintain well in plastic bags if you spray them with water, but they should be pressed as soon as possible. Pressing flattens the plants so that they do not curl or wrinkle, and it also brings the plant parts into direct contact with newspapers and indirect contact with blotters and corrugates, thereby beginning the drying process.

PLANT PRESSES. There are two types of plant presses. One is the temporary field press. It is usually small, lightweight, and easy to carry in a pack. You do not buy a field press. You make your own out of cardboard or press-board end pieces, newspapers, and perhaps a few blotters, held together by rope or a strap or belt. Those of you who are backpackers will find that you can accommodate an amazing number of plants in a small field press. Specimens will last for a few days in such a temporary press until you can transfer them to a regular press.

A standard plant press (12 in. × 18 in.) is too bulky and heavy to carry about in the field. Although you can construct your own, most of them are purchased, usually at great price, from one of the biological supply houses. A regular plant press has wooden or light metal end pieces called frames. Between the two frames is a series of blotters and corrugated cardboards.

FIELD DATA. At the same time that you focus on collecting and preparing high-quality specimens, it is critical that you take down the necessary field data. Without those data, the specimens are scientifically worthless. Data may be recorded in permanent notebooks carried into the field or written in temporary pocket notebooks. Either method has its advantages and disadvantages. The important point, however, is to write down your field data as you obtain it, rather than relying on your memory.

The collection site is probably the single most important element of the field data. This should be as precise as possible. I suggest the following sequence:

- country/state
- county or parish
- latitude and longitude (or similar system)
- reference to a more or less permanent location, such as a town, highway, or river, particularly, one that can be found on generally available maps

Quadrangle names, tier, range and section coordinates, and latitude/longitude are found on topographic maps available from the United States Geological Survey and various websites. Some of this information may also be found on U.S. Forest Service and Bureau of Land Management maps. Hand-held GPS devices allow for very accurate site data.

Other information that you should collect includes:

- habitat (vegetation type, associated species, geology of the site, soil type, etc.)
- elevation
- remarks on the frequency of the plant at that site
- remarks on the plant itself (size, color, odor, etc.)
- date
- your personal collection number for that plant specimen

Pressing Specimens

To press a specimen, first place it in a single fold of newspaper. One of the most common errors is to assume that if a single fold of newspaper is good, then an entire section will be just that much better. All you accomplish by having several layers of wet newsprint is to retard the drying process. Tabloid newspapers 11 in. x 17 in. are just the right size. If you use a full-sized newspaper, then tear it down the middle to yield two single-fold sections. Do not exceed this size or the plant specimens may not fit on the herbarium sheet. Do not use slick, clay-finish paper from magazines or catalogues because that paper will not absorb moisture.

Annuals and small perennials fit nicely in the newspaper and present no particular problem. But some grasses are too tall to be accommodated properly. If the problem is mainly one of height, consider folding the plant. This works well if it is no more than about half a meter tall. Fold the plant in such a way that the parts do not obscure one another. Too much bulk may also impair proper drying. Make sharp bends, not gently rounded ones. These may be held in place during the drying process by using *flexostats*, invented by the eminent agrostologist Richard W. Pohl. You can make your own by cutting an index card or similar material into segments about 4 cm × 8 cm. Cut a slit about 3 cm long in each and slip the folded "knee" of the plant through the opening. After the plant has dried, remove the flexostats and reuse them. Still larger grasses may be subdivided into two or more sections. Such a suite of specimens is often the most practical method of collecting larger grasses. One of my collections of *Saccharum ravennae* from Yolo County required six mounted specimens to do it justice.

It is important that you put only one kind of plant inside the single fold of newspaper. The collection number for that particular plant should be written prominently along one margin. This label will assist you later in sorting material and in finding a particular specimen. After you have labeled the specimen, you can arrange and trim the plant parts. Leaves and stems should be positioned so that they do not overlap unnecessarily. Specimen quality can often be improved by some judicious pruning of excess bulk. This is also a good time to remove the dirt, mud, and insects trapped in the roots, which can ruin the specimen and label if allowed to remain.

Blotters (B) and **corrugated** cardboard (C) are often arranged in one of two sequences: C-B-B-C or C-B-B-B-C. In the first plan, a specimen (S) in a single fold of newspaper is inserted between the two blotters, to form the arrangement C-B-S-B-C. In the second option, two specimens are inserted: C-B-S-B-S-B-C. I have found the second option particularly useful for collecting grasses.

Finally, close the plant press by tightening the straps, belts, or ropes. It must be cinched tight enough to flatten the specimens and bring them into firm contact with the pressing materials. Presses will loosen as plants dry, so they need to be tightened from time to time.

Drying Specimens

Once plants have been put into the press, they must be dried. Presses may be left out in the sunlight or they may be strapped into rooftop racks on automobiles, much to the curiosity and amusement of fellow motorists. But the usual method is to put the plant press in an electric or steam drier.

The plants should remain in the drier until they are dry and no longer. The length of time will depend upon the kind of drier, the plants collected, the arrangement of pressing materials, and how many other presses are in the drier. While 24–48 hours is often sufficient for most grasses, it is critical to check the presses. Are the newspapers still slightly damp? Does the plant still feel and smell wet? Will your thumbnail leave an impression in a stem? If the answer is "yes" to any of these questions, then the plant needs to remain in the drier. If you take the plant out too soon, it will mold. If, however, the plant is dried too long, it will discolor badly and become very brittle. Remember to check and tighten the straps periodically.

Making Labels

If specimens are to be deposited in an herbarium, they must be accompanied by labels that give the pertinent collection data for each plant. Labels should be made from high-quality paper, preferably 100 percent rag content bond paper. Most herbaria supply this paper to collectors. Label information should be typed or word processed. Permanent ink is an acceptable alternative. Do not use ballpoint pen or soft lead pencil. Labels should provide at least the following information: scientific name of the plant, location data, date of collection, your name, and your collection number for the specimen. The simplest numbering scheme is to assign the number 1 to your first collection and to use a new number for each different collection.

Dates should be presented as 12 March 1979 or March 12, 1979, not 3-12-79. In the last example, was the grass collected on March 12 or December 3, in 1979 or 1879? Use your first name or initials, not just your last name, unless you are Carolus Linnaeus, A. S. Hitchcock, Willis Linn Jepson, Asa Gray, or some other equally famous departed botanist. Put the collection number beside your name.

In addition to these essential elements, you may also wish to provide habitat data, along with commentary on the plant itself. Once completed, slip the label inside the newspaper with the plant specimen. Do not glue, tape, or staple either the plant or the label to the newspaper. Both will eventually be removed and mounted on an herbarium sheet for permanent reference.

Here is what a finished label might look like.

HUMBOLDT STATE UNIVERSITY HERBARIUM

Avena barbata Link

California. Humboldt Co. N40.231, W–123.871. Along Salmon Creek Road, 3.4 miles from its junction with U. S. 101. Roadside. Elevation 667 ft.

J. P. Smith & J. O. Sawyer 13,117   23 April 2011

IDENTIFYING GRASSES

I have just made out my first grass, Hurrah, Hurrah! . . . it is a great discovery. I never expected to make out a grass in all my life, so Hurrah! It has done my stomach surprising good.

Charles Darwin, in an 1855 letter to his old friend, Sir Joseph Dalton Hooker

Perhaps the easiest way to identify an unknown grass is to take your specimens to an expert who will name them for you. Unfortunately, such individuals are increasingly rare. Another possibility is the "leaf method." You leaf through a picture book or website until you find an illustration that seems to match your plant. The beautiful drawings in the two grass volumes of the *Flora of North America North of Mexico* come immediately to mind. CalFlora, CalPhoto, and the Plants Database provide photographs. However, the standard method for identifying an unknown is to use a dichotomous key.

Dichotomous Keys

A key is a series of paired statements that describe various aspects of the plants being treated. Because you are presented with paired statements, it is called a dichotomous key (from the Greek, meaning in two + to cut). Such statements may be simple or complex, long or short, employ a combination of floral and vegetative features or be restricted to statements relating to a particular aspect of the plants, such as leaf features. Each statement is called a lead; the two leads together constitute a couplet. The leads of a couplet are written in such a way that they are parallel, exclusive and contrasting statements, as in this example:

1a   Inflorescence subtended by 5–10 bristles; spikelets 1–2 mm long; florets 2.. ***Kikuyuochloa***
1b   Inflorescence not subtended by bristles; spikelets 6–10 mm long; florets 3–5 .... ***Sclerochloa***

In a well-written key, your unknown specimen will fit under only one of those choices. You decide in each case which of the two statements best describes the unknown grass; this will determine a pathway through a series of subsequent couplets.

Here are a few suggestions that I hope will make keys a little easier to use, perhaps minimizing the veracity of the old claim that, "Keys are written by people who don't need them, for people who can't use them."

- Make sure that you are using the right key. It is both a waste of time and an embarrassment to spend several hours attempting to identify a plant in the wrong key. A key to the native grasses of California will be of limited assistance in identifying a roadside weed.
- Check to see if there is a glossary. Authors vary in their use of certain terms and you will have to get used to the eccentricities of the writer.
- Read the key very carefully. Much frustration results from misreading. There is a world of difference in the meaning of "and" and "or." They are not interchangeable.
- Watch for weasel words, such as "mostly" and "usually." We use these words when we do not want to be pinned down.
- Read both leads of the couplet before making your decision. The first lead may sound reasonably good, but the second lead may be perfect.
- Do not base your decision on a single observation, particularly when you are asked about measurements.
- If you are not confident about which lead to take, try them both. One pathway should get you into difficulty fairly quickly.
- If neither lead seems to make any sense at all, you have probably made an error and should not be at that couplet. Go back a step or two and look more carefully.
- If one side of a dichotomy will take you to a relatively small number of plants, check out their descriptions or look at drawings. This additional information may be helpful. Also, as you gain more knowledge, you will be able to eliminate certain leads because they take you to plants that you know.
- Learn to weigh the relative values of characters used in keys. Features of reproductive structures tend to be more important than those of plant height, for instance.
- Do not assume that a key says something that it does not. In the second lead below, the author has not said that the spikelets are awnless.
  1a Plant annual; spikelets awned
  1b Plants perennial
- Verify your determination. Check it against a technical description, illustration, or specimen.

Spikelet Dissection

At some point as you work your way through a key, you will be required to dissect grass spikelets. The plants may be living material or may be pressed, dried, and months or even years old. The authors of most grass keys assume that you are working with pressed specimens. The very first professional taxonomist that I met was horrified when I showed up with living material. He worked only with dried specimens. Luckily, grasses not only retain their essential taxonomic characters in the dried state, but in some instances the dried specimens are superior to living plants for identification because some surface features become more evident when dried.

You will need a good hand lens, or better yet a dissecting microscope. Invest in a pair of decent dissecting needles. I recommend purchasing two dissecting needles, often available at college bookstores, and replacing the needles themselves with sewing machine needles. These typically come to a much finer point than the store-bought dissecting variety. I also recommend a microscalpel blade if you can purchase one. It will be useful in separating spikelet parts from one another. Also buy a reasonably expensive pair of forceps or tweezers; the inexpensive ones do not have the fine tip you will need, they are often bent, and the two tips frequently do not match. Keying is difficult enough without the frustration that comes from poor equipment.

Dried spikelets can be softened and made quite pliable by soaking them in a drop or two of a softening agent. My favorite was called "pohlstoffe" after its inventor, Richard W. Pohl. The recipe is 1 percent Aerosol OT (a brand name for dioctyl sodium sulfosuccinate or docusate sodium), 74 percent distilled water, and 25 percent methyl alcohol. The liquid is applied directly to the plant part. Let it soak in for about 30 seconds. Pohlstoffe leaves no residue. It is also excellent for cleaning lenses and glasses.

A Confession

I do not want to discourage you, but you will not be able to identify every grass that you run through the key in this book or any other, for that matter. Let us stipulate that your unknown grass is included in the key. Here are the potential problems. Your plant is too immature or too old to show you the features used in the key, or you may have top-snatched it so that annual versus perennial or rhizomes-stolons present or absent cannot be determined. Furthermore, you are dealing with living plants that exhibit biological variation. Your plant may be unusually large or stunted, so its spikelet size does not quite fit the description; its lemmas are awned, but they are not "supposed" to be. It seems to have the characters of two species—which may very well be the case because it is a hybrid, and the family is notorious for this phenomenon. I was told a wonderful story about Agnes Chase of the Smithsonian Institution and Ledyard Stebbins of the University of California at Davis. Both were acknowledged experts on grasses. Chase is reported to have said, "Oh, Ledyard, every time you can't identify a grass, you claim that it is a hybrid!"

We also have to admit that the fault might lie with you or me. You misread the key or you were sloppy in your observations or measurements. Or I may be the culprit by constructing key steps that simply do not work properly or by describing the plants incorrectly.

Grass Collections in California

Once you have identified an unknown grass or want to confirm what you believe it to be, check it against technical descriptions and illustrations, or better yet, look at herbarium specimens. An herbarium is a collection of pressed and dried plant specimens, typically stored in metal cases and arranged alphabetically or according to some system of classification. The same term is applied to the room(s) or building(s) that house these specimens. We are blessed here in California in having several world-class herbaria where literally millions of specimens are deposited. Our three largest collections are found at the University of California at Berkeley, at the California Academy of Sciences in Golden Gate Park in San Francisco, and at the Rancho Santa Ana Botanic Garden in Claremont. Other significant grass collections are housed at the University of California at Davis, Humboldt State University in Arcata, and the California Department of Food and Agriculture in Sacramento. A number of other local and regional herbaria, perhaps closer to you, are listed in *Index Herbariorum* (http://sweetgum.nybg.org/ih/).

Selected References

- The most current comprehensive treatment of California grasses will be found in *The Jepson Manual: Vascular Plants of California,* second edition (TJM2) (Baldwin et al. 2012).
- All California grasses are also covered in volumes 24 and 25 of the *Flora of North America North of Mexico* (Barkworth et al. 2003, 2007). The illustrations are beautiful, but this is a full-fledged technical flora and it can be more than a little intimidating. A one-volume condensed edition is also available.
- I still find the classical *Manual of the Grasses of the United States* by A. S. Hitchcock (revised by Agnes Chase) very useful.
- The Consortium of California Herbaria (http://ucjeps.berkeley .edu/consortium/) gives you access to distribution maps and label information for over 1 million specimens deposited in California's major plant collections.
- The United States Department of Agriculture's *Plants Database* (http://plants.usda.gov/java/) allows you to track plant names, see

illustrations and photographs, and see state- and county-level distribution maps.

- Similar information is available on a CD-ROM in the *Synthesis of the North American Flora* by Kartesz and Meacham (1999). A new edition is in preparation.

- A very useful treatment of our weedy grasses is found in *Weeds of California and Other Western States*, volume 2 (2007), by J. M. DiTomaso and E. A. Healy.

- CalFlora (www.calflora.org) and CalPhotos (http://calphotos .berkeley.edu/flora/) are sources of photographs.

- Visit the Humboldt State University Herbarium website (www .humboldt.edu/herbarium) for additional information on California grasses and the grass flora of the conterminous United States.

THE SUBFAMILIES AND TRIBES OF CALIFORNIA GRASSES

Plant families may be subdivided into subfamilies, and subfamilies into tribes. The internal classification of the grass family remains a very active focus of research, but significant differences in the interpretation of data exist. Recent molecular data have been very helpful in some instances, but less so in others. The system of subfamilies and tribes that I will summarize in this chapter is based largely on conclusions reached by the Grass Phylogeny Working Group (2001), Barkworth (2007), and Soreng et al. (2012).

Subfamily *Aristidoideae*

This subfamily is represented in North America by the single genus *Aristida* (three-awn grass). Its 1-flowered spikelets led early workers to put it in the same tribe as *Agrostis*, the bent grasses, along with many others with similar spikelets. Other work suggested that the genus might be allied to the giant reed grass *(Arundo)*. Recent research has shown that alliance to be untenable, and the three-awn grasses do not appear to be very closely related to grasses in any other group. The solution now widely accepted: put the genus in its own subfamily.

SUBFAMILY *ARISTIDOIDEAE:* AN OVERVIEW

HABIT Annual or perennial herbs

INFLORESCENCE An open to contracted panicle of few to many spikelets

SPIKELET 1-flowered, cylindric to laterally compressed; typically with a 3-parted awn (lateral branches sometimes reduced or absent)

FLOWER Stamens 1 or 3; stigmas 2 (red or brown)

DISTRIBUTION Temperate, subtropical, and tropical; often of drier sites

OUR REPRESENTATIVES 1 tribe (*Aristideae*) *Aristida*

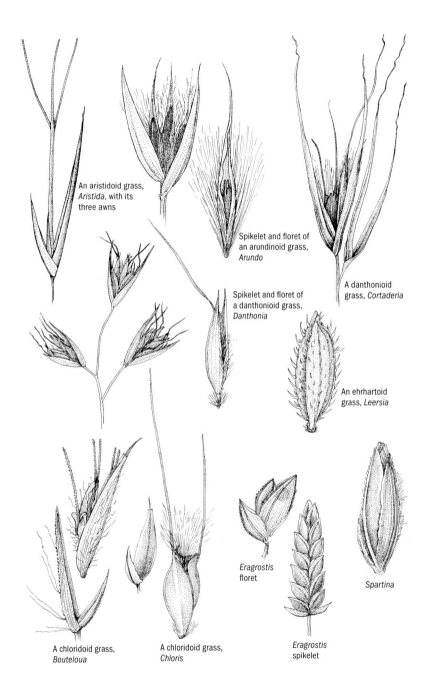

An aristidoid grass, *Aristida*, with its three awns

Spikelet and floret of an arundinoid grass, *Arundo*

Spikelet and floret of a danthonioid grass, *Danthonia*

A danthonioid grass, *Cortaderia*

An ehrhartoid grass, *Leersia*

A chloridoid grass, *Bouteloua*

A chloridoid grass, *Chloris*

Eragrostis floret

Eragrostis spikelet

Spartina

Figure 13. Survey of spikelets and florets in subfamilies *Aristidoideae*, *Arundinoideae*, *Danthonioideae*, *Ehrhartoideae*, and *Chloridoideae*.

Subfamily *Arundinoideae*

It is difficult to provide a general description of the arundinoid grasses. Unfortunately, recent molecular studies have not clarified the matter. The circumscription used here is a narrow one, with all of our North American grasses belonging to a single tribe. Others would interpret the subfamily much more broadly to include the three-awn grasses (*Aristida*), the poverty-oats *(Danthonia)*, and their allies.

SUBFAMILY *ARUNDINOIDEAE:* AN OVERVIEW

HABIT Cane-like, reed-like, or bamboo-like; sometimes perennial herbs

INFLORESCENCE Typically a conspicuous terminal, **plumose** panicle

SPIKELET 1- to several-flowered; upper florets often reduced; in a few, the lower ones unisexual

FLOWER Bisexual or unisexual; stamens 3 [6]; stigmas 2, often densely and minutely plumose

DISTRIBUTION Cosmopolitan, especially southern hemisphere, often of wet sites

OUR REPRESENTATIVES 1 tribe (*Arundineae*) *Arundo* and *Phragmites*

Subfamily *Bambusoideae*

Grasses of this subfamily are typically woody perennials from extensive rhizomes. They range from a few centimeters to more than 40 m tall and can be almost 25 cm in diameter, with internodes that can reach up to 1.5 m long. Leaves on axillary branches have false petioles, while those of the stem itself are typically without blades or fall early. Bamboos produce large, many-flowered panicles, subtended by a few to several bracts. A common error is to assume that any really large grass with what appear to be woody stems must be a bamboo, as in the giant reed grass (*Arundo donax*). But the mature leaves of the *A. donax* that sheath the main stems and its terminal inflorescence tell you instantly that it cannot be a bamboo.

The economic uses of bamboos are almost endless. They include ornamentals and building materials for houses, furniture, ships, aqueducts, carts, umbrella frames, bird cages, tiger cages, chop sticks, musical instruments, springs for carts, food, fibers, cordage, oars, masts, baskets, mats, spear shafts, bows, arrows, knives, ladders, rafts, pails, churns, curtains, tiles for roofs, beehives, fans, fishing poles, medicine ... and several hundred more products.

HABIT Mostly perennial; stems woody (ours) or herbaceous; leaf blades with false petioles

INFLORESCENCE Spikes, racemes, or panicles

SPIKELET Bisexual or unisexual; 1- to many-flowered; glumes 2–5; awned or awnless, breaking apart above the glumes and between the florets

FLOWER Stamens 3, 6, or more; stigmas 3

DISTRIBUTION Asia, Africa, the Americas, and the islands of the Pacific and Indian oceans; abundant in the tropics; absent from Europe; mostly in forests, woodlands, and wet places

OUR REPRESENTATIVES 1 tribe (*Bambuseae*) *Phyllostachys* is clearly naturalized; *Bambusa* and *Pseudosasa* have been reported, but have not been collected in recent years

Subfamily *Chloridoideae*

Chloridoid grasses resemble fescues and bromes in their general spikelet structure and the panic grasses in many of their more technical features. Although there is universal acceptance of the subfamily itself, there is significant disagreement as to its internal classification. It is an area of active research. Many authors recognize two large tribes and several smaller ones. Others argue that the two large tribes are artificial assemblages and should be merged into one large tribe; this is the view that I have tentatively adopted. Distinguishing features are highlighted in the key below.

Key to Tribes

1a Plants sticky; leaf sheaths and blades not clearly differentiated; ligule absent .... ***Orcuttieae***
1b Plants not sticky; leaf sheaths and blades clearly differentiated; ligule present **2**
2a Florets 1 per spikelet; lemmas 1- or 3-veined; seeds falling free from fruit wall ....***Zoysieae***
2b Florets 2 or more per spikelet; lemmas typically 3-veined; seeds not falling free ....***Cynodonteae***

TRIBE CYNODONTEAE. Annuals or perennials. Inflorescence a panicle, spike-like raceme, spike, digitate, or even reduced to a single spikelet.

Spikelets typically bisexual, laterally compressed, 1- to many-flowered; lemmas 1- or 3-veined, or 7- to 13-veined. Our representatives: *Acrachne, Blepharidachne, Bouteloua, Chloris, Cynodon, Dactyloctenium, Dasyochloa, Dinebra, Distichlis, Eleusine, Eragrostis, Erioneuron, Eustachys, Hilaria, Leptochloa, Muhlenbergia, Munroa, Schedonnardus, Scleropogon, Swallenia,* and *Tridens.*

TRIBE ORCUTTIEAE. Grasses of this tribe lack clearly differentiated blades and sheaths, and the spikelets in two of the genera are spirally inserted, a very rare feature in the family. The plants are more or less restricted to vernal pools and similar habitats. Seven of the nine species that comprise *Orcuttieae* are endemic to California. No other tribe of North American grasses is similarly restricted. Caution! Do not collect these grasses. All of them are both state- and federally listed as endangered or threatened. Our representatives: *Neostapfia, Orcuttia,* and *Tuctoria.*

TRIBE ZOYSIEAE. Grasses of this tribe are often found in saline habitats; spikelets 1-flowered, usually laterally compressed; lemmas awnless; and except for *Zoysia,* the fruit wall is not fused to the seed and falls free, so that the fruit is an achene. Our representatives: *Crypsis, Spartina, Sporobolus,* and *Zoysia.*

SUBFAMILY *CHLORIDOIDEAE*: AN OVERVIEW

HABIT Annual or perennial herbs; stem internodes hollow or solid

INFLORESCENCE Panicles, often 1-sided racemes or spikes

SPIKELET 1- to several-flowered; lemmas typically 3-veined, sometimes only 1-veined

FLOWER Stamens 3; stigmas 2

DISTRIBUTION Tropical and subtropical regions, especially of the Old World; particularly in arid and semiarid situations of high light intensity; best represented on this continent in the American Southwest

OUR REPRESENTATIVES See the tribe descriptions for representatives of this subfamily

---

Subfamily *Danthonioideae*

The danthonioid grasses are centered in the southern hemisphere and not well represented in our North American grass flora. When C. E. Hubbard originally described the group in 1948, he created it from genera traditionally assigned to the oat tribe, *Aveneae.* A combination of embryo features, **ciliate** ligules, and a particular photosynthetic pathway define the group. Danthonioid grasses combine features found in the arundinoid, fescucoid, and panicoid subfamilies.

SUBFAMILY *DANTHONIOIDEAE:* AN OVERVIEW

HABIT Annuals to **caespitose** perennials, reed-like in *Cortaderia*; stem internodes often solid

INFLORESCENCE Panicle, sometimes reduced to a raceme or a single spikelet

SPIKELET Glumes longer than the florets, 2- to many-flowered; laterally compressed; breaking apart above the glumes

FLOWER Stamens 3; stigmas 2

DISTRIBUTION Temperate, especially southern hemisphere; only *Danthonia* native to North America

OUR REPRESENTATIVES 1 tribe (*Danthonieae*): *Cortaderia, Danthonia, Rytidosperma, Schismus,* and *Tribolium*

Subfamily *Ehrhartoideae*

Until the mid-1990s, the core of what we now call the ehrhartoid grasses was comprised of rice and its close relatives, and it was called *Oryzoideae*, after *Oryza* (rice). The subfamily was clearly allied to the bamboos and to a little-known tribe that contained the veldt grasses *(Ehrharta)*. Recent studies, particularly at the molecular level, have confirmed their close evolutionary relationship.

Key to Tribes

1a   Plants of dry to moist sites; spikelets with 3 florets, the 2 lower ones
     sterile and the upper fertile ....***Ehrharteae***
1b   Plants aquatic; spikelets with a single well-developed floret
     .... ***Oryzeae***

TRIBE EHRHARTEAE. Terrestrial annuals or perennials. Inflorescence a panicle or 1-sided raceme. Spikelets terete or laterally compressed; glumes 2, shorter or longer than the florets; lemmas 5- to 7-veined. Our sole representative: *Ehrharta.*

TRIBE ORYZEAE. Aquatic annuals or perennials. Inflorescence typically a panicle; spikelets bisexual or unisexual, with what appears at least to be a single fertile floret. Our representatives: *Leersia* and *Oryza; Zizania,* a crop, sometimes escapes from fields, but does not seem to persist.

HABIT Herbaceous annuals and perennials, terrestrial or aquatic

INFLORESCENCE Panicles, racemes, or spikes

SPIKELET 1- or 3-flowered, bisexual or unisexual, laterally compressed or terete; glumes 2, reduced or absent; lemma 5- to several-veined; palea 0- to 5-veined

FLOWER Stamens 6, 3, or 1 (6 and 1 are uncommon numbers in the family); stigmas 1 or 2

DISTRIBUTION Marshy and aquatic sites, especially of the tropics and subtropics

OUR REPRESENTATIVES See the tribe descriptions for representatives of this subfamily

Subfamily *Panicoideae*

The English botanist Robert Brown was the first to recognize this subfamily of grasses in the 19ᵗʰ century. The concept and limits of this group have changed little through the years, unlike those of his other great subfamily of more temperate grasses (the festucoids). Panicoid grasses are centered in the tropical and subtropical regions of the world. If G. Ledyard Stebbins was correct in his observation that grasses are the most advanced of the flowering plants, then panicoid grasses may well be the most advanced of the most advanced.

Key to Tribes

1a   Lower glume shorter than the upper one or absent; upper floret evident, at least as long as the upper glume; fertile lemma leathery to hard...**Paniceae**

1b   Glumes typically ± equal in length; upper and lower florets concealed within the glumes; fertile lemma transparent to membranous ....**Sacchareae**

TRIBE PANICEAE. Inflorescence a panicle or a series of racemose or spicate branches that bear racemes or spikes of spikelets. Lower glume short, sometimes missing; upper glume and sterile lemma both membranous and soft; fertile floret **indurate** or leathery. Spikelets or clusters of them sometimes subtended by bristly or spiny **involucres.** Caution! In spikelets where the lower glume is much reduced or absent, it is easy to misinterpret the spikelet structure, especially when the sterile lemma of the

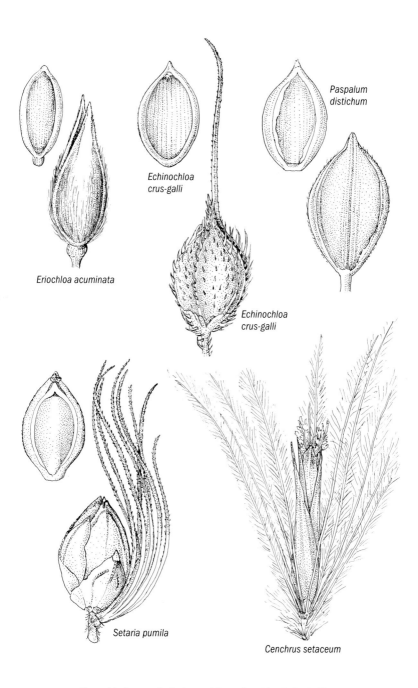

Figure 14. Survey of spikelets and florets in subfamily *Panicoideae*

lower floret is glume-like. The spikelet will appear to be 1-flowered. Our representatives: *Axonopus, Cenchrus, Digitaria, Echinochloa, Eriochloa, Kikuyuochloa, Melinis, Panicum, Paspalum, Setaria, Stenotaphrum,* and *Urochloa.*

TRIBE SACCHAREAE. Stems and leaves often reddish or purplish. Inflorescence a series of paired spikelets (rames), evenly or unevenly pedicellate; stalked spikelet often reduced and sometimes absent. Spikelets 2-flowered, the lower sterile or staminate and the upper bisexual, awnless or awned from fertile lemma, the awn often easily disarticulating. Glumes thick, firm, equal in length. Fertile lemma and palea thin.

Caution! An important diagnostic feature of this tribe is the series of paired spikelets along a central axis or a branch. This pairing will not be evident when the pedicellate spikelet is highly reduced; it is even harder to discern when it is absent. Look carefully for **vestigial** spikelets, especially if a sessile spikelet always seems to be accompanied by a hairy stalk. Our representatives: *Andropogon, Bothriochloa, Heteropogon, Hyparrhenia, Imperata, Miscanthus, Rottboellia, Saccharum, Schizachyrium,* and *Sorghum; Zea* escapes from cultivation, but does not persist. This tribe has been called *Andropogoneae* for many years.

SUBFAMILY *PANICOIDEAE:* AN OVERVIEW

HABIT Mostly herbaceous grasses, although sometimes robust; internodes often solid

INFLORESCENCE Panicles, compound racemes, rames, and spikes

SPIKELET Dorsally compressed, sometimes flat on one side and rounded on the other or terete, breaking apart below the glumes; 2-flowered; glumes 2, 1, or 0; 1 terminal bisexual floret and a staminate or neuter one below it

FLOWER Stamens 3; stigmas 2

DISTRIBUTION Diverse habitats, abundant in the tropics and subtropics; absent from the Arctic

OUR REPRESENTATIVES See the tribe descriptions for representatives of this subfamily

---

Subfamily *Poöideae*

Subfamily *Poöideae,* called *Festucoideae* in the older literature, was recognized by all of the classical workers, but in a much broader sense than we now see it defined. It has always been viewed as the great grouping of temperate and cool climate grasses. Not surprisingly, most California grasses belong here. The number of tribes and their limits remains a lively debate.

When I was a student, the grasses known to occur in the United States were accommodated in two subfamilies, *Festucoideae* and *Panicoideae*. The concept of the subfamily *Panicoideae* survived more or less intact through the decades. The same cannot be said for *Festucoideae*. Six sub-families have been segregated from it with little or no controversy. What remains unsettled is how to deal with the limits of the remaining tribes, in particular the recognition of tribes in the *Poöideae*, as the subfamily is now called. Hitchcock (1951) needed only four tribes for our grasses. Recent treatments have called for as many as 11. Barkworth (2007) and Soreng et al. (2012) put them in six, with the latter recognizing a number of subtribes.

TRIBE BRACHYPODIEAE. Our representative: *Brachypodium*. This genus shares several features with the brome grasses *(Bromus)*. It differs from them in chromosome size and number, and in its nucleic acid content.

TRIBE BROMEAE. Our representative: *Bromus*. In addition to a series of technical features, what sets the these grasses apart is their hairy ovary with an apical appendage and lateral styles.

TRIBE HORDEEAE. Annuals or perennials. Leaf blades usually with well-developed auricles. Inflorescence a balanced spike or rame, its axis remaining intact or breaking apart at maturity. Spikelets commonly 1–3 per node, sometimes as many as 8. Lemmas 5- to 9-veined, awned from the tip or awnless. Caryopsis free from the palea and lemma or adhering to them. Promiscuity and polyploidy are rampant in these grasses. This group was called *Hordeae* in older literature and, more recently, *Triticeae*. Our representatives: *Aegilops, Agropyron,* X *Elyhordeum, Elymus, Hordeum, Secale,* and *Triticum.*

While there is general agreement as to the circumscription of the tribe, defining genera is another matter. *"Abandon hope all ye who enter here"* was the advice offered by Dante Alighieri, writing admittedly on an unrelated, but similarly distressing, topic. Generic delimitations often appear quite arbitrary. To give you some flavor for the difference of opinion as to how to treat this group, G. Ledyard Stebbins, the pre-eminent student of grass evolution, recommended placing all of our North American grasses of this tribe into a single genus. The most liberal alternative would accord generic recognition to each distinct chromosome set or combination of sets, which yields a very large num-ber of segregate genera that are all but impossible to distinguish using traditional morphological characters. Others, myself included, favor a less drastic intermediate solution. I follow Estes & Tyrl (1982) and other recent authors in accepting six genera and in adopting an expanded view of *Elymus.*

TRIBE MELICEAE. Perennials, typically of wet sites. Leaf sheaths closed for all or most of their length. Inflorescence a panicle or raceme. Spikelets several-flowered, laterally compressed, breaking apart above or below the

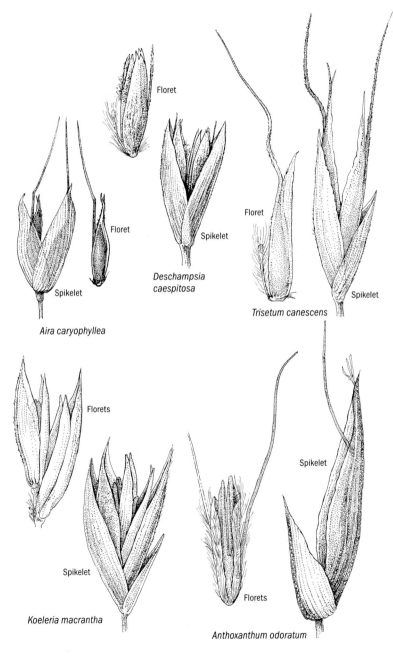

Floret

Spikelet

Aira caryophyllea

Floret

Spikelet

*Deschampsia
caespitosa*

Floret

Spikelet

Trisetum canescens

Florets

Spikelet

Koeleria macrantha

Spikelet

Florets

Anthoxanthum odoratum

Figure 15. Survey of spikelets and florets in subfamily *Poöideae*-I

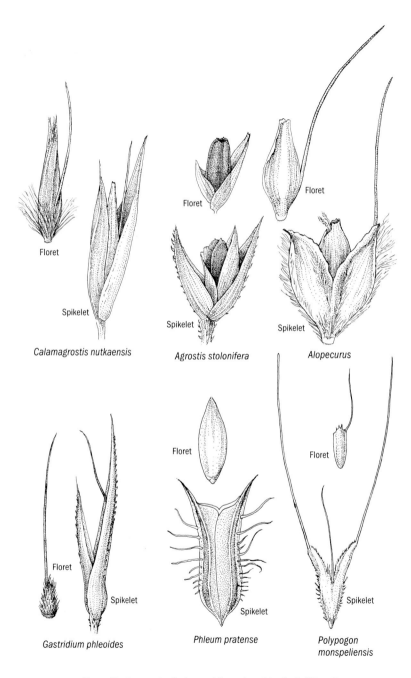

Floret

Spikelet

Calamagrostis nutkaensis

Floret

Spikelet

Agrostis stolonifera

Floret

Spikelet

Alopecurus

Floret

Spikelet

Gastridium phleoides

Floret

Spikelet

Phleum pratense

Floret

Spikelet

Polypogon monspeliensis

Figure 16. Survey of spikelets and florets in subfamily *Poöideae*-II

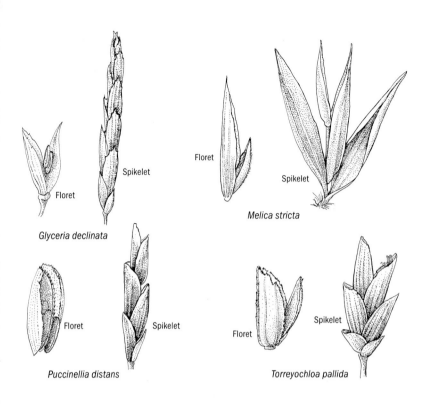

Figure 17. Survey of spikelets and florets in subfamily *Poöideae*-III

glumes. An unusual feature in two of our genera is that the upper 1 to 3 florets overlap to form a knob- or club-shaped **rudiment**. Our representatives: *Glyceria, Melica,* and *Pleuropogon.*

TRIBE POEAE. Annuals or perennials. Inflorescence a panicle, less often a raceme or spike. Spikelets ± laterally compressed, [1-] to several-flowered, reduced florets typically above the fertile ones; glumes [0 or 1] 2, equal or unequal, shorter or longer than the adjacent florets, lemmas usually 1- to 7-veined, awned or awnless. This is by far the largest tribe of California grasses. Our representatives: X *Agropogon, Agrostis, Aira, Alopecurus, Ammophila, Amphibromus, Anthoxanthum, Apera, Arrhenatherum, Avena, Beckmannia, Briza, Calamagrostis, Catapodium, Cinna, Cynosurus, Dactylis, Deschampsia, Festuca, Gastridium, Gaudinia, Hainardia, Holcus, Koeleria, Lagurus, Lamarckia, Melica, Parapholis, Phalaris, Phleum, Poa, Polypogon, Puccinellia, Rostraria, Sclerochloa, Scribneria, Sphenopholis, Torreyochloa, Trisetum,* and *Ventenata.*

TRIBE STIPEAE. There is relatively little discussion of the limits of the needle grass tribe. These plants were once considered closely related to the bent grasses *(Agrostis)* because they exhibited panicles of 1-flowered spikelets, but now we know that they differ in details of spikelet structure as well as in chromosome number. The current focus of attention and controversy is delimitation of genera. The traditional solution was to accommodate our California grasses in only two, as seen in this key adapted from Hitchcock & Chase (1951):

1a. Awn **persistent**, twisted and bent, several to many times longer than the grain; callus sharp-pointed, usually narrow and **acuminate** ....***Stipa***

1b. Awn **deciduous**, not twisted, sometimes bent, rarely more than 3–4 times longer than the grain; callus short, usually **obtuse** .... ***Oryzopsis***

Over the years, species were transferred from one genus to the other. Was this a case of a distinction without a difference? Basic questions arose. Was *Stipa* a genus of closely related species or an artificial construct of grasses that bore only a superficial resemblance to one another? The discovery that we had a third genus of South American stipoid grasses, *Piptochaetium*, added to the complexity. More recent molecular studies confirmed and expanded on the list of differences in these grasses, which also opened new questions. How do we balance the data relating to ancestral differences as seen at the DNA level that argue for dismemberment of *Stipa* with the need to produce a workable taxonomic solution that would allow us to place specimens in genera using ordinary field characters? The stage was set for a classical confrontation between "lumpers" and "splitters." One genus? Three genera? Or, nine genera in California, if we follow the treatment in *Flora of North America*?

I favor placing all of our needle grasses, rice grasses, and porcupine grasses into one genus, *Stipa*. As I used to tell my agrostology students at HSU, going down the pathway of recognizing segregate genera is little bit like eating peanuts or popcorn—once you get started, it's difficult to stop. Many of the new generic names that emerged—such as *Hesperostipa, Jarava,* and *Nassella*—were once recognized as subgenera of *Stipa*. In other words, earlier workers had recognized groupings of species, but had decided to retain them within a broader generic concept. They also treated other generic names, such as *Achnatherum* and *Ptilagrostis*, as synonyms. Since the Barkworth et al. (2007) treatment, additional segregate genera and intergeneric hybrids have been named and generic concepts modified, thereby adding to the complexity. Hybridization is common, as is overlap in many morphological features. Hybrid origin of many taxa has been suggested. It has made constructing a key to genera especially challenging. The recognition of as many as 15 segregate genera in the flora of North America may actually tend to obscure the similarity of these grasses.

HABIT Annual or perennial herbs

INFLORESCENCE Typically a panicle, rarely a spike or raceme

SPIKELET 1- to many-flowered, laterally compressed or terete; bisexual florets 1 to many, the upper usually reduced or aborted; breaking apart usually above the glumes and between the florets; lemmas 5- to many-veined; palea typically 2-keeled

FLOWERS Stamens usually 3; stigmas 2

DISTRIBUTION Herbaceous grasses, primarily of the cool and temperate regions or of the alpine areas of the tropics and subtropics in **both hemispheres**

OUR REPRESENTATIVES See the tribe descriptions for representatives of this subfamily

Selected References

Barkworth, M. E., K. M. Kapels, S. Long, L. K. Anderton, & M. B. Piep (editors). 2007. *Flora of North America North of Mexico.* Vol. 24. *Magnoliophyta: Commelinidae* (in part): *Poaceae,* part 1. New York: Oxford Univ. Press.

Chemisquy, M. A., L. M. Giussani, M. A. Scataglini, & O. Moronne. 2010. "Phylogenetic Studies Favour the Unification of Pennisetum Cenchrus and Odontelytrum (Poaceae): A Combined Nuclear, Plastid and Morphological Analysis, and Nomenclatural Combinations in Cenchrus." *Annals of Botany* 106: 107–130.

Estes, J. R. & R. J. Tyrl. 1982. "The Generic Concept and Generic Circumscription in the Triticeae: An End Paper." *In,* Estes, J. R., R. J. Tyrl, & J. N. Brunken. *Grasses and Grasslands: Systematics and Ecology.* Norman, OK: University of Oklahoma Press. Pp. 145–164.

Grass Phylogeny Working Group. 2001. "Phylogeny and Subfamilial Classification of the Grasses (Poaceae)." *Annals Missouri Botanical Garden* 88(3): 373–457.

Hitchcock, A. S. 1951. *Manual of the Grasses of the United States.* Second edition, revised by Agnes Chase. Misc. Publ. No. 200. Washington, DC: U.S. Department of Agriculture.

Soreng, R. J., G. Davidse, P. M. Peterson, F. O. Zuloaga, E. J. Judziewicz, T. S. Figueiras, O. Morrone, & K. Romaschenko. 2012. *A World-Wide Phylogenetic Classification of Poaceae (Gramineae).* Available at www.tropicos.org.

KEY TO THE GENERA OF CALIFORNIA GRASSES

This key is intended to include all of the genera of grasses reported as growing in California that are native or are otherwise established and persisting without human assistance. Some of these grasses are not at all common and you are not likely to encounter them in the field. Several of them are known only from historic collections. Grasses falling into this category bear an asterisk. They receive only a very short description at the end of the key. All of the other entries are given a more complete treatment later in the book. Although most of the leads in this key end in a generic name, some of them take you to a particular species. This occurs when I am singling out that particular one from others in the genus.

1a   Leaf blades constricted at base to form false petioles; stems woody
      ....*Phyllostachys*
1b   Leaf bases forming tubular sheaths; stems herbaceous to hardened
      (almost woody in *Arundo donax*) **2**
2a   Some or all florets modified into **bulblets** with conspicuous, awn-
      like tails.. *Poa bulbosa*
2b   Florets not modified into tailed bulblets...**3**
3a   Spikelets enclosed in bristly to spiny, bur-like involucre
      ....*Cenchrus*
3b   Spikelets not enclosed in bristly to spiny, bur-like involucre **4**
4a   Leaf blades, at least the upper ones, generally stiff at maturity,
      sharp-pointed, and conspicuously distichous....................................**5**
4b   Leaf blades generally soft, flexible, rounded to acute, but not sharp-
      pointed, nor distichous **6**
5a   Spikelets unisexual, plants generally dioecious; plants of salt
      marshes and moist alkaline sites...*Distichlis*
5b   Spikelets bisexual; plants known only from dunes in Inyo County
      .... *Swallenia*
6a   Spikelets 1 or 2 per inflorescence **7**
6b   Spikelets few to many in a well-developed inflorescence..................**8**
7a   Glumes longer than lowest floret; awns twisted and bent
      .... *Danthonia unispicata*
7b   Glumes shorter than lowest floret; awns (when present) not
      twisted, nor bent ....*Brachypodium*
8a   Leaf blade and sheath undifferentiated; stem internodes solid;
      ligules absent... *Group 1*
8b   Leaf blade and sheath clearly differentiated; stem internodes gener-
      ally hollow; ligules generally present..**9**

9a   Basal or underground internodes swollen, bulb- or corm-like
.... ***Group 2***

9b   Basal or underground internodes not swollen, nor bulb- or corm-
like **10**

10a Perennials, often 2+ m tall; stems tough to woody, typically 0.5
+ cm in diameter; inflorescence a conspicuous terminal panicle;
spikelets or pedicels hairy (less so in *Ampelodesmos*) .... ***Group 3***

10b Low annuals to mid-sized perennials, generally less than 1.5 m
tall; stems generally only a few mm wide, strictly herbaceous and
generally dying back annually; inflorescence axillary, terminal, or
both, but not conspicuously plume- or fan-like................................ **11**

11a Plants generally less than 15 cm tall; mature inflorescence not
clearly elevated above leaves on obvious peduncles, often ±
enclosed in upper sheaths... ***Group 4***

11b Plants generally much taller; mature inflorescence clearly elevated
above upper leaves **12**

12a Spikelets subtended by 1 or more bristles, sterile branches, or long,
silky hairs .... ***Group 5***

12b Spikelets neither subtended by bristles nor by long, silky hairs.... **13**

13a Glume and/or lemma bodies covered with prominent, silky hairs
.... ***Group 6***

13b Glumes and lemma bodies **glabrous** to short-hairy **14**

14a Glumes or lemmas (sometimes only in a unisexual spikelet) bearing [2] 3–9 awns or awn-like segments (lateral awns sometimes
much shorter than the central one).. ***Group 7***

14b Glume or lemma awns 0–2 .... **15**

15a Spikelets generally dorsally compressed [cylindrical or flat on one
side and rounded on the other]; florets 2, lower sterile or staminate, often reduced to sterile lemma, upper floret bisexual; glume
and fertile lemma texture noticeably dissimilar (often thin and
membranous versus leathery to hard); spikelets breaking apart
below the glumes, falling singly or in pairs with segments of the
inflorescence axis attached.. **16**

15b Spikelets generally laterally compressed or cylindrical; florets 1
to many, lower one(s) generally fertile, upper reduced and sterile;
glume and fertile lemma texture generally similar; spikelets generally breaking apart above glumes and between florets or floret
clusters **17**

16a Glumes leathery to hardened, ± equal, one or both generally longer
than the upper floret (except for awn); fertile and sterile lemmas
generally translucent .... ***Group 8***

16b Glumes membranous, flexible, the lower generally shorter than the
upper and sometimes absent; upper glume shorter than or equal
to the upper floret; upper glume and sterile lemma membranous;
fertile lemma leathery to hardened [membranous in *Digitaria*]
.... ***Group 9***

17a Plants bearing markedly dissimilar spikelets in the same or separate inflorescences (excluding those that may be hidden in sheaths) .... *Group 10*

17b Plants bearing similar spikelets, differing only in size and degree of maturity **18**

18a Inflorescence a single spike, raceme, or a combination; spikelets sessile or stalked on an unbranched central axis .... *Group 11*

18b Inflorescence a series of simple branches or more complex open and diffuse to densely cylindrical or head-like panicles (dissection may be needed to reveal branches); spikelets attached to primary or secondary branches **19**

19a Inflorescence a series of 2 or more digitate, racemose, clustered or whorled branches .... *Group 12*

19b Inflorescence a much-branched panicle with secondary or tertiary branching **20**

20a Floret 1 .... *Group 13*

20b Florets 2 to many (look carefully for sterile florets that may be reduced to very small scales or hairy rudiments) **21**

21a Spikelets unisexual; species dioecious .... *Group 14*

21b Spikelets with bisexual florets **22**

22a Fertile floret 1 .... *Group 15*

22b Fertile or florets 2 or more **23**

23a Lemmas (at least one of them) awned or awn-tipped .... *Group 16*

23b Lemmas awnless (sometimes with very short points) .... *Group 17*

Group 1: Leaf blade and sheath undifferentiated; stem internodes solid; ligules absent

1a Spikelets 2-ranked on inflorescence axis .... *Orcuttia*

1b Spiklelets spirally inserted on inflorescence axis *2*

2a Plants glandular-**viscid** at maturity; inflorescence a dense, cylindrical spike, generally fully **exserted** at maturity; spikelets dorsally compressed .... *Neostapfia*

2b Plants not glandular-viscid at maturity; inflorescence club-shaped, often ± enclosed by leaves at maturity; spikelets laterally compressed .... *Tuctoria**

Group 2: Stem bases or subterranean internodes swollen, bulb- or corm-like

1a Some or all florets modified into bulblets with conspicuous, awn-like tails .... *Poa bulbosa*

1b Florets not modified into bulblets *2*

2a Inflorescence a dense, spike-like panicle *3*

2b Inflorescence an open panicle with evident branches *4*

3a Spikelets with a single floret; glumes not winged .... *Phleum pratense*

3b	Spikelets with two or more florets, two of them much reduced; glumes winged...*Phalaris aquatica*
4a	Spikelets with a single floret..*Stipa*
4b	Spikelets with 2 or more florets..**5**
5a	Sheaths closed to near tip; glumes equal to lowest floret; lower lemma awns generally absent or with a straight, untwisted awn ....*Melica*
5b	Sheaths open; glumes ± enclosing florets; lower lemma awns bent and twisted.. *Arrhenatherum*

Group 3: Robust perennials 2+ m tall with conspicuously hairy terminal inflorescences

1a	Inflorescence a series of numerous **ascending** spike-like branches; spikelets in pairs or trios...**2**
1b	Inflorescence a much-branched panicle; spikelets 1 per node **3**
2a	Spikelets unequally stalked ....*Miscanthus**
2b	One spikelet of the pair sessile and the other(s) stalked ....*Saccharum**
3a	Leaves predominantly basal...**4**
3b	Leaves well distributed along stems......................................**5**
4a	Stem internodes hollow; spikelets unisexual; plants pistillate .... *Cortaderia*
4b	Stem internodes solid; spikelets bisexual.................*Ampelodesmos**
5a	Leaf blades conspicuously distichous; rachilla axis glabrous; glumes longer than florets; lemmas densely hairy ....*Arundo*
5b	Leaf blades not distichous; rachilla silky-hairy; glumes shorter than florets; lemmas glabrous...*Phragmites*

Group 4: Plants typically less than 15 cm tall; mature inflorescences not clearly elevated above leaves, often ± enclosed in upper sheaths

1a	Floret 1; lemmas 1-veined ....*Crypsis*
1b	Florets 2 or more; lemmas 3- or more-veined **2**
2a	Lemmas awnless...**3**
2b	Awns 1 or 3 ....**4**
3a	Inflorescence subtended by 5–10 bristles; spikelets 1–2 mm; florets 2 .... *Kikuyuochloa*
3b	Inflorescence not subtended by bristles; spikelets 6–10 mm; florets 3–5 ....*Sclerochloa**
4a	Lemmas 3-lobed; awns 3.. *Blepharidachne**
4b	Lemmas 2-lobed; awns 1 ....**5**
5a	Leaf blades stiff, sharp-pointed; glumes 2–4 mm, shorter than lemmas; lemmas tapering to point ....*Munroa**
5b	Leaf blades not stiff, nor sharp-pointed; glumes 3–9 mm, longer than lemmas; lemmas **bifid**..*Dasyochloa*

Group 5: Spikelets subtended by 1 or more bristles, sterile branches, or long silky hairs

1a   Spikelets subtended by long, silky hairs from their bases, rachis **joints**, or pedicels...**2**

1b   Spikelets subtended by 1 or more generally stiff bristles or sterile branches...**4**

2a   Spikelets dissimilar, the sessile bisexual and the stalked sterile .... ***Bothriochloa***

2b   Spikelets similar, bisexual..**3**

3a   Inflorescence a narrow, spike-like panicle; lemma awnless ....***Imperata*****

3b   Inflorescence broad, fan-like; lemma awned.................***Miscanthus*****

4a   Bristles falling with spikelets at maturity ....***Cenchrus***

4b   Bristles persistent **5**

5a   Bristles conspicuously hairy...***Andropogon***

5b   Bristles ± glabrous...**6**

6a   Ligule absent...***Echinochloa***

6b   Ligule a membrane or set of hairs ....***Setaria***

Group 6: Glume(s) and/or lemmas covered with prominent, silky hairs

1a   Inflorescence dense, ovoid or **oblong**, **capitate** ....***Lagurus*****

1b   Inflorescence open, branching evident **2**

2a   Floret 1, terete in cross-section...***Stipa***

2b   Florets 2, dorsally or laterally compressed...**3**

3a   Spikelets paired on one side of a slender rachis; lower glume glabrous ....***Digitaria californica***

3b   Spikelets single on ends of short **capillary** branches; both glumes **villous** **4**

4a   Plants of disturbed sites; upper floret laterally compressed ....***Melinis***

4b   Plants native to dunes and sandy soils; upper floret dorsally compressed ....***Panicum urvilleanum***

Group 7: Glumes or lemmas bearing 2–9 awns or awn-like segments

1a   Lemma awns 9, plumose...***Enneapogon*****

1b   Lemma awns 0–3, not plumose...**2**

2a   Spikelets forming a wedge-shaped cluster on a zig-zag rachis; glumes fused at base to form an involucre.................................***Hilaria***

2b   Spikelets not forming a wedge-shaped cluster or attached to a zig-zag rachis; glumes not fused at base **3**

3a   Lower glume with 2–9 awns or awn-like segments............................**4**

3b   Lower glume awn 1 or 0...**6**

4a   Spikelets 1 per node...***Aegilops***

4b   Spikelets 2 or 3 [4] per node..**5**

5a   Florets 2–4; lemmas faintly 5- [7-] veined.................................***Elymus***

5b	Floret 1; lemma 3-veined .... ***Lycurus*** *
6a	Floret 1 ....***Aristida***
6b	Florets 2 to several **7**
7a	Inflorescence 1 to many primary branches, each bearing racemes or spikes of spikelets .... ***Bouteloua***
7b	Inflorescence an open panicle **8**
8a	Glumes subtended by a glume-like bract; lemma awns 50+ mm long; florets pistillate .... ***Scleropogon*** *
8b	Glumes not subtended by a glume-like bract; lemma awns less than 15 mm long; lower florets bisexual .... ***Rytidosperma***

Group 8: Glumes leathery to hardened, ± equal, one or both generally longer than the upper floret; fertile and sterile lemmas generally translucent

1a	Spikelets 1 per node, subtended by a hairy bristle ....***Andropogon***
1b	Spikelets 2 or 3 per node, 1 sessile and 1 [2] stalked **2**
2a	Terminal spikelets per branch in trios, 1 sessile and 2 stalked **3**
2b	Terminal spikelets per branch paired, 1 sessile and 1 stalked **4**
3a	Spikelets with a tuft of long, silky hairs at their base ....***Miscanthus*** *
3b	Spikelets not subtended by a tuft of silky hairs ....***Sorghum***
4a	Inflorescence a raceme **5**
4b	Inflorescence a branched panicle **6**
5a	Callus sharp-pointed with golden hairs; awn hairy, 6–10 cm long ....***Heteropogon*** *
5b	Callus absent; awns glabrous, less than 3 cm long ....***Schizachyrium*** *
6a	Inflorescence internodes and spikelet stalks with a translucent longitudinal groove; lowest pair of spikelets per raceme fertile .... ***Bothriochloa***
6b	Inflorescence internodes and spikelet stalks without a translucent longitudinal groove; lowest pair of spikelets per raceme staminate ....***Hyparrhenia*** *

Group 9: Glumes membranous, flexible, the lower generally shorter than the upper or absent; upper glume and sterile lemma membranous; fertile lemma leathery to hardened

1a	Inflorescence a single spike; spikelets attached to one side of a flat-tened, thickened rachis .... ***Stenotaphrum*** *
1b	Inflorescence an open panicle or a series of digitate, paired, or racemose branches **2**
2a	Spikelet subtended by a cup- or ring-like structure ....***Eriochloa***
2b	Spikelet not subtended by cup- or ring-like structure **3**
3a	Ligule absent, at least on the upper leaves ....***Echinochloa***
3b	Ligule present **4**
4a	Inflorescence a much-branched panicle ....***Panicum***

4b   Inflorescence a series of digitate, paired, or racemose branches......**5**
5a   Spikelets 1 per node on each branch **6**
5b   Spikelets in 2s, 3s, or clusters per node on each branch **7**
6a   Lower glume absent; upper glume and sterile lemma of equal
        length .... ***Axonopus****
6b   Glumes 2 ....***Urochloa****
7a   Inflorescence branches 3-sided; fertile floret membranous, flexible
        at maturity..***Digitaria***
7b   Inflorescence branches flat; fertile floret leathery to hardened, rigid
        at maturity..***Paspalum***

Group 10: Spikelets in the same or separate inflorescences markedly dissimilar

1a   Plants bearing staminate and pistillate spikelets in separate
        inflorescences (less frequently on separate plants or with bisexual
        florets in *Scleropogon*)..**2**
1b   Plants bearing bisexual, unisexual, or sterile spikelets in the same
        inflorescence **4**
2a   Plants aquatic; pistillate spikelets on erect upper panicle branches
        and the staminate ones on lower **spreading** branches............***Zizania***
2b   Plants terrestrial..**3**
3a   Plants robust annuals; staminate spikelets in a terminal branched
        panicle ("tassel") and pistillate ones enclosed by enveloping leaves
        on a lateral branch ("ear"); pistillate spikelets awnless............... ***Zea****
3b   Plants low, stoloniferous perennials; spikelets clearly visible, the
        pistillate conspicuously awned .... ***Scleropogon****
4a   Inflorescence a spike or rame...**5**
4b   Inflorescence a panicle, open to condensed and head-like **7**
5a   Spikelets 1 per node..***Aegilops***
5b   Spikelets 3 per node **6**
6a   Stems internodes solid; spikelets sessile....................................***Hilaria***
6b   Stems internodes hollow; central spikelet sessile, laterals stalked
        (except in *H. vulgare*)...***Hordeum***
7a   Lemma awnless; spikelets in clusters of 1 fertile one and 6 or 7
        sterile or staminate ones ....***Phalaris paradoxa***
7b   Lemmas awned; spikelets paired or in pendant clusters...................**8**
8a   Inflorescence a panicle with drooping clusters of 1 fertile spikelet
        and 1 to 3 sterile ones; fertile floret 1; spikelet clusters falling as 1
        unit ....***Lamarckia***
8b   Inflorescence head-like or cylindrical, spikelets generally paired;
        fertile florets 2 or 3; spikelets falling separately .... ***Cynosurus***

Group 11: Inflorescence a solitary spike or raceme; some or all spikelets sessile

1a   All spikelets sessile or nearly so (upper ones sometimes stalked in
        Scribneria) **2**

1b	Some or all spikelets stalked	**17**
2a	Glume 1 (except in uppermost spikelets)	**3**
2b	Glumes 2	**4**
3a	Stem internodes hollow; inflorescence axis remaining intact at maturity; spikelets breaking apart above the glumes; lemma veins 5	***Festuca* subgenus *Lolium***
3b	Stem internodes solid; inflorescence axis breaking apart at maturity, spikelets falling with axis segments; lemma veins 3	***Hainardia***
4a	Spikelet bases ± embedded or fitting into cavities, pits, or curvatures of a thickened rachis or rachis joint	**5**
4b	Spikelet bases not embedded or fitting into cavities, pits, or curvatures of a thickened rachis or rachis joint	**8**
5a	Plants perennial from stolons or rhizomes; spikelets attached to one side of a flattened rachis	***Stenotaphrum***
5b	Plants annual; spikelets attached to both sides of a rounded inflorescence axis	**6**
6a	Spikelets awnless	***Parapholis***
6b	Spikelets awned	**7**
7a	Glumes awnless; lemma awned; floret 1	***Scribneria***
7b	Glumes awned; lemmas awnless; florets 2–5	***Aegilops***
8a	Spikelets borne on one side of inflorescence axis; lemma veins 3	***Bouteloua***
8b	Spikelets 2-ranked; lemma veins 5–9	**9**
9a	Spikelets 2–8 per node	***Elymus***
9b	Spikelets 1 per node	**10**
10a	Lemma keels ciliate	***Secale***
10b	Lemma keels (if present) not ciliate	**11**
11a	Glumes longer than the florets and typically enclosing them	***Danthonia***
11b	Glumes shorter than the florets	**12**
12a	Fertile floret 1, subtended by 2 sterile florets	***Ehrharta***
12b	Fertile florets 2 or more, sterile florets above the fertile ones	**13**
13a	Auricles absent	**14**
13b	Auricles present	**15**
14a	Palea keels strongly ciliate; lemma awns (when present) straight; nodes generally hairy	***Brachypodium***
14b	Palea keels not ciliate; lemma awns bent, twisted; nodes glabrous	***Gaudinia****
15a	Glumes and lemma backs rounded	***Elymus***
15b	Glumes and lemmas keeled	**16**
16a	Plants annual; glumes 6–12 mm long; lemma awns 0–4 cm long	***Triticum***
16b	Plants perennial; glumes 3–6 mm long; lemma awns 1–6 mm long	***Agropyron***
17a	Spikelets 1 per node, stalked; inflorescence a raceme	**18**

17b   Spikelets 3 per node, sessile and stalked, the rachis remaining intact or breaking apart at maturity; inflorescence a spike **22**

18a   Floret 1; lower glume generally absent, the upper enclosing the floret .... ***Zoysia********

18b   Florets several; both glumes present, not enclosing the florets **19**

19a   Lemma veins prominent, parallel; paleas winged on lower half ....***Pleuropogon***

19b   Lemma veins converging at tip; paleas not winged......................... **20**

20a   Upper leaf sheaths closed; lemma tips generally 2-forked or 2-lobed ....***Bromus***

20b   Upper leaf sheaths open; lemma tips obtuse or acute **21**

21a   Upper glume veins 5–9; paleas keeled, ciliate ....***Brachypodium***

21b   Upper glume veins 3 [5]; paleas glabrous or hairy, but not keeled, nor ciliate.. ***Festuca***

22a   Stem internodes solid; auricles absent; central spikelet short-stalked, laterals sessile; glumes awned ....***Hilaria***

22b   Stem internodes hollow; auricles present or absent; central spikelet sessile, laterals stalked; glumes awnless, but sometimes very narrow and awn-like...***Hordeum***

Group 12: Inflorescence branches digitate, racemose, clustered, or in whorls; no further branching evident

1a   Inflorescence branches digitate or clustered at or near the tip of the inflorescence axis **2**

1b   Inflorescence branches racemose, 1+ per node along a central, unbranched axis, or in whorls **5**

2a   Glumes and lemmas awnless **3**

2b   Glumes and/or lemmas awned **4**

3a   Plants perennial; floret 1 per spikelet; rachilla extended behind palea as a slender bristle, rarely bearing a sterile floret .... ***Cynodon***

3b   Plants annual; florets 2 or more per spikelet; rachilla not extended behind palea...***Eleusine***

4a   Spikelets strongly keeled; upper glume awned; end of inflorescence branch extending beyond the last spikelet..............***Dactyloctenium********

4b   Spikelets laterally compressed or terete, but not keeled; upper glume awnless; end of inflorescence branch not extending beyond last spikelet...***Chloris***

5a   Glumes longer than florets ....***Dinebra********

5b   Glumes shorter than or as long as the florets **6**

6a   Floret 1 per spikelet (sometimes with a second floret in *Beckmannia*) **7**

6b   Florets 2 or more per spikelet (except for *Bouteloua aristidoides* in basal spikelets)...**9**

7a   Spikelets somewhat distant on inflorescence branches, breaking apart above the glumes; entire inflorescence breaking away at maturity...***Schedonnardus********

7b   Spikelets clearly overlapping on inflorescence branches, breaking apart below the glumes; plants of coastal marshes and interior wet sites **8**

8a   Spikelets 6–25 mm long, **lanceolate** to oblong......................*Spartina*

8b   Spikelets 2–3 mm long, circular in side view..................*Beckmannia*

9a   Fertile floret 1 per spikelet...**10**

9b   Fertile florets 2 or more per spikelet **13**

10a Inflorescence branches 1 per node..**11**

10b Inflorescence branches 2 or more per node **12**

11a Spikelets laterally compressed; lowest floret bisexual.......*Bouteloua*

11b Spikelets dorsally compressed; upper floret bisexual

....*Echinochloa*

12a Upper glume 2-lobed, awn 0.3–0.6 mm long; lowest lemma awnless

.... *Eustachys**

12b Upper glume acute to acuminate, awnless; lowest lemma generally awned ....*Chloris verticillata*

13a Lemmas 3-veined, sometimes appearing 1-veined **14**

13b Lemmas 5- to several-veined...**15**

14a Leaf blades tapered to a hair-like tip; rachilla and paleas persistent at maturity..*Acrachne**

14b Leaf blades not tapered to a hair-like tip; rachilla and paleas falling at maturity...*Leptochloa*

15a Upper glume 7-veined ....*Sclerochloa**

15b Upper glume 3-veined.. *Festuca*

Group 13: Inflorescence a panicle, open and diffuse to compact, cylindrical or head-like; floret 1 per spikelet

1a   Floret staminate; stem nodes purple-black........................*Ventenata*

1b   Floret bisexual; stem nodes green or straw-colored...........................**2**

2a   Glumes absent; palea 3-veined; plants of wet sites ....*Leersia*

2b   Glumes 1 or 2; palea (when present) 2-veined; plants generally of drier sites (except *Oryza* and some *Phalaris*) **3**

3a   Spikelets ± circular, overlapping in 2 rows on 1 side of inflorescence branch; glumes winged, body transversely wrinkled (a second rudimentary floret sometimes present)...........................*Beckmannia*

3b   Spikelets not circular or overlapping in 2 rows; glumes not winged; body smooth or veined, but not transversely wrinkled.....................**4**

4a   Glumes ciliate-keeled **5**

4b   Glumes glabrous to sparsely hairy, but not ciliate-keeled................**6**

5a   Glumes united at base; lemma awned; palea absent .... *Alopecurus*

5b   Glumes separate at base; lemma awnless; palea present .... *Phleum*

6a   Glumes unequal, tapering to a long point, ± swollen at base

....*Gastridium*

6b   Glumes equal or unequal, but not tapering to long points or swollen at base **7**

7a	Glumes keeled, often winged; floret subtended by a membranous flap or tuft of hairs ....***Phalaris***
7b	Glumes generally rounded, not winged; floret not subtended by a flap or tuft of hairs **8**
8a	Lemma generally hardened at maturity, margins generally overlapping and permanently enclosing palea and grain; grain hardened, round in cross-section; callus well developed, blunt or sharp-pointed **9**
8b	Lemma and grain membranous or firm, but not hardened, generally flattened; callus not especially well developed **10**
9a	Stem internodes ± solid; lemma 3-veined, awns generally straight; ligule of hairs or basal membrane with long cilia ....***Aristida***
9b	Stem internodes hollow; lemma 3- to 7-veined, awns generally 1- or 2-geniculate; ligule generally membranous.................................***Stipa***
10a	Rachilla extended beside or above floret as a glabrous or hairy stub or bristle..**11**
10b	Rachilla not extended beside or above floret (sometimes absent in *Cinna*)..**14**
11a	Spikelets breaking apart below glumes at maturity; stamens 1 or 2 ....***Cinna***
11b	Spikelets breaking apart above glumes at maturity; stamens 3.....**12**
12a	Plants annual; callus glabrous to sparsely hairy.....................***Apera*** *
12b	Plants perennial, often from rhizomes; callus hairy.......................**13**
13a	Inflorescence dense, cylindrical; lemma awnless; coastal dunes ....***Ammophila***
13b	Inflorescence open, branching evident; lemma awn 0.5–17 mm long...***Calamagrostis***
14a	Plants of flooded fields and adjacent ditches; stamens 6 ....***Oryza***
14b	Plants terrestrial; stamens 1 or 3...**15**
15a	Glumes with well-developed awns (except in *P. viridis*); spikelets breaking apart below glumes ....***Polypogon***
15b	Glumes acute, acuminate, or awn-tipped; spiklelets breaking apart above glumes...**16**
16a	Lemma 1-veined, awnless; leaf sheaths generally ciliate at tip; seed ejected from grain at maturity..***Sporobolus***
16b	Lemma 3- or 5-veined, awn present or absent; leaf sheaths not ciliate at tip; seed remaining within grain at maturity **17**
17a	Lemma 3-veined, generally obvious; palea generally well developed ....***Muhlenbergia***
17b	Lemma [3-] 5-veined, faint; palea absent or much shorter than the lemma...***Agrostis***

Group 14: Inflorescence a panicle of unisexual spikelets; species dioecious

1a	Plants 1+ m tall; leaves basal...***Cortaderia***
1b	Plants much shorter; stem leaves well developed **2**

2a Leaf blades with longitudinal grooves on each side of mid-vein, their tips prow-shaped; lemma bases often with cottony or cobwebby tuft of hairs .... **Poa**

2b Leaf tips flat without longitudinal grooves; lemma bases glabrous to **scabrous** **3**

3a Leaves stiffly 2-ranked; lemmas 9- to 11-veined .... **Distichlis**

3b Leaves not stiffly 2-ranked; lemmas 3- or 5- [7-] veined **4**

4a Spikelets 6–12 mm long; florets 3 or 4 .... **Festuca**

4b Spikelets 2–3 cm long; florets 5–10 .... **Scleropogon***

Group 15: Inflorescence a panicle; florets 2 or more per spikelet, but only one of them bisexual

1a Spikelets breaking apart below the glumes; lower floret bisexual, awn absent; upper floret(s) staminate, awned .... **Holcus**

1b Spikelets breaking apart above glumes; staminate or sterile floret(s) below the fertile one (sometimes much shorter than the fertile one and easily overlooked) **2**

2a Fertile floret awned **3**

2b Fertile floret awnless **4**

3a Plants perennial; nodes green or straw-colored; spikelets breaking apart below lowest floret .... **Arrhenatherum**

3b Plants annual; nodes purple-black; spikelets breaking apart above lowest floret .... **Ventenata**

4a Lower florets reduced to sterile lemma less than half the length of the fertile floret .... **Phalaris**

4b Lower staminate or sterile florets equal to or longer than the fertile one **5**

5a Spikelets straw-colored or brown at maturity; stamens 2 or 3; auricles absent (except in *A. odoratum*) .... **Anthoxanthum**

5b Spikelets green or purplish at maturity; stamens 3 or 6; auricles ciliate .... **Ehrharta**

Group 16: Inflorescence a panicle; fertile florets 2 or more; lemmas awned or awn-tipped

1a Lemma awns of upper florets ± terminal or from the tip between or just below 2 teeth or lobes **2**

1b Lemma awns of upper florets arising from the back, often from the midpoint or below (see also *Trisetum*) **10**

2a Lemmas awned from between 2 teeth (these minute in *Erioneuron*) or lobes **3**

2b Lemmas awned from the tip **6**

3a Lemma veins 3, these typically prominent (lateral veins sometimes near margin) .... **Erioneuron***

3b Lemma veins [3] 5 to several, sometimes so faint as to appear veinless **4**

4a Rachilla hairy, extended beyond the upper florets .... **Trisetum**

4b   Rachilla glabrous, not extended **4**

5a   Lemmas hairy, the hairs in 1 or more tufted rows ...... ***Rytidosperma***

5b   Lemmas glabrous or, if hairy, the hairs on margins or evenly
      distributed ....***Danthonia***

6a   Glumes thin, papery, their margins typically translucent; upper
      1–4 florets sterile, overlapping, and forming a club-shaped or
      knob-like rudiment ....***Melica***

6b   Glumes membranous to leathery, but without translucent margins;
      upper florets not overlapping to form a rudiment **7**

7a   Glumes dissimilar in width, the lower narrower than the upper
      ....***Rostraria***

7b   Glumes similar in width **8**

8a   Spikelets in dense, 1-sided clumps toward the ends of spreading to
      erect branches; glumes awn-tipped; lemma keels typically stiffly
      ciliate ....***Dactylis***

8b   Spikelets not in dense, 1-sided clumps at ends of panicle branches;
      glumes not awn-tipped; lemmas generally rounded, if keeled, not
      ciliate **9**

9a   Leaf sheaths closed; spikelets generally 15–70 mm long; lemma tips
      2-toothed; palea adhering to the caryopsis; ovary tip hairy
      ....***Bromus***

9b   Leaf sheaths open (mostly closed when young in *F. rubra*); spikelets
      typically 3.5–12 mm long; lemma tip tapering to a point [minutely
      2-toothed]; palea not adhering to the caryopsis; ovary tip glabrous
      [hairy] .... ***Festuca***

10a   Glumes shorter than the florets ....***Amphibromus****

10b   Glumes longer than the florets and enclosing them........................ **11**

11a   Spikelets 18–50 mm long..***Avena***

11b   Spikelets 2–15 mm long...**12**

12a   Florets 3, the lowest staminate and the upper bisexual; stem nodes
      purple-black... ***Ventenata***

12b   Florets 2 [3], bisexual; nodes green or straw-colored **13**

13a   Plants annual; stem leaves present; lemma tip 2-cleft; rachilla not
      extended beyond the upper floret..***Aira***

13b   Plants perennial (except *D. danthonioides*); leaves basal; lemma tip
      2- to 4-cleft or irregularly toothed; rachilla hairy, extended beyond
      the upper floret and sometimes bearing a rudimentary floret
      .... ***Deschampsia***

Group 17: Inflorescence a panicle; fertile florets 2 or more; lemmas awnless (sometimes with very short points)

1a   Spikelets 2–8 per node (to 40 if those on branches included);
      glumes **awl-shaped** ....***Elymus***

1b   Spikelets 1 per node; glumes broad to narrow, but not awl-shaped
      ....**2**

2a	Spikelets **ovate** to oblong or triangular; glumes and lemmas attached ± right angle to the rachilla, their backs strongly rounded giving them an inflated appearance..*Briza*
2b	Spikelets generally longer than wide, nor triangular; glumes and lemmas not attached at right angles and spikelets not appearing inflated **3**
3a	Glumes thin, papery, their margins typically translucent; upper 1–4 florets sterile, overlapping, and forming a club-shaped or knob-like rudiment ....*Melica*
3b	Glumes membranous to leathery, but without translucent margins; upper florets not overlapping to form a rudiment...........................**4**
4a	Glumes dissimilar; the lower linear to lanceolate, the upper elliptical to ovate, 3–4 times wider when spread flat........... ***Sphenopholis*** *
4b	Glumes similar in shape **5**
5a	Lemma veins 3, these typically prominent (lateral veins sometimes near margin) **6**
5b	Lemma veins [3] 5 to several, sometimes so faint as to appear veinless **8**
6a	Florets 2 ....***Muhlenbergia***
6b	Florets several **7**
7a	Lemma veins glabrous; lemma apex generally **entire**....... ***Eragrostis***
7b	Lemma veins hairy; lemma apex entire or slightly notched ....***Tridens***
8a	One or both glumes as long or longer than the lowest floret; see also *Trisetum*..**9**
8b	Glumes shorter than the lowest floret **14**
9a	Rachilla extended beyond the fertile florets as a slender bristle, sometimes with a reduced floret at its tip **10**
9b	Rachilla not extended...**12**
10a	Plants annual; spikelets 25–50 mm long ....*Avena*
10b	Plants perennial; spikelets 2.5–12 mm long **11**
11a	Spikelets shiny; glume keels ciliate; lemma tip acute............*Koeleria*
11b	Spikelets not shiny; glume keels not ciliate; lemma tip bifid (look carefully)...*Trisetum*
12a	Plants perennial...*Tribolium**
12b	Plants annual **13**
13a	Florets 2 [3]; known in California only from the Channel Islands ....*Dissanthelium**
13b	Florets [4] 5–7 [10]; weedy on sandy soils, especially in Southern California .... *Schismus*
14a	Lemma veins ± prominent, equally spaced, parallel (at least below) **15**
14b	Lemma veins not unusually prominent, converging toward the tip **17**
15a	Leaf sheath closed to near tip; upper glume vein 1 ....*Glyceria*
15b	Leaf sheath open; upper glume veins 3...**16**

16a Rhizomes absent; lemma veins 5, faint; plants of saline or alkaline
soils..***Puccinellia***

16b Rhizomes present; lemma veins 5–9, distinct; plants of freshwater
sites..***Torreyochloa***

17a Leaf blades with a longitudinal groove on each side of the mid-
vein, their tips prow-shaped; callus and/or lemma base generally
cottony-hairy ....***Poa***

17b Leaf tips flat; callus or lemma base glabrous to scabrous; longitudinal groove absent.. **18**

18a Rachilla segments thickened, falling with florets; lemmas ± round
in cross-section...***Catapodium****

18b Rachilla segments not thickened, not falling with florets; lemmas
flattened **19**

19a Leaf sheath closed; lemma tip 2-toothed; spikelets generally 15–70
mm long; palea adhering to the caryopsis; ovary tip hairy
....***Bromus***

19b Leaf sheath open; lemma tip tapering to a point [minutely
2-toothed]; spikelets generally 3.5–12 mm long; palea not adhering
to the caryopsis; ovary tip glabrous [hairy]...........................***Festuca***

Brief Accounts of Infrequently Encountered Genera

† = *presumed extinct or extirpated based on the lack of recent collections*

Acrachne racemosa   **Monsoon Grass**
Naturalized (?) annual. Stems to 50 cm tall. Panicle branches 1.5–10 cm
long. Spikelets 5.5–13 mm long. Known from a single 1991 collection in
Riverside County. †

Ampelodesmos mauritanicus   **Mauritanian grass, dis grass**
Sparingly naturalized perennial. Stems to 3 m tall. Panicles lax, to 50
cm long. Spikelets 10–15 mm long. Napa County. Recent research has
demonstrated that *Ampelodesmos* should be included in *Stipa* and our
representative would then be renamed *Stipa mauritanica.*

Amphibromus nervosus   **Australian Wallaby Grass**
Naturalized (?) perennial. Stems to 1+ m tall. Panicles 15–40 cm long.
Spikelets 10–16 mm long. Known from a single 1996 collection in Sonoma
County. †

Apera   **Silky Bent Grass**
Naturalized annuals. Stems to 120 cm tall. Panicles to 35 cm long. Spike-lets 2–3 mm long.

Axonopus fissifolius   **Carpet Grass**
Naturalized (?) perennial. Stems to 75 cm tall. Panicles 5–11 cm long. Spikelets ± 2 mm long. Last collected in Tulare County in 1969. †

Blepharidachne kingii   **King's Eyelash Grass**
Native annual. Stems to 8 cm tall. Panicles 10–25 cm, subcapitate. Spike-lets 6–9 mm long. Mostly Inyo and Mono counties.

Catapodium rigidum   **Fern Grass**
Naturalized annual. Stems to 60 cm tall. Panicles 1–12 cm long. Spikelets 4–10 mm long. Also treated as a species of *Desmazeria*.

Dactyloctenium aegyptium   **Durban Crowfoot,**
                                                        Egyptian Grass
Naturalized annual. Stems to 1+ m. Panicle branches to 6 cm. Spikelets 3–4.5 mm long. Most of our collections are from San Diego County.

Dinebra retroflexa   **Viper Grass**
Naturalized (?) annual. Stems to 1.2 m tall. Inflorescence 8–34 cm long. Spikelets 6–9 mm long. Known from two collections in Orange and Riverside counties.

Dissanthelium californicum   **Catalina Grass**
Native annual. Stems to 25 cm tall. Panicles 5–15 cm long, with contracted branches. Spikelets 2.5–4 m long. Until its rediscovery in 2005, this grass was thought to be extinct in California, known only from Santa Catalina and San Clemente islands. It was last collected in 1903. Recent studies have demonstrated that *Dissanthelium* should be treated as a section of *Poa* and that Catalina grass would then be renamed *P. thomasii*, in honor of Thomas Nuttall.

Enneapogon desvauxii   **Spike-pappus Grass,**
                                                  Nine-awned Pappus Grass
Native annual-perennial. Stems to 45 cm tall. Panicles 2–10 cm long. Spikelets 5–7 mm long. San Bernardino county.

Erioneuron pilosum var. pilosum   **Hairy-tridens,**
                                                     Hairy Woolly Grass
Native perennial. Stems to 40 cm tall. Panicles 1.5–4 cm long. Spikelets
6–15 mm long. All of our specimens are from San Bernardino County.

Eustachys distichophylla   **Chicken-foot Grass,**
                                        Finger Grass, Windmill Grass
Naturalized (?) annual. Stems to 140 cm tall. Digitate panicles with
branches to 17 cm long. Spikelets 2.4–3 mm long. Last collected in 1941 in
San Diego County. †

Gaudinia fragilis   **French oat Grass, Fragile oat**
Naturalized (?) annual. Stems to 80 cm tall. Spikes 6–15 cm long. Spike-
lets 9–20 mm long. Known from a single 2002 collection in Sonoma
County. †

Heteropogon contortus   **Twisted Tanglehead**
Naturalized perennial. Stems to 150 cm tall. Rames 3–10 cm long. Spikelets 6–10 mm long. Imperial and San Diego counties.

Hyparrhenia hirta   **Thatching Grass**
Naturalized perennial. Stems to 1 m tall. Panicles 10–30 cm long. Spikelets 4–6.5 mm long. Los Angeles and San Diego counties.

Imperata brevifolia   **California Satintail Grass**
Native perennial. Stems to 1.3 m tall. Panicles 16–34 cm long. Spikelets
3–4 mm long.

Lagurus ovatus   **Hare's Tail**
Naturalized annual. Escaped ornamental. Stems to 50 cm tall. Panicles
1.5–3 cm long. Spikelets 8–10 mm long.

Lycurus setosus   **Wolf's-tail**
Native perennial. Stems to 60 cm tall. Panicles 3–10 cm long, spike-like.
Spikelets 1–2 mm long, paired. Rare in California. Known from the New
York Mountains. Recent research suggests that *Lycurus* is part of *Muhlen-
bergia* and would be renamed *M. alopecuroides*.

Miscanthus sinensis   **Eulalia, Plume Grass, Zebra Grass**
Naturalized (?) perennial. Escaped ornamental. Stems to 2 m tall. Panicles 15–25 cm long. Spikelets 3.5–7 mm long. Last collected in 1969 in El Dorado County. †

Munroa squarrosa   **False Buffalo Grass**
Native annual. Stems 3–15 cm tall. Panicles of 2 or 3 spikelets partially hidden within sheaths. Spikelets 6–10 mm long.

Saccharum ravennae   **Ravenna Grass**
Naturalized perennial. Stems to 4+ m tall. Panicles to 70 cm long, plumelike. Spikelets 3.5–7.5 mm long. Most of our collections are from Imperial County.

Schedonnardus paniculatus   **Tumble Grass**
Naturalized (?) perennial. Stems to 55 [70] cm tall. Inflorescence a panicle of spike-like racemes 10–20 [30] cm long. Spikelets 3–5.5 mm long. Known in California from a single 1980 collection in Siskiyou County. Recent research suggests that the genus should be merged with *Muhlenbergia* and that tumble grass would then be renamed *M. paniculata*. †

Schizachyrium cirratum,   **Beard Grass, Bluestem**
S. scoparium
Native and naturalized perennials. Stems to 2+ m tall. Rames 2–8 cm long. Spikelets 6–11 mm long.

Sclerochloa dura   **Hard Grass**
Naturalized annual. Stems to 15 cm tall. Racemes 1–4 cm long. Spikelets 5–12 mm long. Most of our collections are from Siskiyou County.

Scleropogon brevifolius   **Burro Grass**
Native perennial; spikelets unisexual, plants monoecious or dioecious. Stems to 20 cm tall; stolons to 50 cm. Staminate inflorescence 3–7 cm long; pistillate inflorescence 10–20 cm long. Staminate spikelets 1–2.5 cm long; pistillate spikelets with awns to 15 cm long.

Sphenopholis obtusata   **Wedge-scale Grass, Bunch Grass**
Native perennial. Stems to 130 cm tall. Panicles 5–14 cm long. Spikelets 2–4 mm long.

Stenotaphrum secundatum   **St. Augustine Grass**
Naturalized perennial. Escaped lawn grass. Stems to 30 cm, **decumbent**, rooting at nodes. Spikes 4.5–10 cm long. Spikelets 3.5–5 mm long.

Tribolium obliterum   **Cape Grass or Capetown Grass**
Naturalized perennial. Stems to 40 cm tall; stolons to 30 cm long. Panicles 1–5 cm long. Spikelets 3.5–4.5 mm long. Our only North American location is the former U. S. Army base at Ford Ord in Monterey County, where it is now a widespread and aggressive weed. Eradication efforts have been unsuccessful. It may become one of California's next major weeds.

Tuctoria   **Spiral Grass**
Native annuals. Stems 5–15 cm tall, ascending to erect, fragile at maturity; internodes solid. Leaf blade and sheath not differentiated. Inflorescence a spike, the spikelets spirally inserted, often partially enveloped by upper leaves. Spikelets 7–15 mm long. Endemic to vernal pools and grasslands in California and Baja California, Mexico. The generic name is an anagram of *Orcuttia*, the genus in which these species were originally described. Listed: CDFG and USFWS.

Urochloa   **Signal Grass**
Native and naturalized annuals. Stems to 2 m tall. Panicles 6–24 cm long. Spikelets 3.2–6 mm long. Last collected in 1992. †

Zea mays   **Maize, Corn, Indian Corn**
Not naturalized in the usual sense, in that plants do not perpetuate themselves.

Zoysia japonica   **Japanese Lawn Grass**
Naturalized (?) perennial; escaped lawn grass. Stems to 15 cm long. Racemes to 8 cm. Spikelets 3–4 mm long. Last collected in Santa Barbara County in 1988.

ACCOUNTS AND DESCRIPTIONS
Selected Genera and Species

Aegilops   **Goat Grass**

Caespitose annuals. Stems to 80 cm tall. Inflorescence a single, balanced spike, the spikelets solitary at each node, typically with 1–3 rudimentary spikelets at the base. Spikelets typically oblong to ovate in side view, attached flatwise and fitting into the rachis, 2- to 8-flowered, rounded to ± laterally compressed, bisexual (the upper sometimes sterile), breaking apart below the glumes with a rachis segment attached or at the base of the spikes. Glumes 2, several-veined, 0- to 3-awned; lemmas usually 5- to 7-veined, awnless, mucronate, or 1- or 2-awned; palea keels ciliate.

Plate 1. _Aegilops cylindrica_ (left) and _Ae. neglecta_ (right).

TABLE 43. A comparison of *Aegilops*, *Hainardia*, *Parapholis*, and *Scribneria*

Characteristic	Aegilops	Hainardia	Parapholis	Scribneria
Habitat	drier, weedy	coastal marshes	coastal marshes	dry to wet
Auricles	present	absent	absent	absent
Spikelet position	flatwise to rachis	edgewise	flatwise to rachis	flatwise to rachis
Glume number	2	1	2	2
Glumes awned	yes	no	no	no
Floret number	2-7	1	1	1
Lemmas awned	yes	no	no	yes
Stamen number	3	1-3	3	1

5 • 7 • 21.* Mediterranean area and Asia. Goat grasses are completely interfertile with wheat and the two genera are often merged. Two of its chromosome sets contributed to the evolution of modern bread wheat.

1a   Spikes narrowly cylindrical; glumes 1-awned or -toothed
....***Ae. cylindrica***
JOINTED GOAT GRASS (pl. 1). Stems to 50 cm tall. Spikes 2–12 cm long. Spikelets 9–12 mm long. Aggressive weed of disturbed sites. Cascades foothills, Sacramento Valley, South Coast, Southwestern California. Listed: CDFA.

1b   Spikes subcylindrical to ovoid; glumes 3- or 2- awned......................**2**

2a   Upper spikelets 4–5 mm long, much narrower than the lower ones; fertile lemma with 2 or 3 awns..***Ae. neglecta***
THREE-AWNED GOAT GRASS (pl. 1). Stems to 35 cm tall. Spikes 3–6 cm long. Spikelets 8–12 mm long. While herbarium specimens document the presence of this species in the state, it has been overlooked and misidentified as *Ae. triuncialis*. It sometimes occurs in large populations.

2b   Upper spikelets 7–9 mm long, their width similar to the lower ones; fertile lemma toothed or with 1 awn...................***Ae. triuncialis***
BARBED GOAT GRASS. Stems to 45 cm tall. Spikes 2–6 cm long. Spikelets 6–10 mm long, the upper ones shorter. Aggressive weed disturbed sites, especially roadsides. North Coast ranges, Cascades and Sierra Nevada foothills, Sacramento Valley, South Coast. Listed: CDFA and Cal-IPC.

---

* For each genus, these three numbers tell you the number of species found in California, in the conterminous United States, and in the world.

Agropyron   **Crested Wheat Grass**

Caespitose or rhizomatous perennials. Stems to 1 m tall. Auricles usually present. Inflorescence a balanced spike, the spikelets strongly overlapping, 1 per node, inserted flatwise to axis. Spikelets 3- to 16-flowered, laterally compressed, bisexual, breaking apart above the glumes and between the florets. Glumes 2, ± equal, 1- to 5-veined, shorter than the florets, broad or narrow, acute, awned or awnless; lemmas 5- or 7-veined, acute, awned or awnless; palea shorter than or slightly longer than the lemma.

1 • 2 • 2–20. Mediterranean area and Asia. Crested or desert wheat grass (*A. cristatum*) (pl. 2). Naturalized. Stems to 1 m tall. Spikes 1–10+ cm long. Spikelets 7–16 mm long. Along roadsides at scattered locations. Cascades, Warner Mountains, Sierra Nevada, mountains of Southern California.

Plate 2. *Agropyron cristatum*

Planted for erosion control and to restore damaged areas, this is also a valuable forage grass. Includes *A. desertorum*, which is often treated as a separate entity. Other species reported in earlier floras have been transferred to *Elymus* or to segregates of that genus.

Agrostis   **Bent Grass, Bent, Redtop, Tickle Grass**
Annuals to rhizomatous-stoloniferous perennials. Stems to 1 m tall. Inflorescence an open to contracted panicle. Spikelets small (small spikelet size causes anguish and gastrointestinal disturbances), 1-flowered, laterally compressed, bisexual, breaking apart above [below] the glumes. Glumes 2, ± equal, the lower typically 1-veined and the upper 1-[3-] veined, as long as or longer than the floret; lemma typically 5-veined, veins not convergent, glabrous or hairy at base, awned dorsally from or below the middle or awnless; palea typically small or absent to ± equal to lemma. Stamens [1] 3.
22 • 30 • 200. Temperate and cooler regions of both hemispheres. These are of considerable economic importance as forage and lawn grasses. A number of them are also weedy. Creeping bent grass is carefully nurtured as the substrate on which some of us play a game that involves using expensive sticks to knock little white balls into small holes in the ground. You may confuse *Agrostis* with *Muhlenbergia* and *Sporobolus*, two other grasses with small, 1-flowered spikelets. You will be in good company. If you look at the nomenclatural history of these genera, you will discover that noted botanists also found them difficult to distinguish. The grasses may be separated as follows.

TABLE 44. A comparison of *Agrostis*, *Muhlenbergia*, and *Sporobolus*

Characteristic	*Agrostis*	*Muhlenbergia*	*Sporobolus*
Lemma vein number	3–5	3	1 [3]
Palea	poorly developed or 0	well-developed	well-developed
Leaf sheath	glabrous	glabrous	ciliate at apex
Ligule	membranous	membranous or **hyaline**	hairs
Seed	fused to pericarp	fused to pericarp	free from pericarp

With a little practice, you will soon be able to recognize this genus in the field. Determining species is another matter, however. A realistic, if not altogether satisfying, option is to decide that the grass is an *Agrostis* and to declare victory at that point. For those who enjoy the challenge, I offer the following key modified from M. J. Harvey (Hickman 1993: 1228, 1229).

CREEPING BENT GRASS, REDTOP. (pl. 3). Naturalized perennial, introduced in North America prior to 1750. Rhizomatous and often stoloniferous, stolons to 1 m long, often forming dense mats. Stems to 1.2 m tall, sometimes rooting at the nodes. Panicles 3–25 cm tall, narrowly contracted, branches ascending to ± erect. Spikelets 2–3

Plate 3. *Agrostis stolonifera*

mm long. Marshes, lake margins, streams, moist meadows, and lawns. Widespread. Valuable for livestock forage and provides cover for game birds and waterfowl. Ornamental uses in gardens and landscaping. Most authors treat *A. gigantea* (redtop) and *A. stolonifera* (creeping bent grass) as distinct species. Redtop is seen as a rhizomatous plant with panicles that remain open after flowering. Creeping bent is a stoloniferous plant with panicles that contract after flowering. Because rhizome and stolon production can be influenced by environmental conditions, and open and contracted panicles have been found in the same population, I join in the minority opinion that the two species should be combined under the older name, *Agrostis stolonifera*. Listed: Cal-IPC.

3b   Stolons less than 5 cm long; panicle branches bearing spikelets on upper half only ....**A. capillaris**
COLONIAL BENT OR BROWNTOP (pl. 4). Naturalized perennial from rhizomes or stolons. Stems to 75 cm tall, ascending or spreading. Panicles to 20 cm long, broadly ovate in outline. Spikelets 2–3.5 mm long. Roadsides and disturbed sites. A popular lawn grass. Klamath Region, Cascade Range, and Sierra Nevada south through the Central and South coasts.

4a   Floret callus hairs 1.5–2 mm long...**A. hallii**
HALL'S BENT GRASS. Native perennial. Rhizomes to 50 cm. Stems to 1 m tall. Panicles 7–22 cm long, open to dense, branches ascending to **appressed**. Spikelets 3.2–4.2 mm long. Oak woodlands and conifer forests. Northern California, Central and South coasts.

4b   Floret callus hairs 0–0.3 [1] mm long..**5**

5a   Palea absent or nearly so..**A. pallens**
DUNE OR SEASHORE BENT GRASS. Native perennial. Rhizomes present. Stems to 70 cm tall. Panicles 5–20 cm, open to contracted, branches generally ascending. Spikelets ± 3 mm long. Sea level to the subalpine in open meadows and forests. Widespread, except warm desert. The common name is misleading, in that it suggests a more restricted habitat.

5b   Palea at least half as long as the lemma...**6**

6a   Rhizomes thick, scaly; panicle branches bearing spikelets to their base ....**A. stolonifera complex**
See 3a.

6b   Rhizomes slender, not noticeably scaly; panicle branches bearing spikelets on upper half ....**A. capillaris**
See 3b.

7a   Lemma awned..**8**

7b   Lemma awnless (occasionally awned in *A. densiflora*)..................**11**

8a   Inflorescence open, branches clearly visible; spikelets not crowded **9**

8b   Inflorescence dense (rarely open in *A. exarata*), branches not clearly visible; spikelets overlapping..**10**

Plate 4. *Agrostis capillaris* (left) and *A. exarata* (right).

9a   Rachilla extended beyond lemma ± 1 mm; palea 1.2–1.5 mm long
....***A. avenacea***
PACIFIC BENT GRASS. Naturalized annual-perennial. Stems to 65 cm
tall. Panicles 7–30 cm long, ovate, open, branches spreading. Spikelets ± 2.5 mm long, lemma 2-toothed with an awn to 7.5 mm. Disturbed sites. North Coast Ranges, Sierra Nevada foothills, Central
Valley, South Coast Ranges.
9b   Rachilla not extended beyond lemma; palea 0–0.2 mm long
....***A. scabra***
TICKLE GRASS, ROUGH BENT GRASS. Native annual-perennial. Caespi-
tose, rhizomes and stolons lacking. Stems to 75 cm tall. Panicles 8–

25 cm long, diffuse, almost as wide as long; its roughened branches giving rise to the common name. Spikelets 2.2–3 mm long. Various habitats, especially on moist soils. North Coast Ranges, Sierra Nevada at medium to high elevations, Southern California. Valuable for livestock forage before flowering and for revegetation.

10a Plants annual ....**A. microphylla**
   SMALL-LEAVED BENT GRASS. Native annual. Stems to 45 cm tall. Panicles 2–12 cm long, dense, cylindric, branches ascending to appressed. Spikelets 3.5–4 mm long. Rocky, sandy areas on cliffs, vernal pools; sometimes on serpentine. North Coast, Central Valley, Central and South coasts.

10b Plants perennial...**A. exarata**
   SPIKE BENT GRASS (pl. 4). Native perennial. Caespitose, but sometimes rhizomatous. Stems to 1 m tall. Panicles 5–30 cm long, open to dense, branches ascending to appressed. Spikelet 2.5–3.5 mm long; lemma awn rudimentary to well-developed. Generally on moist sites below 3,000 m. Widespread. Valuable forage grass. Our most commonly collected bent grass.

11a Inflorescence dense, branches not clearly visible, spikelets crowded, overlapping (sometimes more open in *A. variabilis*) **12**

11b Inflorescence open, branches clearly visible, spikelets not crowded **13**

12a Leaf blades 2–10 mm wide; palea about 1/3 as long as the lemma; plants of coastal bluffs...**A. densiflora**
   CALIFORNIA BENT GRASS. Native perennial. Rhizomes and stolons absent. Stems to 85 cm tall. Panicles 2–10 cm long, dense and ± cylindrical, branches appressed. Spikelets ± 3 mm long. Sandy soils on coastal bluffs, dunes, and adjacent meadows. North, Central, and South coasts.

12b Leaf blades less than 1 mm wide; palea less than 1/3 the length of the lemma or absent; plants of subalpine-alpine meadows and forests .... **A. variabilis**
   MOUNTAIN BENT GRASS. Native perennial. Stems to 30 cm tall, erect or bent at the base. Panicles to 6 cm long, dense, cylindrical, the branches appressed. Spikelets ± 2.5 mm long. Northern California south through the Sierra Nevada.

13a Inflorescence about as wide as long; spikelets [2.2] 2.5–3.2 mm long ....**A. scabra**
   See 9b.

13b Inflorescence about twice as long as wide; spikelets 1.6–2.4 mm long...**A. x idahoensis**
   IDAHO BENT GRASS. Native perennial. Plants to 30 cm tall. Panicles to 13 cm long, lanceolate to ovate, the primary branches ascending. Conifer forests and wet subalpine and alpine meadows. Northern California through the Sierra Nevada to the mountains of Southern California.

Aira   **Hair Grass**

Delicate, caespitose annuals. Stems to 25 cm tall. Inflorescence an open
or contracted panicle. Spikelets 2-flowered, laterally compressed, bisexual, breaking apart above the glumes and between the florets. Glumes
2, ± equal, as long as or longer than the florets, 1- or 3-veined; lemmas
5-veined, a bent, hair-like awn arising from below the middle, apex with
2 slender teeth; palea relatively long. (Fig. 15)

2 • 2 • 8. Temperate regions of the Old World. Of no economic importance.

1a   Panicle open, 1.5–10 cm wide, the branches **divergent** to ascending
      ....**A. caryophyllea**
      SILVER HAIR GRASS (pl. 5). Stems to 60 cm tall. Spikelets 1.7–3.3 mm
      long. Low and medium elevations, especially on disturbed sites.
      Widespread. Two varieties in California, differing slightly in pedicel
      length and spikelet size.

1b   Panicle spike-like, less than 0.7 cm wide, the branches appressed
      .... **A. praecox**
      LITTLE HAIR GRASS, SHIVER GRASS. Stems to 40 cm. Spikelets 3–4 mm
      long. Mostly at low elevation along the North Coast.

Plate 5. *Aira caryophyllea*

Alopecurus   **Meadow Foxtail**

Annuals and caespitose or rhizomatous perennials. Stems to 1 m tall. Inflorescence a dense, spike-like panicle. Spikelets 1-flowered, strongly laterally compressed, bisexual, breaking apart below the glumes. Glumes 2, their lower edges united, ciliate-keeled, equal, 3-veined, equaling the floret; lemma 5-veined, its lower margins typically joined, awned from below the middle; palea absent or much-reduced. (Fig. 16)

6 • 11 • 36. Northern temperate regions of both hemispheres, especially Europe. Of economic significance as a source of fodder, pasture grasses, and weeds.

1a   Plants annual; lemma awn bent.. ***A. saccatus***
      PACIFIC MEADOW FOXTAIL (pl. 6). Native. Stems 12–45 cm tall. Panicles 1.5–6.5 cm long. Spikelets 4–5 mm long. Moist, open meadows, plains, and vernal pools. North Coast, Cascades and Sierra Nevada foothills, Central Valley, South Coast, Southwest California.

1b   Plants perennial; lemma awn straight.......***A. aequalis var. aequalis***
      SHORT-AWNED FOXTAIL. Native. Stems 9–75 cm tall. Panicles 1–9 cm long. Spikelets 2–2.5 mm long. Wet places from the coast to 3500 m. Widespread. Larger plants with longer lemmas from Marin County and Sonoma County marshes have been named *A. aequalis* var. *sonomensis*. Do not collect! Listed: USFWS.

Plate 6. *Alopecurus saccatus*

Ammophila   **Beach Grass, Marram**

Coarse, rhizomatous perennials. Stems to 1.5 m tall. Inflorescence a dense, spike-like panicle, 10–35 cm long. Spikelets large, 1-flowered, laterally compressed, bisexual, rachilla prolonged as a hairy bristle beyond the floret, breaking apart above the glumes. Glumes 2, ± equal, the lower 1-veined and the upper 1- to 3-veined, as long as or longer than the floret; lemma 5-veined, awnless, with long hairs at the base; palea relatively long, 2- or 4- to several-veined.

2 • 2 • 2. North America and Europe. European beach grass or marram (***A. arenaria*** **var.** ***arenaria***) (pls. 7 & 8). Naturalized. Stems to 1.2 m tall. Panicles 15–30 cm long. Spikelets 10–13 mm long. Native from the North

Plate 7. *Ammophila arenaria*

Sea to the Mediterranean and Black Sea. Here naturalized on sand dunes and extends for a short distance inland. North, Central, and South coasts. Beach grass may be confused with wild-ryes *(Elymus* spp.) growing in the same habitat, but they have more than one floret per spikelet. Listed: Cal-IPC.

Beach grass was first introduced into California at Golden Gate Park in the late 1800s, and later it was planted for dune stabilization and to protect highways and railroads from moving sand. It has become an invasive species that forms dense patches that crowd out native plants. This negatively affects the nesting habitat of the western snowy plover, a federally threatened bird. The Nature Conservancy and Humboldt Bay National Wildlife Refuge have been successful in eradicating plants using

Plate 8. *Ammophila arenaria*

mechanical and chemical means. European beach grass has also been used for thatching, brooms, and mats.

Andropogon   **Bluestem, Broom Sedge, Beard Grass**

Coarse, caespitose or rhizomatous perennials; less frequently annuals. Stems to 2 m tall, the internodes solid. Inflorescence a series of 2 to several rames, the flowering stems much-branched, subtended by a **spathe**-like sheath in some species. Spikelets 2-flowered (the lower floret sterile and the upper bisexual) and dorsally compressed. Sessile spikelet well developed and fertile, breaking apart with a section of rachis and pedicel; pedicellate spikelet reduced or absent in our representatives. Glumes 2, ± equal, firm, the lower keeled and 1- to several-veined and the upper 1- to 3-veined, awnless; sterile lemma hyaline, 2-veined, ± equaling the fertile lemma; fertile lemma hyaline, narrow, 1- to 3-veined entire or bifid, usually bearing a bent and twisted awn; palea hyaline, veinless, reduced or absent. Stamens 1–3.

2 • 15 • 120. Warmer regions of both hemispheres, especially well adapted to savannas. Of limited importance as pasture and fodder grasses, thatching, and erosion control.

1a   Inflorescence a series of 2–5 [7] aggregations of silky-white rames of spikelets scattered along the flowering stem; leaf sheaths glabrous...*A. virginicus* var. *virginicus*
       BROOM SEDGE BLUESTEM. Naturalized perennial. Stems to 2 m tall. Panicles with numerous dense clusters of spikelets; rames 2–3 cm long, silky white, flowering in the fall. Spikelets 3.5–4 mm long. Weed of disturbed moist sites. North Coast ranges, Cascades, Sierra Nevada foothills, Sacramento Valley.

1b   Inflorescence a series to 10 to numerous aggregations of tawny rames in dense spreading clusters; leaf sheaths minutely scabrous
       ....*A. glomeratus* var. *scabriglumis*
       BUSHY BLUESTEM, BUSHY BEARD GRASS (pl. 9). Native perennial. Stems to 1.5 m tall. Panicles densely clustered, plume-like; rames 1–3 cm long. Spikelets 4–4.5 mm long. Moist soils of open areas, springs, and seeps. Sierra Nevada, Sacramento Valley, South Coast, Southern California. Native only in the southern portion of its range.

Anthoxanthum   **Sweet Vernal Grass, Holy Grass, Sweet Grass**

Caespitose or rhizomatous perennials or annuals, plants pleasantly fragrant. Stems to 1+ m tall. Inflorescence an open to contracted panicle. Spikelets laterally compressed, bisexual, 3-flowered, with a single fertile floret subtended by two staminate or sterile ones reduced to awned lemmas, breaking apart above the glumes (the three florets falling as a group). Glumes 2, equal or unequal, the lower 1- to 5-veined and the upper 3- to

Plate 9. *Andropogon glomeratus*

5-veined, as long as or slightly shorter than the florets; lemmas of staminate florets awnless or with a short awn from a notched apex, 5-veined;
lemma of fertile floret 3- to 5-veined, awnless; palea 1- or 3-veined. Stamens 2 in bisexual florets or 3 in staminate ones. (Fig. 15)

5 • 6 • 50. Temperate and cooler regions of both hemispheres. As treated
here, the genus includes *Hierochloë*. Admittedly, our California grasses
traditionally assigned to that genus appear quite distinct from *Anthoxanthum*, but this is not the case when the Old World species are examined.
The vanilla-like odor of these grasses is from coumarin. It is the scent
you associate with newly mown hay. Coumarin is also found in sweet
clover, cinnamon, the tonka bean, and several other plants. The action
of naturally occurring fungi converts this compound into a very potent

anticoagulant. As such it can cause hemorrhaging and death from internal bleeding, which explains its use in products to kill rodents. Given in precise doses, it can also be an effective blood thinner to prevent clots after surgery. While coumarin has a very pleasant odor, it has a decidedly bitter taste that animals avoid. These grasses have been strewn on church floors, burned as incense, and used in Native American medicine and basketry.

1a Lower glume shorter than the upper; 2 lower florets awned
.... ***A. odoratum***
SWEET VERNAL GRASS (pl. 10). Naturalized perennial. Stems to 60 cm tall. Panicles 2–14 cm long. Spikelets 7–10 mm long. Meadows,

Plate 10. *Anthoxanthum odoratum*

pastures, lawns, and openings in forests. North Coast ranges, Sierra Nevada foothills, Central Coast. Listed: Cal-IPC. (Fig. 15)

1b   Glumes more or less equal; 2 lower florets awnless
.... ***A. occidentale***
VANILLA GRASS, CALIFORNIA SWEET GRASS (pl. 11). Native perennial. Stems to 1 m tall. Panicles 7–13 cm long. Spikelets 5–6 mm long. Moist to dry forests. Northern California, Central Coast, South Coast ranges.

Plate 11. *Anthoxanthum occidentale*

Aristida   Three-awn Grass

Caespitose annuals or perennials. Stems to 1 m tall, the internodes hollow or solid. Inflorescence an open or contracted panicle, sometimes reduced and raceme-like. Spikelets 1-flowered, terete to laterally compressed, bisexual, breaking apart above the glumes. Glumes 2, thin and narrow, 1-veined, as long as or longer than the floret; lemmas tough, terete, 3-veined, with a sharp-pointed callus, tapering gradually to an awn column that usually bears 3 awns (the lateral ones sometimes reduced or obsolete); palea relatively short to reduced. Stamens 1 or 3. (Fig. 13)

8 • 29 • 300. Drier grasslands, savannas, woodlands, and deserts of both hemispheres; their presence often indicating land abuse. Awns and calluses can be mechanically injurious to animals.

1a   Plants annual **2**
1b   Plants perennial...**3**
2a   Lower glumes 3- to 7-veined; lemma awns generally 12–70 mm
      long ....***A. oligantha***
      OLD FIELD THREE-AWN, PRAIRIE. Naturalized. Stems to 70 cm tall. Panicle raceme-like, 12–25 cm long. Spikelets 18–25 mm long. Disturbed places; fields, grasslands, woodlands. Northern California, Central Valley, South Coast. Flowers in the summer and fall, unusual for an annual.
2b   Lower glumes 1- or 2- [3-] veined; lemma awns 3–15 mm long
      ....***A. adscensionis***
      SIX-WEEKS THREE-AWN (pl. 12). Native. Stems to 80 cm tall. Panicles 2–22 cm long. Spikelets 6–12 mm long. Dry, often disturbed open rocky places, hillsides, often on sandy soils. Central and South coasts, Southern California.

(account continued)

Plate 12. *Aristida adscensionis*

3a Upper side of leaf blade glabrous or with hairs no longer than 0.5 mm long at its base ....***A. purpurea* complex** **PURPLE THREE-AWNS** (pl. 13). Natives. Stems to 1 m tall. Panicles 3–24 cm long, branches erect to drooping. Spikelets 11–15 mm long. Six intergrading or overlapping varieties, differing in position of panicle branches and pedicels, lemma apices, and glume color. Sandy to rocky soils, slopes, and plains. Great Basin, South Coast, Southern California.

3b Upper side of leaf blade with scattered hairs 1.5–3 mm long at its base...***A. ternipes* var. *gentilis*** **HOOK THREE-AWN, SPIDER GRASS.** Natives. Stems to 1+ m tall, prostrate to erect. Panicles 15–40 cm long, its branches spreading. Spikelets 9–15 mm long. Dry slopes, plains, roadsides. North Coast ranges, Sierra Nevada, Central Valley, South Coast, Southern California.

Plate 13. *Aristida purpurea*

Arrhenatherum   **Tall Oat Grass**

Caespitose perennials. Stems to 2 m tall; corms sometimes present. Inflorescence a narrow panicle 7–30 cm long. Spikelets 7–11 mm long, typically 2-flowered (the lower larger and staminate, the upper bisexual), laterally compressed, breaking apart above the glumes (florets falling together); rachilla extended as a bristle beyond the uppermost floret. Glumes 2, very unequal, the lower 1-veined and the upper 3-veined, awnless; lemmas 5- to

Plate 14. *Arrhenatherum elatius* (inflorescence)

9-veined, the lower with a dorsal bent, twisted awn, the upper awnless or with a short straight awn.

1 • 1 • 6. Europe and the Mediterranean. Tall oat grass or tuber oat grass *(A. elatius)* (pls. 14–16). Roadsides, disturbed places, and fields. Mostly northern half of state. Planted for pasture, erosion control, and as an ornamental; it escapes readily from cultivation.

Plate 15. *Arrhenatherum elatius* (spikelet detail)

Plate 16. *Arrhenatherum elatius* (corms)

Arundo   Giant Reed

Rhizomatous perennials. Stems 2–10 m tall, woody. Leaf blades to 80 cm long and 7 cm wide. Inflorescence a terminal, plumose, silvery to purplish panicle 30–60 cm long. Spikelets 10–15 mm long, 2- to several-flowered, bisexual, laterally compressed, breaking apart above the glumes and between the florets; rachilla glabrous. Glumes 2, ± equal, 3-veined, tapering to a point, awnless; lemmas 5- to 9-veined, long-hairy on their lower half, tapering to a point or awn. (Fig. 13)

1 · 1 · 3. Cosmopolitan in tropical, subtropical, and warm temperate regions. Giant reed *(A. donax)* (pls. 17 & 18). Naturalized. Weedy along waterways. North, Central, and South coasts, Central Valley, Southern

Plate 17. *Arundo donax*

Plate 18. *Arundo donax*

California. Of economic importance as an ornamental and for erosion control. Its stems are also used in construction and for canes, fishing rods, and arrow shafts, and as a source of industrial cellulose. Stem tissue has been used for 5,000 years to make the musical reeds for wind instruments and organs. The Environmental Protection Agency has approved the giant reed as a biofuel. Young shoots were eaten by Native Americans. Because of its size and woody stems, the giant reed is our most bamboo-like grass. It is easily distinguished from true bamboos by its terminal panicles and leaves with sheathing bases. Listed: Cal-IPC. You might confuse the giant reed with two other robust grasses with plume-like inflorescences. They are compared in Table 45.

TABLE 45. A comparison of *Arundo*, *Cortaderia*, and *Phragmites*

Characteristic	Arundo	Cortaderia	Phragmites
Leaves mainly basal	no	yes	no
Lemma	densely hairy	hairy	glabrous
Glumes	longer than florets	longer than florets	shorter than florets
Rachilla segments	glabrous	upper part hairy	silky-hairy

Avena **Oat**

Caespitose annuals. Stems to 1 m tall. Inflorescence an open panicle, the branches capillary and pendulous, sometimes reduced to a raceme or even a solitary spikelet in **depauperate** material. Spikelets large, typically 2- or 3-flowered, bisexual, laterally compressed, breaking apart above the glumes and between the florets (except in cultivated oats). Glumes 2, unequal to ± equal, 3- to 11-veined, as long as or longer than the florets, awnless; lemmas rounded, 5- to 7-veined, with a stout, bent awn from at or below its middle (reduced or absent in cultivated oats), tip 2-toothed or with bristle-like extensions.

5 • 8 • 25–30. Temperate and cold regions of Europe, North Africa, and Asia. Of considerable economic importance, both positive and negative, as a source of food and noxious weeds.

1a   Awn straight to curved or absent; callus glabrous; spikelets not breaking apart at maturity ....***A. sativa***

     OAT, CULTIVATED OAT (pl. 19). Naturalized. Stems to 2+ m tall. Panicles 15–40 cm long. Spikelets 25–32 mm long. Widespread, especially near cultivated fields and along roadsides. Grains used in a variety of food products (oatmeal, cakes, crackers, cookies, etc.), in cosmetics (soaps, shampoos, etc.), and to reduce cholesterol. The cultivated oat is a domesticated form of *A. fatua* and it is sometimes treated as a variety of that species.

1b   Awn bent above and twisted below; callus bearded; breaking apart above the glumes at maturity..**2**

(account continued)

Plate 19. *Avena sativa*

2a   Lemma apex bristle-tipped, the teeth 2–6 mm long.........**A. *barbata***
SLENDER OAT, SLENDER WILD OAT (pl. 20). Naturalized. Stems to 80+ cm tall. Panicles 15–35 cm long. Spikelets 21–30 mm long. Widespread, especially at low elevations. Listed: Cal-IPC. An important forage grass, particularly when young.

Plate 20. *Avena barbata*

2b   Lemma apex bifid, the teeth about 1 mm long .... **A. fatua**
WILD OAT (pl. 21). Naturalized. Stems to 2 m tall. Panicles 7–40 cm long. Spikelets 18–32 mm long. Widespread pernicious weed here and worldwide. First collected in California in 1882. Listed: Cal-IPC. Its panicles of large, drooping spikelets are sometimes gathered for dried floral arrangements.

Plate 21. *Avena fatua*

Beckmannia   Slough Grass

Annual (ours) or rhizomatous perennial. Stems to 1.5 m. Inflorescence a panicle or raceme of appressed or ascending spikes. Spikelets 1- or 2-flowered, ± circular in side view, laterally compressed, sessile, breaking apart below the glumes, the rachilla often prolonged. Glumes 2, equal, broad, inflated, 3-veined, strongly keeled, transversely wrinkled, and apiculate at apex; lemma ± equal to glumes, narrow, inconspicuously 5-veined, awnless, tapering to a slender tip. Palea narrow, shorter than lemma.

1 • 1 • 2. Eurasia and North America. American slough grass *(B. syzigachne)* (pl. 22). Native annual. Stems to 1.5 m tall. Panicles 7–30 cm long. Spikelets 2–3 mm long. Marshes and wet places over much of the northern half of California. It is sometimes frequent enough to use for hay or forage. Its spikelet shape is highly diagnostic.

Plate 22. *Beckmannia* syzigachne

Bothriochloa   **Bluestem**

Caespitose-rhizomatous-stoloniferous perennials. Stems to 2 m tall, erect or decumbent, the internodes solid. Inflorescence a series of a few to several rames, silvery-white in our species. Pedicels and upper rachis branches with a central groove or membranous area. Spikelets paired, one sessile and the other stalked, dorsally compressed. Sessile spikelet 2-flowered, the lower reduced to a hyaline scale, the upper floret fertile and awned; some with a pit (depressed glandular area) on the middle or upper portion of the lower glume, dorsally compressed; upper glume ± keeled, 3-veined. Pedicellate spikelet well-developed or reduced, staminate or sterile, unawned. Spikelet pairs and a section of rachis breaking away as a unit.

4 • 13 • 35. Warmer parts of both hemispheres. Used for forage and range rehabilitation; a few are popular ornamentals. Cane bluestem *(B. barbinodis)* (pl. 23). Native. Stems to 1.2 m tall. Leaf blades 20–30 cm long. Panicles 7–14 cm long. Common on dry slopes and open hillsides. Southern California. Used as an ornamental.

Plate 23. *Bothriochloa barbinodis*

Bouteloua   **Grama Grass**

Annuals or caespitose, rhizomatous, or stoloniferous perennials. Stems to 1 m tall, internodes hollow or solid. Inflorescence a panicle of 1 to many short, spicate branches attached along a common axis, each bearing sessile, overlapping spikelets in 2 rows along a flattened or angular rachis. Spikelets with 1 fertile floret and 1–3 rudimentary ones above it, laterally compressed, breaking apart either above the glumes (subgenus *Chondrosum*) or at the base of a branch, the subunit of the inflorescence falling at maturity (subgenus *Bouteloua*). Glumes 2, equal or unequal, 1-veined, awned or awnless; lemmas 3-veined, the veins often extended as awns; palea sometimes 2-awned. (Fig. 13)

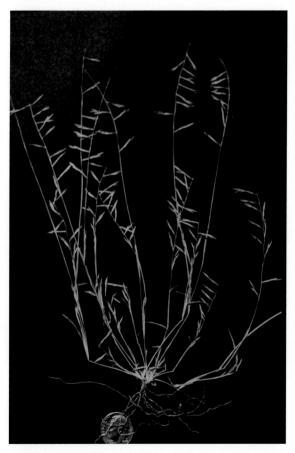

Plate 24. *Bouteloua aristidoides*

6 • 23 • 40–50. New World from Canada through South America; the American Southwest and Mexico are major centers of diversity. Several are important forage grasses and major components of North American grasslands, especially the western part of the Great Plains.

1a   Panicle branches extending beyond the last spikelet, deciduous, bearing 1–5 spikelets, these appressed to the branch
....**B. aristidoides**
      NEEDLE GRAMA (pl. 24). Native annual. Stems to 35 cm tall. Panicles 2.5–10.5 cm long, with 4–16 branches. Spikelets 6–8 mm long; awns unequal. Dry, open slopes, washes. Mojave and Sonoran deserts.

1b   Panicle branches terminating in a spikelet, persistent, bearing [7] 20–100+ closely crowded spikelets **2**

2a   Plants annual; upper glumes glabrous.........**B. barbata var. barbata**
      SIX-WEEK'S GRAMA (pl. 25). Native. Stems to 30 cm tall, erect to prostrate and sometimes rooting at the nodes. Panicles 1–25 cm long, with 2–8 branches. Spikelets 2.5–3.5 mm long; awns ± equal. Sandy to rocky places; scrub, woodlands, pine forests, disturbed sites. San Joaquin Valley, Peninsular ranges, Mojave and Sonoran deserts.

Plate 25. *Bouteloua barbata*

2b Plants perennial; at least some upper glumes with swollen-based hairs...***B. gracilis***

BLUE GRAMA (pl. 26). Native. Stems to 60 cm tall. Panicles 2–9 cm long, with 1–3 branches. Spikelets 5–6 mm long; awns ± equal. Sandy to rocky sites in woodlands and pine forests. San Bernardino Mountains, Mojave and Sonoran deserts. An important forage grass and popular ornamental.

Plate 26. *Bouteloua gracilis*

Brachypodium   **False Brome, Purple-brome**

Mostly perennials. Stems to 2 m tall. Inflorescence a series of linear racemes on stiffly erect branches. Spikelets 1 per node, ± sessile, divergent. Spikelets 2- to 20-flowered, ± terete to slightly laterally compressed, bisexual, breaking apart above the glumes and between the florets. Glumes 2, 5- to 9-veined; lemmas membranous, sometimes leathery at maturity, 7- to 9-veined, acute to awned from the tip; paleas keeled, ciliate to minutely toothed.

5 • 5 • 18. Temperate regions of Europe and Asia, especially of woodlands and open grasslands of the Mediterranean. Annual or purple false brome *(**B. distachyon**)* (pl. 27). Stems to 35+ cm tall. Racemes 2–7 cm long.

Plate 27. *Brachypodium distachyon*

Spikelets 15–40 mm long. Low elevations on dry slopes, disturbed fields and grasslands, and edges of thickets. North Coast ranges, Cascades, Sierra Nevada foothills, Central Valley, South Coast to Southern California. Although sometimes abundant, it is a poor forage grass. The other species are naturalized on a much more limited basis. Heath false brome or tor grass *(B. pinnatum)* is thriving on sand dunes in Sonoma County.

TABLE 46. A comparison of *Brachypodium* and *Bromus*

Characteristic	*Brachypodium*	*Bromus*
Leaf sheath	open	closed
Inflorescence	spike-like raceme	panicle
Lemma apex	obtuse or acute	2-toothed

Briza   **Quaking Grass, Rattlesnake Grass**

Tufted annuals (ours) or perennials. Stems to 50 cm tall. Inflorescence an open panicle, the spikelets appearing inflated and often dangle on hair-like pedicels. Spikelets 2- to several-flowered, florets crowded and spreading at right angles to the rachilla, bisexual, laterally compressed, breaking apart above the glumes and between the florets. Glumes 2, ± equal, thin and papery, rounded, 3- to 15-veined; lemmas rounded, similar to glumes in texture, 5- to 9-veined, awnless.

3 • 3 • 16–20. Europe, Mexico, and principally South America. Two European species are naturalized in California. Their scientific and common names provide an excellent clue as to their comparative sizes.

1a   Spikelets oval to oblong, 10–20 mm long .... *B. maxima*
      LARGE QUAKING GRASS OR RATTLESNAKE GRASS (pl. 28). Stems to 80
      cm tall. Panicles 3.5–10 cm long. Coastal dunes, roadsides, pastures,
      and woodlands. North Coast, Sierra Nevada foothills, Central and
      South coasts. It is gathered for dried arrangements, especially when
      the glumes become tinged with purple. Listed: Cal-IPC.

(account continued)

Plate 28. *Briza maxima*

Plate 29. *Briza minor*

1b Spikelets triangular to oval, 2–5 mm long ....***B. minor***
    SMALL QUAKING GRASS (pl. 29). Stems to 40 cm tall. Panicles 4–14 cm
    long. Various habitats, especially moist sites. Widespread, mostly in
    the northern half of the state.

Bromus   **Brome Grass, Rescue Grass, Chess, Ripgut**

Annuals or rhizomatous-stoloniferous perennials. Stems to 2 m tall, the
internodes hollow [solid]. Leaf sheaths closed. Inflorescence an open to
contracted panicle, sometimes reduced to a raceme or even to 1- to a few
spikelet(s). Spikelets several-flowered, laterally compressed to rounded,
bisexual, breaking apart above the glumes and between the florets.

Plate 30. Inflorescences of six *Bromus* species

Glumes 2, typically unequal in length and shorter than the lowest floret, the lower 1- to 7-veined, the upper 5- to several-veined, rounded to keeled, awnless; lemmas 5- to several-veined, awned from a bifid tip or awnless; palea often fused to the caryopsis; ovary hairy, with an apical appendage and lateral styles.

35 • 51 • 150 (100–400!) (pl. 30). Temperate regions of both hemispheres, and in cooler, mountainous regions of the tropics and subtropics. Most of our perennials are native; most of our annuals are European introductions. Controversy continues as to species definitions, as seen in the numbers just cited. Of considerable economic significance as a source of fodder, hay, and invasive weeds. The stout awns and sharp florets of some plants can cause mechanical injury to the eyes, nostrils, and ears of grazing animals, leading to inflammation and infection. You may confuse *Bromus* with *Brachypodium* (see preceding table) or, more likely, with *Festuca*.

TABLE 47. A comparison of *Bromus* and *Festuca*

Characteristic	*Bromus*	*Festuca*
Leaf sheaths	closed to near top	open [closed]
Spikelet length	[5] 10–70 mm	3–20 mm
Lemma vein number	5–13	5 [7]
Lemma apex	entire, notched, toothed	acute to **attenuate**
Apical appendage on ovary	present	absent

1a Spikelets strongly laterally compressed, glumes and lemmas distinctly keeled **2**

1b Spikelets terete to slightly compressed, glumes and lemmas rounded to flattened, but not keeled **3**

2a Plants annual [perennial]; lemmas 9- to 13-veined, prominent, often raised, awn 0–3.5 mm long...................................**B. catharticus**
RESCUE GRASS (pl. 31). Naturalized annual-perennial. Stems to 1+ m tall. Sheaths usually densely hairy. Panicles 9–28 cm long, erect or nodding, lower branches spreading or ascending. Spikelets 20–40 mm; lemma margins whitish or purplish. Introduced as a forage grass and now widely naturalized in open, disturbed areas. Wide-

Plate 31. *Bromus catharticus*

spread. The common name refers to plants providing forage after droughts or severe winters.

2b   Plants perennial; lemma 7- to 9-veined, veins faint; awns 4–17 mm long ....***B. carinatus***

CALIFORNIA OR MOUNTAIN BROME (pl. 32). Native annual-perennial. Stems to 1+ m tall. Panicles 5–40 cm long, lower branches ascending to **reflexed**. Spikelets 2–4 cm long. Woodlands, meadows, grasslands from coastal areas to the subalpine. Widespread. Valuable forage grasses. Mountain brome (*B. carinatus* var. *marginatus*) is often recognized, based primarily on spikelets with shorter awns. This and other features intergrade completely with the typical variety.

Plate 32. *Bromus carinatus*

3a   Awns generally 15–55 mm long; lemma apex bifid, the teeth 3–7
     mm long (except in *B. sterilis*)..**4**
3b   Awns generally 0–15 mm long; lemma apex entire to bifid, the
     teeth less than 1 mm **8**
4a   Lemma 2–3 cm long, teeth 3–7 mm; awn 30–65 mm long
     ....***B. diandrus***
     RIPGUT OR NEEDLE BROME (pl. 33). Naturalized annual. Stems to 90
     cm. Sheaths with soft hairs. Panicles 6–25 cm long, branches stiffly
     erect to ascending or spreading, bearing 1 or 2 spikelets. Spikelets [2]
     3–6 cm long; lower glume linear, the upper lanceolate; callus with
     sharp point; florets mostly self-fertilized. An abundant weed along
     our roadsides, and in fields, vacant lots, and waste areas. A source
     of good forage when plants are young, but its sharp-pointed florets
     and long awns cause mechanical injury to wild animals and pets
     by penetrating the eyes, mouth, ears, and nostrils. Listed: Cal-IPC.
4b   Lemma 9–20 mm long, teeth 1–3 mm long; awn 8–30 mm long......**5**
5a   Spikelets shorter than or as long as the panicle branches **6**
5b   Spikelets mostly longer than the panicle branches **7**
6a   Lemma 14–20 mm long, awn 18–30 mm; primary inflorescence
     branches with 1–3 spikelets...***B. sterilis***
     POVERTY BROME OR STERILE BROME. Naturalized annual. Stems to
     1 m. Sheaths densely **pubescent**. Panicles 10–20 cm long, branches
     ascending, spreading, or drooping. Spikelets 20–35 mm, awns 15–30
     mm. Roadsides, fields, overgrazed rangelands, waste areas at low
     elevations. Widespread.

(account continued)

Plate 33. *Bromus diandrus*

6b   Lemma 9–12 mm long; awn 8–18 mm; primary inflorescence
      branches bearing 4 or more spikelets .... ***B. tectorum***
      CHEAT GRASS, DOWNY BROME (pl. 34). Naturalized annual. Stems to
      90 cm. Sheaths usually densely hairy. Panicles 5–20 cm long, open,
      branches hair-like, typically drooping to one side. Spikclets 10–20
      mm long, awns 10–18 mm long. Naturalized on disturbed sites, such
      as overgrazed rangelands. Widespread. Provides good forage when
      young. Highly invasive and quickly becomes dominant after fires.
      The common name comes from western farmers believing they had
      been sold impure seed or that this grass had cheated them by sud-
      denly replacing wheat in their fields. *Bromus tectorum* is probably
      the worst weedy grass in the western United States, where it now is
      dominant over about 100 million acres. It is particularly adept at
      colonizing burned soils, where it can then outcompete native grasses
      and shrubs. Recent research suggests that a fungal pathogen, *Pyre-
      nophora semenperda*—known affectionately as the "black fingers
      of death"—may prove effective in killing cheat grass seeds. Listed:
      Cal-IPC.

7a   Inflorescence loose, some branches spreading, visible
      ....***B. madritensis* subsp. *madritensis***
      SPANISH BROME, MADRID BROME, OR COMPACT BROME. Naturalized
      annual. Stems to 70 cm. Panicles 3–15 cm long, branches ascend-
      ing to spreading, bearing 1 or 2 spikelets. Spikelets 30–50 mm long;
      awns 12–23 mm long. Roadsides and disturbed places. North Coast
      ranges, Sierra Nevada foothills, Central Valley, South Coast, and
      deserts. Often a pioneer on disturbed soils, forming dense stands.

(account continued)

Plate 34. *Bromus tectorum*

7b Inflorescence dense, spikelets clustered, ascending to erect, often reddish-brown, branches not readily visible
....*B. madritensis* subsp. *rubens*
FOXTAIL OR RED BROME (pl. 35). Naturalized annual. Stems to 40 cm tall. Panicles 2–10 cm long. Spikelets 18–25 mm long. Widespread at low and medium elevations; much more common than subsp. *madritensis*. Often treated as distinct species, but the two entities are scarcely distinguishable when examined world wide. Listed: Cal-IPC.

8a Plants perennial...**9**

8b Plants annual **11**

9a Plants rhizomatous; lemma awn 0–2.5 [3] mm long .... *B. inermis*
SMOOTH BROME OR HUNGARIAN BROME. Naturalized. Stems to 1+ m tall. Panicles 10 cm to 25 cm long, open to somewhat contracted. Spikelets 2–4 cm long; lemmas 9–13 mm long, glabrous, sometimes hairy below. Widespread along roadsides and on disturbed sites. Valuable for forage and revegetation after fires.

9b Rhizomes absent; lemma awn 3–7 [9] mm long...............................**10**

10a Stems erect; sheaths **pilose** or ± velvety; upper glume 3- [5-] veined
....*B. orcuttianus*
ORCUTT'S BROME. Native. Stems 80–150 cm tall. Panicles 7–15 cm long. Spikelets 2–4 cm long. Dry places, meadows, open woods; mostly below 2500 m. Widespread.

10b Stems decumbent, often rooting at the lower nodes; sheaths glabrous; upper glume 5-veined ....*B. laevipes*
CHINOOK BROME OR WOODLAND BROME. Native. Stems to 1.6 m. Panicles 8–20 cm long, branches ascending, to spreading, eventually drooping. Spikelets 1.5–4 cm long; margins of glumes and lemmas often bronze-tinged; awns 4–6 mm long, straight. Woodlands and slopes at low to medium elevations. North Coast ranges, Cascades, Sierra Nevada foothills, Central Valley, South Coast, Southern California.

(account continued)

Plate 35. *Bromus madritensis* subsp. *rubens*

11a Panicle dense, all spikelets ascending to erect; lemmas papery, their veins prominently raised.....................................**B. hordeaceus**
SOFT BROME, SOFT CHESS, LOP GRASS (pl. 36). Naturalized. Stems to 70 cm. Lower sheaths densely hairy. Panicles 1–13 cm long (sometimes reduced to 1 or 2 spikelets), branches ascending to erect. Spikelets 14–20 mm long; awns 6–8 mm long, straight or curved at maturity. An abundant weed of disturbed sites at low elevations. Widespread. Listed: Cal-IPC.

11b Panicles open, at least the lower spikelets spreading to nodding; lemmas ± leathery, their veins not raised **12**

12a Glumes hairy ....**B. arenarius**

Plate 36. *Bromus hordeaceus*

AUSTRALIAN CHESS. Naturalized. Stems to 40 cm. Panicles 10–15 cm long, open, branches spreading or ascending, wavy. Spikelets 10–20 mm long; glumes and lemmas densely hairy; awns 10–16 mm long, straight or slightly spreading. Dry slopes, fields, and waste areas. An important forage species. Widespread.

12b Glumes glabrous...**13**

13a Lemma awn twisted at base, arising 2–5 mm below the apex
....**B. japonicus**
JAPANESE BROME. Naturalized. Stems to 85 cm. Panicles 10–26 cm long, branches slender, flexuous and wavy, ascending, spreading, or drooping. Spikelets 20–40 mm long, awns strongly divergent when mature. Disturbed sites, fields, and roadsides. Widespread.

13b Lemma awn not twisted at base, arising less than 1.5 mm below the apex..**B. commutatus**
MEADOW BROME, HAIRY CHESS. Naturalized. Stems to 1+ m tall. Leaf sheaths and blades hairy. Panicles 6–18 cm long, open, branches drooping and bearing a few spikelets toward the ends. Spikelets 1.5–2 [3] cm long; awns 4–10 mm long. Meadows, moist slopes, streams. Widespread, especially in the northern part of the state.

(Key based in part on D. Wilken & E. Painter in Hickman 1993: 1,240, 1,242.)

Calamagrostis   **Reed Grass, Bluejoint**

Caespitose, rhizomatous, or stoloniferous perennials, often of wet and marshy sites. Stems to 2 m tall, sometimes reed-like. Inflorescence an open to contracted panicle. Spikelets 1-flowered, laterally compressed, bisexual, breaking apart above the glumes, rachilla often extended as a slender, hairy bristle. Glumes 2, ± equal, longer than the floret, the lower 1-veined and the upper 3-veined; lemma 3- or 5-veined, generally tapering into 4 teeth, bearing a slender, bent dorsal awn from below its middle; callus hairs long.

11 • 23 • 250. Temperate and cooler regions of both hemispheres. Of limited economic importance; a few are range forage grasses; Foerster's reed grass *(C. x acutiflora)* is a widely planted ornamental. Although the genus is not difficult to recognize in the field, hybridization, asexual reproduction, and the formation of polyploids make species identification a challenge.

1a Lemma awn 4–5.5 mm long, generally extended beyond the tip of the glumes ....**C. koelerioides**
FIRE REED GRASS, TUFTED PINE GRASS. Rhizomes to 5 cm long. Stems to 1 m+ tall. Panicles 10–13 cm long, generally dense, straw-colored to pale purple, branches appressed. Spikelets 4.5–6 mm long; awn stout and easily distinguished from callus hairs. Meadows, slopes, hills, and ridges. North Coast ranges, Central Coast, South Coast and Peninsular ranges.

1b   Lemma awn 1–3 mm long, generally not extended beyond the tip of the glumes **2**

2a   Lemmas 2–3.1 mm long; callus hairs nearly as long as the lemma .... ***C. canadensis***

BLUEJOINT. Rhizomes to 15+ cm long. Stems 1+ m tall. Panicles 9–25 cm long, nodding, often purplish, contracted when young, but opening at maturity. Spikelets 2–4.5 mm long, rachilla hairs to 3 mm, silky; awn often difficult to distinguish from callus hairs. Moist meadows, bogs, and forest openings at medium to high elevations. Klamath Region, Cascades, Sierra Nevada.

Plate 37. *Calamagrostis nutkaensis*

2b   Lemmas 4–4.5 mm long; callus hairs less than ½ as long as the
lemma...**C. nutkaensis**
PACIFIC REED GRASS (pls. 37 & 38). Rhizomes generally shorter than
3 cm. Stems to 1.5 m tall. Panicles generally 12–23 cm long, erect to
nodding, contracted to ± loose, greenish-yellow to purplish. Spikelets 4.5–6.5 mm long; awn easily distinguished from callus hairs.
Usually at or near immediate coast in meadows, fens, dunes, and on
cliffs; occasionally inland. North and Central coasts. (Fig. 16)

Plate 38. *Calamagrostis nutkaensis*

Cenchrus   **Sandbur, Sandspur, Fountain Grass**

Annuals or caespitose-rhizomatous-stoloniferous perennials. Stems erect or weak, decumbent, internodes hollow or solid, to 4 m tall. Inflorescence a spike-like panicle bearing **fascicles** of spikelets subtended by sets of bristles or a series of spike-like or racemose burs. Spikelets 2-flowered (the lower sterile or staminate and the upper fertile), dorsally compressed to ± rounded, bisexual, hidden within burs (involucres of bristles or spines) (pl. 39), the entire structure falling from the plant at maturity (*Cenchrus* in the traditional sense) or solitary or in clusters of 2 or 3, subtended by an involucre of bristles (often plumose), these united at their base and falling with the spikelet (*Pennisetum* in the traditional sense). Glumes

Plate 39. *Cenchrus* burs

2, unequal, the lower 0- to 5-veined and the upper 0- to 11-veined; sterile lemma 1- to 15-veined, ± equal to fertile lemma, awnless; fertile lemma 3- to 12-veined, thin, membranous or firmer than the glumes.

12 • 23 • 96. Warmer regions of both hemispheres, but mostly American. Transitional species have made the distinction between sandburs *(Cenchrus)* and fountain grasses *(Pennisetum)* seem arbitrary. A recent paper (Chemisquy et al., 2010, Annals of Botany 106: 107–130) presents the arguments for combining the two genera, as adopted here. Sandbur spines can be injurious to the mouths of animals that consume them. We are able to identify sandburs with relative ease when we encounter them with our bare feet or remove them from our skin, clothing, shoes, pets, and so on. The backwardly barbed spines are painful to remove. Sandbur seeds may remain viable in the soil for many years. Of economic importance as a source of grains, pasture and lawn grasses, ornamentals, paper fibers, and weeds. Kikuyu grass, traditionally treated as *P. clandestinum*, now resides in *Kikuyuochloa.*

1a   Spikelets in fascicles of 1–4 surrounded by and mostly concealed within a bur formed of sharp-pointed, fused, flattened bristles **2**

1b   Spikelets subtended by sets of free or only partially fused bristles that are not fused to form sharp-pointed burs....................................**4**

2a   Sheaths strongly keeled ....***C. longispinus***
     MAT SANDBUR, LONG-SPINED SANDBUR. Naturalized annual. Stems to 90 cm tall, often decumbent, often forming large mats. Panicles 1.5–8 cm long; bristles 45–75, the outer shorter than the inner. Spikelets 6–8 mm long. Disturbed places, Modoc Plateau, Central Valley, South Coast ranges, Southern California. Listed: CDFA.

2b   Sheaths rounded to compressed, but not keeled................................**3**

3a   Burs with 1 whorl of flattened, united inner spines subtended by 1 to several whorls of smaller, finer bristles......................***C. echinatus***
     SOUTHERN SANDBUR. Naturalized annual. Stems to 1 m tall. Panicles 2.5–12 cm long. Spikelets 5–7 mm long. Disturbed sites. Southern California. Listed: CDFA.

3b   Burs with several whorls of flattened spines, these at irregular intervals ....***C. incertus***
     COASTAL SANDBUR, COMMON SANDBUR, FIELD SANDBUR. Naturalized annual-perennial. Stems 10–50+ cm tall. Panicles 3–5+ cm long. Spikelets 3.5–6 mm long. Disturbed woods, fields, and waste areas. Central Valley, South Coast, Southern California. Listed: CDFA.

(account continued)

4a   Panicles white to light brown; spikelets 9–12 mm long
    .... ***C. villosus***
    FEATHERTOP (pl. 42). Naturalized perennial. Escaped ornamental.
    Stems to 75 cm tall. Panicles 2–10 cm long. Spikelets 9–12 mm long.
    Lawns and other disturbed areas. Sierra Nevada, San Francisco Bay
    Area, South Coast, Southern California.

Plate 40. *Cenchrus setaceus*

4b   Panicles pink to dark burgundy; spikelets 2.5–7 mm long
....***C. setaceus***

CRIMSON OR TENDER FOUNTAIN GRASS (pls. 40 & 41). (Fig. 14) Naturalized perennial. Stems to 1.5 m tall. Panicles 8–30 cm long. Spikelets 4.5–7 mm long. Escaped ornamental and aggressive weed. Central Valley, San Francisco Bay Area, South Coast, Southern CA. Listed: Cal-IPC.

Plate 41. *Cenchrus setaceus* (inflorescence detail)

Plate 42. *Cenchrus villosus*

Chloris   **Windmill Grass, Finger Grass**
Caespitose annuals or perennials from rhizomes or stolons. Stems to 3 m
tall, internodes hollow or solid. Leaf sheaths keeled. Inflorescence a series
of racemose or digitate branches, each bearing 2 rows of sessile spikelets.
Spikelets with 1 [2] fertile floret and 1 or more rudimentary ones above it,
laterally compressed, bisexual, breaking apart above the glumes. Glumes
2, equal or unequal, the lower 1-veined and the upper 1- to 4-veined; fertile lemma 3-veined, awned from the tip. (Fig. 13)

4 • 20 • 70. Warmer regions of the Old World and New World, especially
in the southern hemisphere. Of some economic importance as pasture
grasses, several are invasive weeds, a few are grown as ornamentals. Table
48 compares grasses with digitate inflorescences. The crab grasses *(Digitaria)* have digitate or racemose branching, but the dorsally compressed
spikelets that break apart below the glumes set them apart.

1a   Plants annual; florets 2, the lower bisexual and the upper sterile
     .... ***C. virgata***
     FEATHER FINGER GRASS OR SHOWY CHLORIS (pl. 43). Naturalized. Stems
     to 70 cm tall. Inflorescence 5–10 cm long, of 4–20 digitate branches.
     Spikelets 1.5–4.5 mm long, strongly overlapping. An increasingly com-
     mon annual weed of summer and fall along roadsides and in agricul-
     tural fields throughout the state. Younger inflorescences are attractive,
     but older ones, when they begin to fade and break apart, far less so.

1b   Plants perennial, typically from thick, leafy stolons; florets 3–5, the
     lowest fertile and the others staminate or sterile .... ***C. gayana***
     RHODES GRASS. Naturalized. Stems to 2+ m tall. Inflorescence 8–20
     cm long, of 7–30 digitate branches. Spikelets 2.5–5 mm long, strongly
     overlapping. Moist, disturbed sites and irrigated pastures in the
     Central Valley and South Coast. It is a major forage grass in the
     tropics and subtropics. The common name commemorates Cecil
     Rhodes of South Africa, where the grass is native.

TABLE 48. A comparison of grasses with digitate inflorescences

Characteristic	*Chloris*	*Cynodon*	*Dactyloctenium*	*Eleusine*
Spikelets strongly keeled	no	no	yes	no
Floret number	2+	1	2+	2+
Glumes awned	no	no	yes	no
Lemmas awned	yes	no	yes	no
Rachilla extended	no	yes	no	no

Plate 43. *Chloris virgata*

Cinna **Wood Reed**

Caespitose or rhizomatous perennials, often of moist, shady sites. Stems to 2 m tall. Inflorescence an open or congested panicle, 3–46 cm long, the branches spreading to ascending. Spikelets 1-flowered, laterally compressed, bisexual, and breaking apart below the glumes, the rachilla extended above the floret as a stub or bristle. Glumes 2, equal or the lower shorter, the lower 1-veined and the upper 1- or 3-veined; lemmas 3- to 5-veined (these sometimes faint), the mid-vein extended as a short, straight awn; palea 1-veined. Stamens 1 or 2.

2 • 3 • 4. Temperate regions of both hemispheres, often in damp woods and meadows or beside streams. Of no economic importance.

1a   Florets ± sessile within the spikelet; stamens 2..............**_C. bolanderi_**
      BOLANDER'S OR SIERRAN WOOD REED. Endemic. Stems to 2+ m tall.
      Panicles 7–43 cm long. Spikelets 4–5.5 mm long. Meadows and along
      streams in Madera, Mariposa, and Tulare counties.
1b   Florets on a **stipe** 0.1–0.7 mm long within the spikelet; stamen 1
      ....**_C. latifolia_**
      DROOPING OR SLENDER WOOD REED (pl. 44). Native. Stems to 1 m tall.
      Panicles 3–46 cm long. Spikelets 2.5–4 mm long. Stream banks and
      other moist sites. Northwest California, Cascades, Sierra Nevada.

Plate 44. *Cinna latifolia*

Cortaderia   **Pampas Grass**

Robust, caespitose, dioecious perennials. Stems to 4 m tall. Leaf blades to 2 m long, 2–14 mm wide, mostly basal, the blades often with harsh, toothed margins. Inflorescence a terminal panicle (conspicuously plumose in female plants). Spikelets 2- to 8- flowered, unisexual, laterally compressed, breaking apart above the glumes and between the florets, the rachilla extended beyond the uppermost floret. Glumes 2, ± equal, glabrous, 1- to 3-veined, awnless; lemmas 3- to 7-veined, conspicuously hairy on back and base in pistillate spikelets, tapering to a point, awned or awnless. (Fig. 13)

2 · 2 · 27. New Zealand and South America. At first, you may confuse pampas grass with _Arundo_ and _Phragmites_, two other similarly robust perennials. The resemblance is entirely superficial; they are not closely related. See Table 45 for a comparison.

1a   Sheaths hairy; leaf blades deep green, their tips not curled; immature inflorescence deep violet, well elevated above the foliage at maturity; stems 4–5 times longer than the inflorescences; plants with pistillate spikelets only; 2n = 108* .... **_C. jubata_**
      PURPLE OR ANDEAN PAMPAS GRASS, JUBATA GRASS (pls. 45 & 46). Naturalized. Stems to 4 m tall, densely clumped. Leaf blades to 1+ m long, 4–12 mm wide. Panicles 30–60 cm long. Spikelets 14–16 mm long. A pernicious weed of coastal California. Jubata grass presents us with an interesting reproductive life style. We find only female plants in California, yet these plants form viable seed. What is the source of the pollen needed to produce seed? Our other pampas grass, _C. selloana_, can produce pollen-bearing spikelets, but _C. jubata_ sets seed in its absence. The answer is simple, even if somewhat disconcerting. Pampas grass is just one of many grasses that have evolved mechanisms for producing viable seeds without the union of egg and sperm that you were told in high school biology was the essential step. Grasses are masters of this form of asexual reproduction, called **apomixis**. Listed: CDFA, Cal-IPC.

                                                              (account continued)

---

*A really good hand lens will be needed for an accurate count!

Plate 45. *Cortaderia jubata*

Plate 46. *Cortaderia jubata*

Plate 47. *Cortaderia selloana*

1b   Sheaths glabrous or somewhat hairy; leaf blades bluish-green, their tips curled; immature inflorescence light violet to white, elevated only slightly above the foliage at maturity; stems 2–4 times as long as the inflorescences; plants staminate or pistillate; 2n = 72*

....***C. selloana***

URUGUAYAN OR SILVER PAMPAS GRASS (pl. 47). Naturalized. Stems to 4+ m tall. Leaf blades to 2 m long, 3–12 mm wide. Panicles 25–130 cm long. Spikelets 15–17 mm long. North Coast, Sierra Nevada foothills, Central and South coasts, Transverse ranges. A popular ornamental in warm areas of the country. Once thought to be the "good pampas grass," it has become a more aggressive weed in recent years. Listed: Cal-IPC.

Crypsis   **Prickle Grass, Swamp-timothy**

Prostrate to ascending annuals. Stems to 75 cm tall, ascending to erect, internodes hollow or solid. Leaf sheaths often inflated. Inflorescence a terminal or axillary, ovoid to capitate spike-like panicles, often ± enclosed in bract-like sheaths. Spikelets 1-flowered, keeled, strongly laterally compressed, bisexual, breaking apart above or below the glumes. Glumes 2, acute or short-awned, 0- or 1-veined; lemma 1-veined, awnless; palea 1- or 2-veined. Stamens 2 or 3. Fruit an achene, the seed free from the **pericarp**. **3 • 3 • 8.** Mostly Middle Eastern and Mediterranean, mainly on the moist soils of bottom lands, stream banks, and reservoirs.

---

*A really good hand lens will be needed for an accurate count!

1a   Sheaths hairy; many leaves bladeless at maturity.........**C. vaginiflora**
      SHARP-LEAVED CRYPSIS. Naturalized. Stems to 30 cm tall, often pro-
      fusely branched. Bladeless leaves distinctive in mature plants. Pan-
      icles generally 3–15 mm long. Spikelets 2.5–3.2 mm long. Clay and
      sandy soils, wet sites. Northern California, Sierra Nevada foothills,
      Central Valley, South Coast, Southwest California.
1b   Sheaths glabrous; blades not falling at maturity.......**C. schoenoides**
      PRICKLE GRASS, SWAMP-TIMOTHY (pl. 48). Naturalized. Stems to 75
      cm tall, decumbent, generally mat-forming. Panicles 0.3–4 cm long,
      often pink to purple, bases typically enclosed in uppermost sheaths.
      Spikelets 2.7–3.2 mm long. Sandy and clay soils at margins of lakes

Plate 48. *Crypsis schoenoides*

and pools. Northern California, Sierra Nevada foothills, Central Valley, South Coast to Southern California.

Cynodon   Bermuda Grass

Low, mat-forming, stoloniferous and/or rhizomatous perennials. Stems to 40 cm tall. Inflorescence a series of 2 to several digitate branches, spikelets sessile, in 2 rows on a ± triangular rachis. Spikelets 1- [2-] flowered, rachilla extended beyond floret and sometimes bearing a rudiment, laterally compressed, bisexual, breaking apart above the glumes. Glumes 2, ± equal, 1-veined, the upper about as long as the floret; lemmas 3-veined, hairy on keel and lateral veins, awnless; palea 2-keeled.

3 · 7 · 10. Tropical areas of the Old World. A source of lawn, pasture grasses, and turf for putting greens. Bermuda grass *(C. dactylon)* (pl. 49). Naturalized perennial. Stems to 40 cm tall. Panicles typically of 4–7 digitate branches, these 2.5–5 cm long. Spikelets ± 2 m long. Disturbed areas, especially roadsides. Widespread, except for Modoc Plateau. Important pasture grass, lawn grass, and aggressive weed. It is now being studied for its possible antimicrobial and antiviral properties and in the treatment of diabetes. Its pollen is a significant cause of hay fever. See Table 48 for a comparison of grasses with digitate inflorescences.

Plate 49. *Cynodon dactylon*

Cynosurus   **Dogtail**

Caespitose annuals or perennials. Stems to 1 m tall. Inflorescence a 1-sided, head-like or cylindrical, condensed panicle of conspicuously dissimilar fertile and sterile spikelets. Fertile spikelets sessile, 1- to 5-flowered, bisexual, laterally compressed, and breaking apart above the glumes and between the florets. Glumes 2, ± equal; lemmas 5-veined, awned. Sterile spikelets pedicellate, 6- to 18-flowered, reduced to rigid, linear-lanceolate, 1-veined, awnless or awned lemmas that ± conceal the fertile ones.

2 • 2 • 8. Europe and Africa, in open, grassy disturbed sites. Of limited economic importance as a fodder or pasture grass.

Plate 50. *Cynosurus cristatus*

1a   Plants perennial; inflorescence a narrow, cylindric spike-like panicle; fertile lemma awn less than 1 mm ....***C. cristatus***
CRESTED DOGTAIL (pl. 50). Stems to 80 cm tall. Panicles 3–14 cm long. Spikelets 3–7 mm long. Less common than *C. echinatus*. North, Central, and South coasts. When first encountered, its spike-like inflorescence and much shorter awns may not suggest that it is in the same genus as hedgehog dogtail, but its dimorphic spikelets provide a clue. A well-known cause of hay fever.

1b   Plants annual; inflorescence a head-like panicle; fertile lemma awn 3–10 mm long..***C. echinatus***
HEDGEHOG DOGTAIL (pl. 51). Stems to 70 cm tall. Panicles 1–4 cm long. Spikelets 7–14 mm long; awns give the inflorescence a bristly appear-

Plate 51. *Cynosurus echinatus*

ance. North, Central, and South coast ranges, Sierra Nevada foothills, Sacramento Valley. Presence often indicates deteriorated range conditions. Sometimes gathered as an ornamental. Listed: Cal-IPC.

Dactylis   **Orchard Grass**

Tall, densely caespitose perennials, often forming large clumps. Stems to 2 m tall. Leaf sheaths keeled and closed for at least half their length; blades with a conspicuous mid-rib and white margins. Inflorescence a panicle, 4–20 cm long, with spikelets clumped at ends of otherwise naked panicle branches. Spikelets 5–8 mm long, 2- to 5-flowered, bisexual, laterally compressed, and breaking apart above the glumes and between the florets. Glumes 2, shorter than or equaling the florets, 1- or 3-veined, awn-tipped; lemmas 5-veined, awned or awnless; palea tip notched.

1 · 1 · 1. Temperate Eurasia. Orchard grass or cock's-foot *(D. glomerata)* (pl. 52). Pasture and fodder grass throughout much of the cool-temperate parts of the world. Also used as a soil stabilizer. Escapes from cultivation. Widespread weed. Livestock, deer, rabbits, and rodents eat its foliage and seeds. It also causes pollen allergies and cattle poisoning from a fungal endophyte. Listed: Cal-IPC.

Plate 52. *Dactylis glomerata*

Danthonia   **Poverty-oat, Oat Grass**

Caespitose perennials. Stems to 1+ m tall. Leaf sheaths with tuft of api-cal hairs; ligule hairy. Inflorescence a few-flowered panicle or raceme, sometimes reduced to a single spikelet; self-pollinated spikelets hidden within the leaf sheaths. Spikelets 3- to 12-flowered, bisexual, ± laterally compressed, breaking apart above the glumes and between the florets. Glumes 2, 1- to 7-veined, much longer than the florets; lemmas hairy, 7- to many-veined (often indistinctly so), its apex 2-toothed or cleft, with a flat, twisted, bent awn from its mid-vein (unawned in *D. decumbens*). (Fig. 13) **4 • 8 • 20**. Mesophytic to xerophytic habitats of Europe, North Africa, and the Americas. Several are important pasture species. Some species traditionally assigned to *Danthonia* now reside in the genus *Rytido-sperma*. The report of South African oat grass (*D. purpurea* or *Karroo-chloa purpurea*) being in California persists in the literature, based solely on a single historic collection from the University of California, Berkeley Botanical Garden.

1a   Upper leaf blades sharply spreading to reflexed; lower inflorescence branches flexible, spreading to reflexed .... **D. californica**
   CALIFORNIA OAT GRASS (pl. 53). Native. Densely tufted. Stems to 1+ m tall. Racemes 2–6 cm long. Spikelets 14–26 mm long. Moist, open places in meadows and open woods. Northern California, Sierra Nevada, Central Coast, South Coast ranges, Peninsular ranges.

1b   Upper leaf blades ascending to erect; lower inflorescence branches stiff and erect **2**

2a   Leaf sheaths densely hairy; stems breaking away at maturity; spikelets 1 [2 or 3] per inflorescence; lemmas 5.5–11 mm
   ....**D. unispicata**
   ONE-SPIKE OAT GRASS (pls. 54 & 55). Native. Densely tufted. Stems to 30 cm tall. Spikelets 12–26 mm long. Dry rocky slopes, flats, and meadows, especially those in open coniferous forests. Northwest California, Sierra Nevada, Cascades, San Joaquin Valley, Southwest California. Perhaps better treated as a variety of *D. californica*.

2b   Leaf sheaths typically glabrous; stems not breaking away at matu-rity; spikelets 4–10 per inflorescence; lemmas 3–6 mm
   ....**D. intermedia**
   TIMBER OR INTERMEDIATE OAT GRASS. Native perennial. Stems 10–50 cm tall. Panicles 2–5 cm long. Spikelets 11–15 mm long. Dry to moist boreal and alpine meadows, bogs, forests. Northern Cali-fornia, Sierra Nevada. Abortive stamens suggest that it reproduces asexually.

Plate 53. *Danthonia californica*

Plate 54. *Danthonia unispicata*

Plate 55. *Danthonia unispicata*

Dasyochloa   **Fluff Grass**

Low, stoloniferous perennial, sometimes mat-forming. Stems [1] 4–15 cm tall, erect at first, but eventually bending and rooting at the nodes. Leaf sheaths with a tuft of hairs at the **throat**; blades **involute**. Inflorescence a terminal, dense panicle with spike-like branches, subtended by leafy bracts and partially concealed by upper leaves. Spikelets 6–9 mm long, bisexual, 4- to 10-flowered, laterally compressed, breaking apart above the glumes and between the florets. Glumes 2, ± equal, 1-veined, glabrous;

lemmas similar to glumes in texture, densely hairy on the margins and the lower half, 3-veined, 2-lobed, the mid-vein extended as an awn.

1 • 1 • 1. Southwestern United States and Mexico. Rocky, arid sites, especially in the desert scrub and woodland. Fluff grass *(D. pulchella)* (pls. 56 & 57). Native. Sandy to rocky soils of desert flats and shrub lands and woodlands. Desert mountains, Mojave and Sonoran deserts. This species has traditionally been included in *Erioneuron.* That genus is represented in California by hairy woolly grass *(E. pilosum),* known from relatively few collections, all from San Bernardino County.

Plate 56. *Dasyochloa pulchella*

Plate 57. *Dasyochloa pulchella*

Deschampsia   **Hair Grass**

Mostly caespitose perennials. Stems to 1 m tall. Inflorescence an open or congested panicle, often with hair-like branches. Spikelets small, 2- [3-] flowered, laterally compressed, bisexual, breaking apart above the glumes and between the florets, the rachilla hairy and prolonged above the upper floret (sometimes with a rudiment at its tip). Glumes 2, ± equal, the lower 1-veined and the upper 3-veined, as long as or longer than the lower floret; lemmas [3] 5- to 7-veined (often obscurely so), its apex several-toothed or cleft, and with an awn from or below the middle. (Fig. 15)

4 · 6 · 40. Temperate and cooler portions of both hemispheres. Of no economic importance.

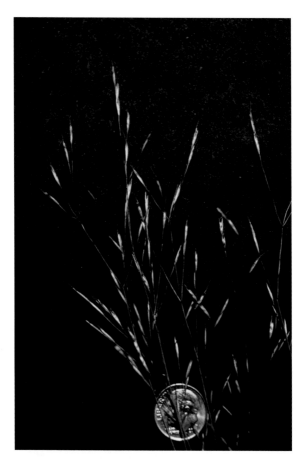

Plate 58. *Deschampsia danthonioides.*

1a Plants annual; basal leaves not tufted ....**D. danthonioides**
ANNUAL HAIR GRASS (pl. 58). Native annual. Stems to 60 cm tall.
Panicles 5–15 cm long. Spikelets 4–9 mm long. Open, wet to dry
meadows, streambanks; striking in vernal pools when spikelets
reddish-purple. Widespread, except for the deserts.

1b Plants perennial; basal leaves tufted **2**

2a Leaf blades soft, hair-like, 0.2–2 mm wide, often longitudinally
rolled inward; panicles 0.5–2 cm wide ....**D. elongata**
SLENDER HAIR GRASS. Native perennial. Stems to 1+ m tall. Panicles
5–30 cm long. Spikelets 3–7 mm long. Moist to wet habitats at lower
to higher elevations. Northern California, Sierra Nevada, South
Coast ranges, Southwest California.

2b   Leaf blades firm, with at least some flat, 1–4 mm wide; panicles
      generally open, sometimes ovate or contracted, 4–30 cm wide
      ....***D. caespitosa* complex**

TUFTED HAIR GRASS (pls. 59 & 60). Native perennials. Stems to 1.5 m
tall. Panicles 8–30 cm long, open to contracted, the branches usually
strongly divergent, but sometimes strongly ascending to erect. Spikelets 2–8 mm long. Variability in this group of grasses has led to the
description of about 24 taxa in North America. We have three freely
intergrading entities in California, which are sometimes treated as
species, varieties, or subspecies. They range from 0 to almost 4,000
m, from coastal marshes to alpine areas. In Pacific hair grass *(D. c.
subsp. holciformis)*, the panicle is contracted, its branches ascending

Plate 59. *Deschampsia caespitosa*

to erect. It occurs primarily in coastal marshes and meadows, but also at higher elevations from the North Coast, Sacramento Valley, and the Central Coast. Bering tufted hair grass *(D. c.* subsp. *beringensis)* is distinguished from the typical subspecies in being **glaucous**. It occurs mainly in coastal marshes and meadows of the North Coast, especially Humboldt County, south to the San Francisco Bay Area. Tufted hair grass *(D. c.* subsp. *caespitosa)*, our most widely encountered subspecies, ranges from Northern California, Sierra Nevada, Central Coast, to Southern California. Morphological, ecological, and geographic distinctions are not as sharp as this brief discussion might suggest. There is even some doubt as to whether this species is native in North America. More study is clearly in order.

Plate 60. *Deschampsia caespitosa* (inflorescence detail)

You may confuse this genus with *Trisetum*. They are compared in the Table 49.

TABLE 49. Distinguishing *Deschampsia* and *Trisetum*

Characteristic	Deschampsia	Trisetum
Lemma apex	ragged or 2- to 4-toothed	bifid [entire]
Lemma awn insertion	typically below middle	typically above middle
Palea	without 2 apical bristles	with 2 apical bristles

Digitaria   Crab Grass

Caespitose annuals or rhizomatous-stoloniferous perennials. Stems to 2 m tall, often decumbent and rooting at the nodes, the internodes solid or hollow. Inflorescence a series of racemose or digitate branches bearing subsessile or short-pedicellate spikelets or a panicle. Spikelets in pairs or trios [solitary or in groups of 5], alternating in 2 rows on one side of a 3-angled winged or wingless rachis. Spikelets 2-flowered (the lower sterile and the upper fertile), bisexual, dorsally compressed, breaking apart below the glumes. Glumes 1 [2], the lower minute or absent, the upper resembling the sterile lemma in size and texture, 3- to 7-veined, glabrous to long-ciliate; sterile lemma as long as fertile floret, 3- to 7-veined, often hairy; fertile lemma ± narrow, acute or acuminate, cartilaginous or leathery, its margins thin and flat, not clasping the palea as in other genera of the tribe.

6 • 27 • 300. Warmer regions of both hemispheres. A source of grains, pasture and lawn grasses, and weeds. At first, you may confuse *Digitaria* with windmill grass *(Chloris),* Bermuda grass *(Cynodon),* or goose grass *(Eleusine).* See Table 48 for a comparison.

1a Spikelets conspicuously hairy; inflorescence a panicle, the branches appressed to ascending.. *D. californica*
   ARIZONA COTTONTOP. Native perennial. Stems to 1 m tall. Panicles 5–10 cm long, primary branches 3–6 cm long. Spikelets 3–5.5 mm long. Desert areas of San Diego and San Bernardino counties.

1b Spikelets glabrous or with short marginal hairs; inflorescence branches digitate, spreading **2**

2a Spikelets generally 3 per node; lower glume vestigial or missing; leaf sheaths and blades typically glabrous...................***D. ischaemum***
   SMOOTH CRAB GRASS (pls. 61 & 62). Naturalized annual. Stems to 50+ cm tall. Sheaths glabrous [pubescent]. Panicles both terminal and axillary (often partially concealed in sheaths) of 2–7 branches, these 1.5–7 cm long. Spikelets 1.7–2.3 mm long. Disturbed areas. Widespread.

Plate 61. *Digitaria ischaemum*

2b   Spikelets generally 2 per node; lower glume 0.2–0.8 mm; leaf
sheaths and blades typically pubescent, the hairs with swollen
bases .... **D. sanguinalis**
HAIRY CRAB GRASS. Naturalized annual, often purplish. Stems to 70
cm tall. Panicles with 4–13 branches, these 3–18 cm long. Spikelets
2.5–3.5 mm long. Disturbed areas. Widespread.

Plate 62. *Digitaria ischaemum*

Distichlis   **Salt Grass, Alkali Grass, Shore Grass**

Low, rhizomatous-stoloniferous, dioecious [monoecious] perennials, often mat-forming. Stems to 60 cm tall, mat-forming to ascending and erect, rigid, the internodes solid. Leaf blades flat, rigid to lax or stiff and needle-like, typically distichous. Inflorescence a reduced panicle or raceme, or a single spikelet. Spikelets 3- to 20-flowered, generally laterally compressed, unisexual, breaking apart above the glumes and between the florets. Glumes 0 or 2, unequal, 3- to 9-veined, shorter than the florets, awnless; lemmas several-veined, those of the staminate spikelet thinner in texture, awnless; palea 2-keeled, ± winged.

2 • 2 • 8. North and South America, and Australia in coastal salt marshes and interior alkaline or saline sites. A source of forage grasses and sand-binders.

1a   Spikelet 1 per inflorescence, ± concealed by upper leaf sheaths; glumes 0 .... **_D. littoralis_**
      SHORE GRASS (pl. 63). Native. Stems to 15 cm tall, erect and mat-forming with wiry stolons. Inflorescence unique in North American grasses. Spikelets ± 10 mm long. Moist, sandy maritime coastal flats. Santa Barbara to San Diego counties. You may have walked past shore grass thinking that it was a young heath plant that had not flowered. In TJM2 and older floras, shore grass was placed in the genus _Monanthochloë_.

Plate 63. _Distichlis littoralis_

Plate 64. *Distichlis spicata*

1b Spikelets 2–20 per inflorescence, clearly exserted at maturity;
glumes 2 .... ***D. spicata***
SALT GRASS (pls. 64 & 65). Native. Stems to 5 cm tall; extensive yellow
rhizomes are diagnostic. Panicles 2–8 cm long, those of staminate
plants typically elevated above the leaves; pistillate ones at or below
the blades. Spikelets 5–20 mm long. This grass occurs in almost
every county in California on alkaline or saline flats from the coast
inward. A valuable range forage grass and an important food for
birds and insects. Native Americans extracted salt by crushing or
burning plants.

Plate 65. *Distichlis spicata*

Echinochloa   Barnyard Grass, Cockspur, Water Grass

Coarse, caespitose annuals or perennials. Stems to 5 m tall, often succulent, the internodes hollow or solid. Leaf sheaths compressed. Inflorescence a contracted to more or less open panicle, the branches simple to rebranched. Spikelets subsessile, solitary, or in irregular clusters on one side of the branch, 2-flowered (the lower sterile and the upper fertile), bisexual, flat on one side and rounded on the other, breaking apart below the glumes (remaining intact in domesticated forms). Glumes 2, unequal, the lower 0- to 3-veined and the upper 5- to 7-veined; sterile lemma similar to upper glume, 5-veined, awned; fertile lemma 5-veined, smooth and shining, pointed, its margins enrolled below (enclosing the palea at that point), the upper portion flat; palea similar to fertile lemma in texture, narrowing to a point that is free from the lemma margins.

7 • 12 • 40–50. Warmer regions of both hemispheres. A source of minor cereals (millets), grains, pasture grasses, and weeds. Although the genus is easy to recognize, the species are not. Characters tend to overlap and there is often a lack of geographic and ecological separation.

1a Panicle branches unbranched; spikelets 2.5–3 mm long, awnless ....***E. colona***
JUNGLE-RICE, SHAMA MILLET. Naturalized annual. Stems to 70 cm tall. Panicles 2–12 cm long. North Coast and Cascade Range through the Great Valley and South Coast to the Sonoran Desert.

1b Panicle branches generally branched, these sometimes inconspicuous; spikelets 3–5 mm long, awned .... ***E. crus-galli* complex**
BARNYARD GRASS (pls. 66 & 67). Naturalized annual. Stems to 2 m tall. Panicles 5–35 cm long. (Fig. 14) The species in this complex, which includes *E. crus-pavonis* and *E. muricata,* are widespread weeds of our lawns, gardens, irrigated fields, and waterways, and are especially abundant during the summer months. They are distinguished, should you wish to do so, by subtle and overlapping differences in the shape of the upper lemma and by the presence or absence of a line of minute hairs just below the tip of the lemma, visible under 25× magnification. Another member of the group is early barnyard grass *(E. oryzoides),* an attractive weed of the rice fields in the Central Valley.

Plate 66. *Echinochloa crus-galli*

Plate 67. *Echinochloa crus-galli*

Ehrharta **Veldt Grass**

Annual or perennial herbs. Stems woody or herbaceous (in ours), to 2 m tall. Inflorescence a panicle, sometimes reduced to a raceme. Spikelets 3-flowered (the lower 2 reduced to sterile lemmas), bisexual, laterally compressed or terete, breaking apart above the glumes but not between the florets. Glumes 2, 5-veined, shorter or much longer than florets; sterile lemmas often transversely wrinkled; fertile lemma 5- to 7-veined; palea 2-keeled, 0- to 5-veined. Stamens 3, 4, or 6.

3 • 3 • 27. Old World, most of them native to southern Africa. Of economic importance as pasture grasses, soil-binders, and weeds. The common name derives from an Afrikaans word now used for open areas of grass or low scrub in South Africa.

1a   Plants annual; spikelets 8–18 mm long; sterile lemma awns 2–20 mm; stamens 3 ....***E. longiflora***
      LONG-FLOWERED VELDT GRASS, ANNUAL VELDT GRASS (pl. 69). Stems to 1 m tall, erect or bent at the base. Panicles 9–15 cm long, branches ascending or spreading, sometimes raceme-like. Disturbed sites, often on sandy or loamy soils. South Coast and Peninsular Range. Common weed at Torrey Pines State Reserve. Listed: Cal-IPC.

1b   Plants perennial; spikelets 3–9 mm long; sterile lemma awns 0; stamens 6 ....**2**

2a   Glumes purplish at maturity; sterile lemmas soft-hairy, the upper smooth ....***E. calycina***
      PERENNIAL VELDT GRASS (pls. 68 & 69). Stems to 75 cm tall. Panicles 7–22 cm long, nodding and sometimes partially enclosed in upper sheaths. Spikelets 4–9 mm long. North Coast ranges, Sacramento Valley, South Coast, Southwestern California. Especially common on coastal dunes around San Luis Obispo and San Diego. Listed: Cal-IPC.

2b   Glumes greenish at maturity; sterile lemmas ± glabrous, the upper wrinkled cross-wise .... ***E. erecta***
      UPRIGHT VELDT GRASS (pl. 69). Stems to 1 m tall. Panicles 5–21 cm long, erect or nodding. Spikelets 3–5 mm long. Disturbed, often shady, moist sites. North, Central, and South coasts, Southern California. Especially common in the San Francisco Bay Area where it has become an aggressive weed. Listed: Cal-IPC.

Plate 68. *Ehrharta calycina*

Plate 69. *Ehrharta calycina* (left), *E. erecta* (center), and *E. longiflora* (right)

Eleusine   **Goose Grass**

Low, spreading annuals or perennials. Stems to 20 cm tall, weak, flattened. Inflorescence a series of 2 to several ± digitate branches clumped at the stem apex. Spikelets sessile in 2 rows, 3- to 15-flowered, laterally compressed, bisexual, breaking apart above the glumes and between the florets (except in cultivars). Glumes 2, unequal, the lower 1- to 3-veined and the upper 3- to 5-veined, shorter than the florets; lemmas 3-veined, acute, awnless to mucronate; palea tip notched.

Plate 70. *Eleusine indica*

3 · 3 · 9. Mesic to dry sites in Africa (8) and South America (1). A source of grains in the Old World. Goose grass *(E. **indica**)* (pl. 70). Naturalized annual. Stems to 50 cm tall. Panicles of 4–10 digitate branches, these 4–15 cm long. Spikelets 5–8 mm long. Disturbed places. Central Valley to the San Francisco Bay Area, South Coast, Southwest California. African finger millet *(E. **coracana** subsp. **africana**)* is becoming weedy in Southern California. Its lower glume has 2 or 3 veins, versus 1 in goose grass.

X *Elyhordeum*   **Elymus x Hordeum Hybrids**

Plants perennial, caespitose or rhizomatous. Inflorescence a terminal spike or rame, with 1–3 [7] spikelets per node; lateral spikelets sessile or on short pedicels. Spikelets laterally compressed, with 1–4 florets. Glumes narrowly lanceolate to tapering to a fine point, typically awned; lemmas typically awned. Plants are usually sterile. When you run across a grass that seems to combine features of *Elymus* and *Hordeum,* it might be doing exactly that. Three named hybrids are reported for California, none of them common.

Elymus   **Wild-rye**

Caespitose or rhizomatous-stoloniferous perennials (annual in *E. caput-medusae*). Stems to 2 m tall. Leaf auricles generally present; blades flat, folded, or rolled. Inflorescence a balanced spike [raceme], sometimes branched at base, the rachis remaining intact at maturity. Spikelets typically [1] 2 or 3 [7] at all or most nodes; [1-] 3- to 7- [11-] flowered, laterally compressed, bisexual, breaking apart above the glumes and between the florets. Glumes 2 [0], equal or unequal, 3- to 7-veined, broad to quite narrow, almost awn-like in some, sometimes awned; lemmas 5- to 7-veined, tapering to a straight or outwardly curved awn [awnless].

31 • 66 • c. 235. Temperate and cooler regions of both hemispheres (pl. 71). Of economic importance as a source of forage, grains, sand-binders, and fibers for a variety of uses. As treated here, the genus includes *Agropyron* (in part), *Sitanion,* and various segregate genera. Hybridization within the genus is common and confounds identification. Hybrids with *Hordeum* are also found in California. See X *Elyhordeum.*

1a   Plants annual; fertile floret 1....................................***E. caput-medusae***
      MEDUSA HEAD (pl. 72). Naturalized. Stems 10–50 cm tall, slender, erect to reclining. Spikes 2–6 cm long, excluding awns. Spikelets 5–80 mm long; glumes to 80 mm, awl- or awn-like; lemma awn to 10 cm. Widespread, especially the northern half; absent from desert areas; often forming dense patches that crowd out other plants. An aggressive invader of disturbed areas. Listed: CDFA and Cal-IPC.

1b   Plants perennial; fertile florets 2 or more..**2**

2a   Inflorescence branched, at least at its base (see also *E. cinereus*)
                                                                    E. condensatus
      GIANT WILD-RYE (pl. 73). Endemic. Stems to 3+ m, typically in large clumps. Inflorescence a panicle 17–44 cm long, spike-like above and branched below. Spikelets 9–25 mm, sessile or stalked; lemma tip acute, awn-tipped or with an awn to 4 mm. Dry slopes, open woodlands. San Francisco Bay area, South Coast Ranges, Southern California.

Plate 71. Inflorescences of five species of *Elymus*

2b   Inflorescence unbranched, spikelets sessile or nearly so...................**3**

3a   Rachis breaking apart at maturity; glumes divided into 2–9
     segments [entire]..**4**

3b   Rachis remaining intact at maturity; glumes entire.........................**5**

4a   Glumes cleft into 3–9 awn-like segments; leaf auricles generally
     present..***E. multisetus***

     BIG SQUIRRELTAIL (pl. 74). Native. Stems to 65 cm tall. Spikes 5–20
     cm long. Spikelets 10–15 mm long. Dry, open, rocky places, from sea
     level to 3000 m. Widespread.

Plate 72. *Elymus caput-medusae*

4b   Glumes cleft into 2 [3] awn-like segments; leaf auricles generally
      absent ....***E. elymoides***
      SQUIRRELTAIL. Native. Stems to 65 cm tall. Spikes 3–20 cm long.
      Spikelets 10–20 mm long. Dry, open, often rocky habitats, from des-
      ert to the alpine. Widespread.
5a   Lemma awn curved outward at maturity ....***E. spicatus***
      BLUE BUNCH WHEAT GRASS. Native. Forming dense clumps; stems
      to 1 m tall. Spikes slender, 8–15 cm long. Spikelets 8–22 mm long.
      Sagebrush steppe, woodlands. Mainly Klamath Region and Modoc
      Plateau. A valuable forage grass.

Plate 73. *Elymus condensatus*

    BLUE WILD-RYE, WESTERN WILD-RYE. Native. Stems to 1.4 m tall. Spikes
    5–21 cm long. Spikelets 8–25 mm long. Dry to moist places in mead-
    ows, woods, and chaparral. Widespread, especially in the foothills
    and slopes below 8500 ft, and variable.
    BEARDLESS WILD-RYE. Native. Spikes 5–20 cm long. Spikelets 10–22
    mm long, glumes awl-like. Moist, often saline meadows. Widespread.

Plate 74. *Elymus multisetus*

ASHY WILD-RYE, GREAT BASIN WILD-RYE (pl. 75 & 76). Native. Spikes 10–29 cm long, rarely branched at lower nodes. Spikelets 9–25 mm long, glumes awl-like. Along streams, roadsides and in sagebrush and open woodlands. Cascades, Sierra Nevada, Sacramento Valley, Southern California.

9a   Glumes rounded to truncate at tip......................................***E. hispidus***
INTERMEDIATE WHEAT GRASS. Naturalized. Stems to 1 m tall. Spikes stiff, 8–20 cm long. Spikelets 10–18 mm long; lemmas awnless. Widespread. Planted for forage and to control soil erosion.

9b   Glumes acute, acuminate or awned at tip.. **10**

10a Plants strongly rhizomatous; anthers 4–7 mm long............***E. repens***
QUACK GRASS. Naturalized. Stems to 50–100 cm tall. Spikes 5–20 cm long. Spikelets 10–20 mm long, glumes and lemmas awned or awnless. Widespread weed in disturbed areas and cultivated fields.

Plate 75. *Elymus cinereus*

10b. Plants densely tufted [weakly rhizomatous]; anthers 1.2–2.5 mm long...***E. trachycaulus***
SLENDER WHEAT GRASS. Native. Stems to 1.5 m tall. Spikes slender, 4–30 cm long. Spikelets 10–20 mm long. Widespread on moist to dry soils. A valuable forage grass. A similar grass with larger spikelets and a less crowded spike is Stebbins' wild-rye (***E. stebbinsii***). It is endemic to dry slopes, chaparral, and conifer forests along the North Coast Ranges, Sierra Nevada, South Coast, Southwest California.

Plate 76. *Elymus cinereus*

Eragrostis   **Love Grass**

Caespitose annuals or perennials, often with wart-like **glands**. Stems to 1 m tall, internodes hollow or solid. Inflorescence an open or contracted panicle. Spikelets often lead-gray, dark olive, or pale green, 3- to many-flowered, the florets usually strongly overlapping, bisexual [unisexual and the species dioecious], laterally compressed, breaking apart above the glumes and between the florets. Glumes 2, unequal, shorter than the lowest floret, 1-veined; lemmas 3-veined, keeled or rounded, acute or acuminate, awnless; palea usually curved or bowed-out by the grain, strongly 2-keeled, often remaining attached after the lemmas have fallen. Stamens 2 or 3. (Fig. 13)

13 • 49 • 350. Warmer regions of the United States and worldwide in the tropics and subtropics. Of little value for forage. A few introduced species have been used for erosion control. The generic name translates from the Greek as love grass, but the derivation is obscure. Plants are not known to have eros-inducing properties. Other interpretations suggest the name means an early-invading or many-flowered *Agrostis*.

1a   Plants perennial; rachilla breaking apart at maturity........***E. curvula***
      WEEPING LOVE GRASS. Naturalized. Stems to 1.5 m tall, densely tufted. Panicles 7–18 cm long, branches flexible, generally nodding. Spikelets 4–8 [10] mm long, generally gray-green. Grown as an ornamental and used for erosion control. Roadsides, ditches, and other disturbed areas. Cascades, Central Valley, South Coast ranges to the Mojave Desert.

1b   Plants annual; rachilla remaining intact at maturity.........................**2**

(account continued)

2a Leaf margins (and often glumes and lemmas) with conspicuous wart-like glands..***E. cilianensis*** **STINK GRASS** (pl. 77). Naturalized. Stems to 50 cm tall, spreading or erect. Panicles 5–20 cm long. Spikelets 2.5–3 mm long. Glands give plants an unpleasant odor. Disturbed sites. Widespread, especially in agricultural areas.

2b Leaf margins without wart-like glands...**3**

3a Sheath hairs with swollen bases; pedicels stiff; grain with a shallow to deep groove..***E. mexicana*** **MEXICAN LOVE GRASS.** Native. Stems 1+ m tall, spreading or erect. Panicles 10–35 cm long. Spikelets ± 2 mm long. Disturbed open sites, roadsides, and agricultural areas. Widespread.

Plate 77. *Eragrostis cilianensis*

3b   Sheath hairs without swollen bases; pedicels flexible; grain without a groove **4**

4a   Lowest inflorescence branches whorled; palea deciduous ....***E. pilosa* var. *pilosa***

   INDIAN LOVE GRASS. Naturalized. Stems 8–70 cm tall. Panicles 4–20 cm long. Spikelets 3.5–6 [10] mm long. Disturbed sites, roadsides, gardens, agricultural fields. Most collections are from Central Valley.

4b   Lowest inflorescence branches alternate or opposite; palea persistent ....***E. pectinacea***

   TUFTED LOVE GRASS (pl. 78). Native. Stems to 80 cm tall. Panicles 10–25 cm long. Spikelets 5–8 mm long. Along roadsides and in agricultural areas. Widespread.

Plate 78. *Eragrostis pectinacea*

Eriochloa   **Cup Grass**

Annuals or perennials, often of moist sites. Stems to 1 m tall, erect or decumbent. Inflorescence a sparingly branched, contracted panicle, spikelets 1 or 2 per node, on one side of the branch. Spikelets 2-flowered (the lower sterile and the upper bisexual), dorsally compressed, breaking apart below the glumes. Glumes 2, the lower reduced to minute sheath or strip that is fused to the thickened ring- or cup-like callus, the upper 3- to 9-veined, awned or awnless; sterile lemma 5-veined, similar to upper glume, longer than fertile floret; fertile lemma 5-veined, glabrous, indurate, mucronate to awned.

Plate 79. *Eriochloa acuminata*

4 • 11 • 25. Warmer parts of both hemispheres. A minor source of forage. The lower glume surrounding the darkened, thickened callus at the base of the spikelet is diagnostic and is the basis of the common name.

1a   Spikelets 1 per node at middle of inflorescence branch; inflorescence branches closely appressed to central axis; leaf blades generally densely pubescent.. ***E. contracta***
     PRAIRIE CUP GRASS. Naturalized annual. Stems to 1 m tall, erect or decumbent, often rooting at the nodes. Panicle 6–20 cm long. Spikelets 3.5–4.5 mm long, fertile lemma short-awned (to 1 mm). Moist places, roadside ditches, and a summer weed of irrigated fields. Central Valley, South Coast, Southern California.

1b   Spikelets 2 or 3 per node at middle of inflorescence branch; inflorescence branches ascending to slightly divergent; leaf blades glabrous to sparsely hairy...***E. acuminata***
     SOUTHWESTERN CUP GRASS, SUMMER GRASS (pl. 79). (Fig. 14) Native annual. Stems to 1.2 m tall. Panicles 7–16 cm long. Spikelets 3.8–5 mm long, fertile lemma with a minute tip. Although native, often seen typically during the summer months in irrigated fields. Central Valley, Southern California.

Festuca   Fescue, Annual Fescue, Rye Grass

Caespitose, rhizomatous, or stoloniferous perennial or tufted annual herbs. Stems to 2 m tall, internodes hollow or solid. Leaves mostly basal; sheaths open; auricles present or absent. Inflorescence an open to contracted panicle, spike or raceme. Spikelets 2- to several-flowered, bisexual, laterally compressed, breaking apart above the glumes and between the florets. Glumes 2 [1], unequal, the lower 1- to 3-veined, the upper 3- to 5-veined, shorter than the lowest floret; lemmas similar to glumes in texture or much firmer, typically [3-] 5- to 9-veined, awned from an entire to minutely bifid apex, acuminate or awnless; palea apically notched. Stamens 3 or 1; flowers open- or self-pollinated.

22 • 46 • 500+. Temperate and mountainous regions worldwide. Of economic importance as a source of fodder, lawn grasses, erosion control, ornamentals, and major weedy species. As treated here, *Festuca* includes four genera accepted by other authors: *Leucopoa* (dioecious grasses with glumes thinner than lemmas), *Schedonorus* (clasping auricles, caryopsis adhering to palea), *Vulpia* (self-pollinated annuals), and *Lolium* (inflorescence a simple spike). Grasses in all four genera are interfertile. For those who have some familiarity with grasses, merging *Lolium* with *Festuca* might seem unexpected. The two genera hybridize freely and some species of *Festuca* have already been transferred to *Lolium* by some authors, thereby breaching the panicle vs. spike boundary, which some find worrisome. The acceptance of the genus *Vulpia* has waxed and waned. Our California annual and perennial fescues do have a very different appearance. But when viewed worldwide, those differences do not hold. I invite your attention to the following comparison.

TABLE 50. Distinguishing *Festuca* and *Vulpia*

Characteristic	Festuca	Vulpia
Duration	perennial [annual]	annual or perennial
Stamen number	3 or 1	3, 1, or 2
Pollination	open [closed]	closed [open]

1a   Inflorescence a spike; spikelets (except the uppermost) with 1 glume (subgenus *Lolium*)..**2**

1b   Inflorescence a panicle; spikelets with 2 glumes.................................**3**

2a   Glume as long or longer than the upper florets ....***F. temulenta*** **DARNEL, TARES, POISON RYE GRASS** (pl. 80). Naturalized annual. Stems to 1 m. Spikes 2–40 cm. Spikelets 10–30 mm long. Open, disturbed sites, roadsides. Widespread at low elevations. Toxins produced by fungi living within the tissues of the grass can cause central nervous system disturbances in humans and "rye grass staggers" in animals. Traditionally placed in *Lolium*. Listed: Cal-IPC.

2b   Glume shorter than the upper florets ....***F. perennis*** **RYE GRASS** (pl. 80). Naturalized annual or perennial. Stems to 1+ m tall. Spikes 3–45 cm long, sometimes a branched panicle. Spikelets 5–30 mm long. Dry to moist disturbed sites, roadsides, lawns, meadows, and pastures. Widespread at low to medium elevations. As treated here, the species includes *L. multiflorum* and *L. rigidum*. The annual vs. perennial character and the presence or absence of lemma awns are not reliable features and appear to be environmentally influenced.

3a   Plants annual; stamen 1; plants self-pollinated (subgenus *Vulpia*) **4**

3b   Plants perennial; stamens 3; plants cross-pollinated **7**

4a   Lower glume 0.5–2 mm, less than ½ the length of the upper glume ....***F. myuros*** **RAT-TAIL FESCUE, FOXTAIL FESCUE, SIX-WEEKS GRASS.** Naturalized annual. Stems to 75 cm. Panicles dense, 3–25 cm long, often curved, or spike-like racemes. Spikelets 5–12 mm; lemmas glabrous (except margins sometimes ciliate); awn generally 5–15 mm. Both disturbed and undisturbed sites, often on well-drained, sandy soils and roadsides. Widespread, except for Great Basin areas.

4b   Lower glume 1.7–5.5 mm, ½ to ⅔ the length of the upper glume **5**

Plate 80. *F. temulenta* (left) and *Festuca perennis* (right)

5a Florets generally 7–12, closely overlapping and hiding the inflores-
cence axis..***F. octoflora***
SIX-WEEKS FESCUE (pl. 81). Native. Stems to 60 cm, glabrous or hairy.
Panicles 1–16 cm, branches 1 or 2 per node, appressed to spreading.
Spikelets 4–10 mm long; lemmas glabrous or pubescent, awns to 9
mm. Sandy to rocky soils, grasslands, woodlands, roadsides and
other disturbed sites. Widespread.

5b Florets generally 1–5, loosely overlapping, inflorescence axis visible
....**6**

Plate 81. *Festuca octoflora*

6a   Lower inflorescence branches spreading or reflexed at maturity,
with basal swellings ....***F. microstachys* complex**
SMALL FESCUE (pl. 82). Native. Stems 10–75 cm tall. Panicles 2–24 cm
long, lower branches few, spreading to reflexed. Spikelets 5–10 mm;
lemma awn 3–20 mm long. Disturbed, open, generally sandy soils.
Widespread, mostly below 5,000 ft. A half dozen or so other species
similar to *F. microstachys* have been published, but none appear useful to recognize. Four varieties are often recognized, distinguished
mainly by spelling; their features overlap and they are not ecologi-
cally nor geographically distinct.

Plate 82. *Festuca microstachys*

6b Lower inflorescence branches appressed or erect at maturity, but without basal swellings .... *F. bromoides*
    BROME FESCUE. Naturalized annual. Stems to 50 cm tall. Panicles 1.5–15 cm long, with 1 branch per node. Spikelets 5–10 mm long; lemma awn 2.5–12 mm. Dry, disturbed places, coastal-sage scrub, chaparral. Widespread.

7a Leaf blades with prominent claw-like or clasping auricles at the base; lemma awn absent or poorly developed (subgenus *Schedonorus*) **8**

7b Leaf blades without prominent auricles at the base; lemma awn well developed (subgenus *Festuca*) **9**

8a Auricles glabrous; lemmas generally smooth .... *F. pratensis*
    MEADOW FESCUE. Naturalized. Stems to 1+ m. Leaf auricles glabrous. Panicles 10–25 cm, with longest branches at base. Spikelets 12–15 mm long; lemma awnless or with a sharp point to 0.2 mm. Disturbed places; once an important forage grass. Widespread.

8b Auricles ciliate (sometimes reduced to only 1 or 2 hairs); lemmas with minute hairs or bristles ....*F. arundinacea*
    TALL FESCUE, ALTA FESCUE, REED FESCUE (pl. 83). Naturalized. Plants sometimes rhizomatous. Stems to 1.5+ m. Leaf auricles sparsely hairy. Panicles 12–50 cm long. Spikelets 8–15 mm long; lemma awns 0–2 mm. Roadsides and other disturbed, especially moist, sites. Widespread. Used for forage and soil stabilization. Plants often infected with a fungus that makes alkaloids toxic to cattle. Listed: Cal-IPC.

9a Leaf sheath closed, ± reddish, generally with downward-pointing hairs ....*F. rubra* **complex**
    RED FESCUE. Native and naturalized, often rhizomatous, sometimes stoloniferous. Stems to 1 m. Panicles 3.5–20 cm long, open or somewhat contracted. Spikelets 5–17 mm long; lemma awns to 4.5 mm. Widespread in California, especially dunes, bluffs, salt marshes of the North Coast; grasslands, subalpine forests. There is morphological, ecological, and geographic variation in this complex. The treatment in *Flora North America* recognizes ten subspecies; still others have been proposed. However, hybridization between natives, between natives and introduced cultivated forms, and backcrossing to parents yield numerous intermediates that blur boundaries. Hundreds of forage and turf cultivars are available in the trade.

9b Leaf sheath open for at least half its length, typically green, glabrous **10**

(account continued)

Plate 83. *Festuca arundinacea*

10a Leaf blades [1] 2–6.5 mm wide; junction of sheath and blade
     densely hairy [± glabrous in one variety].....................***F. californica***
     CALIFORNIA FESCUE (pl. 84). Robust, native perennial. Stems to 1.5
     m tall, the tallest of our North American fescues. Panicles 10–30
     cm long, branches spreading or drooping, bearing spikelets toward
     their ends. Spikelets 8–18 mm long; lemma awn [0] 2–3 mm long.
     Three varieties, differing in minor characters of hairiness of collars
     and ligules, occur in California. Dry, open forests, stream banks,
     chaparral, often on serpentine soils. Northwest California, Cas-
     cades, Sierra Nevada, Central Coast, South Coast ranges.

10b Leaf blades less than 2 mm wide; junction of sheath and blade
     glabrous **11**

Plate 84. *Festuca californica*

11a   Leaf blades green; lemma awn as long or longer than the lemma; tip of ovary hairy...***F. occidentalis*** **WESTERN FESCUE.** Native perennial. Stems to 80 cm. Panicles 10–20 cm, branches widely spreading to drooping. Spikelets 6–12 mm long; lemma awns 3–12 mm. Open coniferous forests, oak-pine woodlands, rocky slopes. Northern California, Sierra Nevada, Central and South Coast, Peninsular Range.

11b   Leaf blades glaucous or bluish; lemma awn shorter than the lemma; tip of ovary glabrous ....***F. idahoensis* complex** **IDAHO FESCUE, BLUE BUNCH GRASS** (pl. 85). Densely tufted native perennial. Stems to 1 m tall. Leaf blades often bluish or glaucous. Panicles 6–20 cm long, branches ± appressed to open. Spikelets

Plate 85. *Festuca idahoensis*

7–17 mm long; lemma awn 1–6 mm. Grasslands, forests, dry, open places; sometimes dominant. This is a good forage grass, and also popular as an ornamental. Northern California, Sierra Nevada, Central and South Coast ranges. Boundaries of this species remain controversial. *F. idahoensis* was once included in *F. ovina* (sheep fescue), along with the very similar *F. arizonica* (Arizona fescue). Another member of the complex is *F. idahoensis* subsp. *roemeri* or *F. roemeri* (Oregon fescue). This differs from typical Idaho fescue in the number of ribs over the major veins on the leaf blade (3–5 vs. 5–9) and subtle differences in the position of inflorescence branches.

Gastridium   **Nit Grass**

Caespitose annuals. Stems to 70 cm tall. Inflorescence a dense, spike-like panicle, 2–17 cm long. Spikelets 3–4.8 mm long, 1-flowered, bisexual, laterally compressed, breaking apart below the glumes, the rachilla extended above the floret as a bristle. Glumes 2, unequal, enclosing the floret, somewhat swollen at the base, 1-veined, gradually tapering to its tip; lemma pubescent, 5-veined, ours with a 3–6 mm awn from below the toothed apex. (Fig. 16)

1 • 1 • 2. Western Europe and the Mediterranean. Of no economic importance. Nit grass *(G. phleoides).* Annual grasslands below about 1,400 m. Widespread. Of minor forage value to livestock. Our plants have traditionally been misidentified as *G. ventricosum.*

Glyceria   **Manna Grass**

Rhizomatous-stoloniferous or caespitose perennials [annuals] of wet sites. Stems to 2.5 m tall, often decumbent and rooting at the nodes. Leaf sheaths closed for at least ¾ of their length. Inflorescence an open to contracted panicle 15–50 cm long, sometimes reduced to a raceme. Spikelets fragile, linear or oval in side view, awnless, 2- to 16-flowered, bisexual, laterally compressed or almost terete, breaking apart above the glumes and between the florets. Glumes 2, unequal, 1- [3-] veined, shorter than the lowest floret; lemmas broad, with [5] 7 [9] conspicuous, parallel veins, the apex acute, obtuse, or **truncate**; palea broad, shorter to slightly longer than the lemma, keels winged or not. Stamens [1] 2 or 3.

8 • 21 • 35. Wet areas in the temperate regions of both hemispheres; 13 species are native to North America. Several species are important sources of food for livestock and waterfowl. Native Americans ate the grains of various species. The common name makes reference to the Hebrew, Arabic, and Persian word for a sweet-tasting food provided by their deities. The grain of this species of *Glyceria* is sweet to the taste; the name itself is from the Greek word for sweet.

1a   Spikelets cylindrical to terete, 9–24 mm long ....**G. declinata**
       WAXY MANNA GRASS (pl. 86). (Fig. 14) Naturalized annual-perennial.
       Stems to 1 m tall. Panicles 6–30 cm long, narrow. Wet places, includ-
       ing vernal pools. North Coast ranges, Cascades, and Sierra Nevada,
       Central Valley, South Coast. Northern or boreal manna grass *(G.
       borealis)* has a very similar appearance, but its lemmas are glabrous
       between the veins and it does not range as far south.

Plate 86. *Glyceria declinata*

1b   Spikelets laterally compressed, 3–6 mm long.........................***G. elata***
      FOWL OR TALL MANNA GRASS (pl. 87). Native. Stems to 1.5 m tall.
      Panicles 15–25 cm long, branches gracefully nodding. Wet places
      and shady forests. Northwest California, Cascades, Sierra Nevada,
      mountains of Southern California. Very palatable to wildlife. This is
      our most commonly collected manna grass.

The manna grasses are perhaps most easily confused with alkali
grasses (*Puccinellia*) and false manna grasses (*Torreyochloa*), which
reside in a different tribe, *Poeae*. A comparison of the three genera is
presented in Table 51.

TABLE 51. A comparison of *Glyceria, Puccinellia,* and *Torreyochloa*

Characteristic	Glyceria	Puccinellia	Torreyochloa
Saline-alkaline habitat	no	yes	no
Leaf sheath	closed	open	open
Upper glume veins	1	[1] 3 [5]	[1] 3 [5]
Lemma vein number	[5] 7 [9], prominent	[3] 5 [7], faint	[5] 7–9, prominent

Plate 87. *Glyceria elata*

Hainardia — Thintail

Caespitose annuals. Stems to 50 cm tall, internodes solid. Inflorescence a single spike 8–25 cm long. Spikelets 5–8 mm long, 1 per node, ± embedded in notches in a thickened, cylindrical rachis. Spikelets 1-flowered, bisexual, dorsally compressed, breaking apart below the glume, with a rachis segment attached. Glume 1, the lower absent in all except the terminal spikelet, the upper firm to indurate, acute, 3- to several-veined, longer than the floret, acute, sometimes with a mucro, closing over the cavity in the rachis; lemma 3-veined, thin, awnless.

1 • 1 • 1. Mediterranean area. Hard grass or thintail (*H. cylindrica*)

Plate 88. *Hainardia cylindrica*

(pl. 88). Primarily in coastal salt marshes and on interior alkaline soils below 500 m. Sierra Nevada foothills, Central Valley, South Coast, Southern California. See Table 43 for a comparison with other grasses with similar inflorescences.

Hilaria   **Galleta, Tobosa, Curly-mesquite**

Caespitose or rhizomatous perennials. Stems to 2+ m tall, herbaceous to almost woody, internodes solid. Inflorescence a condensed spike, the zig-zag rachis remaining intact at maturity (pl. 89); spikelets in wedge-shaped, overlapping trios at each node, falling as a unit. Central spikelet subsessile, 1- or 2-flowered, bisexual or the upper staminate, laterally

Plate 89. *Hilaria* (zig-zag rachis)

compressed, breaking apart along with the lateral pair as a group. Glumes 2, equal, shorter than the floret, keeled, the apex deeply 2-lobed, bearing 1 dorsal awn and 2–8 terminal ones; lemma 3-veined, ciliate, 2-lobed, generally with a terminal awn. Lateral spikelets sessile, 1- to 4-flowered, sterile or staminate, laterally compressed, breaking apart along with the central one as a group. Glumes 2, dissimilar, the lower bearing an awn near its margin, the upper awnless; lemmas 3-veined, ciliate at its tip, awnless.

2 • 5 • 10. Desert areas and dry grasslands of southwestern United States to Guatemala. A source of important forage grasses and soil-binders.

Plate 90. *Hilaria rigida*

1a Plants shrubby, caespitose, 35 cm to 2.5 m tall; lower stem inter-
nodes sparsely to densely hairy ....***H. rigida***
BIG GALLETA (pls. 90 & 91). Native. Spikes 4–10 cm long. Spikelet
clusters 7–11 mm long. Fertile and sterile spikelets 6–12 mm long.
Dry, open, sandy, rocky flats, washes, scrub, woodlands. Peninsular
ranges, desert mountains, Mojave and Sonoran deserts. An important forage grass.

1b Plants herbaceous, strongly rhizomatous or stoloniferous, 20–65
cm tall; lower stem internodes glabrous..............................***H. jamesii***
GALLETA. Native. Spikes 3–7 cm long. Spikelet clusters 6–9 mm long.
Fertile spikelets 6–8 mm long; the sterile slightly shorter. Habitats
similar to *H. rigida*. Great Basin, desert mountains, Mojave Desert.

Plate 91. *Hilaria rigida*

Holcus   Velvet Grass

Caespitose perennials. Stems weak, succulent, to 1 m tall. Leaves velvety-pubescent, especially the sheaths. Inflorescence a contracted panicle, 6–15 cm long. Spikelets 2- [3-] flowered, the lower bisexual, the upper(s) staminate or sterile, laterally compressed, rachilla sometimes prolonged above the uppermost floret, breaking apart below the glumes. Glumes 2, as long as or longer than the florets, the lower 1-veined and the upper

Plate 92. *Holcus lanatus*

3-veined; lemmas faintly 3- to 5-veined, the lower awnless, the upper with a short, hooked or bent awn from near its apex.

2 • 2 • 8. Europe, North Africa, and the Middle East. Velvet grass *(H. lanatus)* (pls. 92 & 93). Naturalized. Stems to 1 m tall. Panicles 7–15 cm long. Spikelets 3–6 mm long. Moist disturbed sites from low to medium elevation. Widespread. Its hooked awn is diagnostic. Listed: Cal-IPC.

Plate 93. *Holcus lanatus*

Hordeum   **Barley**

Annuals or caespitose perennials. Stems to 1+ m tall. Leaf auricles present or absent. Inflorescence a dense, balanced, often bristly spike, shattering at maturity (except in cultivated barley). Spikelets typically 3 per node, the central sessile and fertile. Lateral spikelets 1-flowered, often stalked and sterile (all three fertile in barley), often reduced to awn-like glumes; lemmas usually awned. Central spikelet 1-flowered, the rachilla extended above it and bearing a rudiment, laterally or dorsally compressed, bisexual, breaking apart below the glumes or not breaking apart in cultivars. Glumes 2, narrow to bristle-like, rigid, 1-veined, subulate or awned; lemma dorsally flattened, 5-veined (often difficult to distinguish), tapered to an awn or awn-point; palea often fused to caryopsis.

10 · 10 · 32. Temperate regions of both hemispheres; a number are weedy. Of considerable economic importance because of the many uses for cultivated barley (*H. vulgare*).

1a   Auricles present at base of upper leaves **2**
1b   Auricles absent from upper leaves...**3**
2a   Inflorescence axis remaining intact at maturity; glumes not ciliate
     ....**H. vulgare**
     BARLEY (pl. 94). Naturalized annual. Stems to 1 m tall. Spikes 5–10
     cm long, green to purple, variable in the number of spikelets per
     node that will produce grain (2-, 4-, and 6-rowed barleys). Spike-
     lets 10–15 mm long. Roadsides, disturbed places, and fields. Wide-
     spread. Grains eaten directly or used to make bread and soups. Also
     sprouted to make malt for the brewing and distilling industries—
     including especially the production of single malt Scotch, which
     must be viewed as one of the major accomplishments in our cultural
     evolution. An important source of fodder for domesticated animals
     and sometimes planted for erosion control.
2b   Inflorescence axis breaking apart at maturity; glumes of the
     central spikelet ciliate...**H. murinum**
     WALL, HARE, SMOOTH, OR MOUSE BARLEY. Naturalized annual. Stems
     to 1+ m tall. Spikes 3–8 cm long, pale green to reddish. Fertile spike-
     lets 7–12 mm long. Weedy at low elevations. Widespread. Valuable
     for forage. Three subspecies occur here, varying in hairiness of the
     palea and size of anthers. Listed: Cal-IPC.

(account continued)

Plate 94. *Hordeum vulgare*

3a   Glumes strongly divergent at maturity ....***H. jubatum***
SQUIRRELTAIL OR FOXTAIL BARLEY (pl. 95). Native perennial. Stems to 80 cm. Spikes 3–15 cm long, whitish green to light purple. Glumes and florets of the lateral spikelets reduced to hair-like awns. Fertile spikelets 4–7 mm long. Disturbed areas, meadows, and marshes; sometimes forming dense stands. Widespread from low to high elevations.

3b   Glumes straight [spreading slightly] at maturity ***4***

Plate 95. *Hordeum jubatum*

4a Plants perennial; spikes fully exserted at maturity
....***H. brachyantherum***

MEADOW BARLEY (pl. 96). Native perennial. Stems to 95 cm. Spikes 3–9 cm, green to purple. Fertile spikelets 7–12 mm long. Moist soils from sea level to 3,500 m. Widespread, especially along the North Coast. Two subspecies in California; in subsp. *brachyantherum* the basal sheaths are typically glabrous, while in the endemic subsp. *californicum* they are densely hairy.

4b Plants annual; spikes ± enclosed in upper leaf sheaths at maturity (except in some *H. marinum*)..**5**

5a Lemma awn of lateral spikelet 3–8 mm long
....***H. marinum* subsp. *gussoneanum***

Plate 96. *Hordeum brachyantherum*

MEDITERRANEAN BARLEY (pl. 97). Naturalized annual. Stems to 50 cm. Spikes 1.5–7 cm long, green to purple. Spikelets 6–8 mm long. Dry to moist disturbed sites, especially on clay soils and alkaline flats. Widespread.

5b   Lemma awn of lateral spikelet 0–1.2 mm long **6**

6a   Nodes glabrous; glumes of central spikelet rounded to slightly flattened near base .... ***H. depressum***

ALKALI OR LOW BARLEY. Native annual. Stems to 60 cm. Spikes 2–7 cm long, pale green to reddish. Spikelets 5–10 mm long. Moist sites, vernal pools, generally on alkaline soils. West of Sierra Nevada-Cascades axis.

Plate 97. *Hordeum marinum*

6b Nodes generally hairy; glumes of central spikelet distinctly flattened at base.. ***H. intercedens***
BOBTAIL BARLEY. Native annual. Stems to 40 cm. Spikes 2.5–6.5 cm long, pale green. Spikelets 4.5–7.5 mm long. Vernal pools, saline river beds, and alkali flats. San Joaquin Valley, South Coast ranges, Southwest California.

Kikuyuochloa   **Kikuyu Grass**
Mat-forming stoloniferous-rhizomatous perennial. Stems to 45 cm tall, highly branched. Leaf sheaths glabrous or pubescent; blades 1–15 cm long, 1–6 mm wide. Panicles 2–3 cm long, consisting of 1–6 clusters of spikelets concealed in the sheaths. Spikelets 10–22 mm long, sessile or stalked, subtended by an inner and outer set of bristles, 2-flowered, bisexual, dorsally compressed, breaking apart with bristles remaining attached. Lower glume generally absent; upper glume ± 1 mm long; florets 2, the lower sterile and the upper fertile; lemmas 8- to 13-veined; paleas 2- to 7-veined. Anthers on elongated filaments at flowering.

1 · 1 · 1. Africa. Of economic importance as forage and as a lawn grass. Recently segregated from the fountain grasses *(Pennisetum)*, where it is treated in TJM2, the genus consists of a single species, kiyuyu grass *(K. clandestina)*. The common name derives from the Kiyuyu people of upland Kenya. The specific epithet refers to the spikelets being hidden in the leaf sheaths. This grass was introduced into California around 1918 for forage, as a lawn grass, and for erosion control. It has since become an aggressive weed in orchards and agricultural fields along the coast and in inland valleys. Mostly North, Central, and South coasts, Sacramento Valley, Southern California. In addition to its aggressive vegetative reproduction, kikuyu grass appears to excrete soluble chemicals that can depress the growth of its competitors. Listed: CDFA, USDA.

Koeleria **June Grass**

Caespitose perennials. Stems to 1+ m tall. Inflorescence typically a dense, spike-like panicle. Spikelets 2- to 4-flowered, bisexual, laterally compressed, breaking apart above the glumes and beneath the florets, rachilla extended as a bristle beyond the uppermost floret. Glumes 2, ± equal, as long as or shorter than the lowest floret, dissimilar (lower acute, 1-veined and the upper broader, longer, obscurely 3- to 5-veined); lemmas 5-veined, their margins shiny, awnless or awned from a bifid apex; palea tip notched, sometimes short-awned.

1 • 1 • 35. Temperate regions of both hemispheres. Of economic importance as forage for livestock. June grass *(K. macrantha)* (pl. 98). (Fig. 15) Native. Stems to 85 cm tall. Panicles 4–27 cm long. Spikelets 2.5–6.5 mm long. Widespread in various habitats from 0 to 4,000 m. Its small, shiny tan to purplish spikelets are distinctive. A second annual species often included in the genus is here placed in *Rostraria*.

Plate 98. *Koeleria macrantha*

Lamarckia   Goldentop

Caespitose annual. Stems to 40 cm tall, erect or spreading. Leaf sheaths keeled and closed for ⅔ their length. Inflorescence a contracted panicle 2–8 cm long of drooping clusters of dissimilar fertile and sterile spikelets. Fertile spikelets 3–5 mm long, with a single fertile floret and a stalked rudimentary one, laterally compressed, and breaking apart below the glumes. Glumes 2, ± equal, 1-veined; lemmas papery, 2-lobed, awned from near the tip. Staminate or sterile spikelets 6–9 mm long, 3- to 8-flowered; glumes linear; lemmas awnless. Palea absent.

1 • 1 • 1. Mediterranean area and Asia. Goldentop (*L. aurea*) (pl. 99). Naturalized. A popular garden ornamental and a weed on disturbed, thin, often degraded soils. Mainly in the Sierra Nevada foothills, Central Coast, and Southwest California. The generic name commemorates the famous French naturalist and the epithet is a reference to the golden color of its spikelets.

Plate 99. *Lamarckia aurea*

Leersia   **Cut Grass, Rice Cut Grass, White Grass**

Mostly rhizomatous perennials of wet sites. Stems to 1.5 m tall, erect or rooting at the nodes. Inflorescence a panicle, 4–30 cm long. Spikelets 1-flowered, bisexual, laterally compressed, breaking apart below the glumes. Glumes 0; lemmas 5-veined, usually awnless. Stamens 1–6. (Fig. 13)

2 • 5 • 18. Moist woods and river bottoms to drier sites in the tropics

Plate 100. *Leersia oryzoides*

and warm-temperate regions of the Old and New World. Rice cut grass *(L. oryzoides)* (pls. 100 & 101). Native. Stems to 1.5 m tall. Panicles 10–30 cm long. Spikelets 4–6.5 mm long. Along margins of marshes, streams, and ponds. Widespread. The epithet refers to its rice-like spikelets and its common name to the backwardly barbed leaf margins that can penetrate the skin. I recall noticing a few drops of blood in the water after collecting rice cut grass along the edge of a stream. A second species *(L. hexandra)* has been reported recently as a weed in Central Valley rice fields.

Plate 101. *Leersia oryzoides*

Leptochloa   **Sprangletop**

Caespitose annuals (ours) or perennials, often of marshy or wet sites. Stems to 1+ m tall. Inflorescence a panicle of digitate or racemose branches that bear spikes or spike-like racemes. Spikelets 2- to several-flowered, often overlapping, bisexual, rounded to laterally compressed, breaking apart above the glumes and between the florets. Glumes 2, equal or unequal, 1-veined, shorter than the lowest floret; lemmas 3-veined, often minutely pubescent on the veins, awnless, mucronate, or awned.

4 • 11 • 32. Warmer regions of both hemispheres. Bearded sprangletop

Plate 102. *Leptochloa fusca*

(*L. fusca*) (pls. 102 & 103). Native annual. Stems to 1 m tall. Inflorescence 1–70 cm long, with 3–35 branches. Spikelets 5–12 mm long. In Mexican sprangletop (**var. *uninervia***) the mature lemmas are awnless, often dark green or lead colored. In **var. *fascicularis*** they are often smoky-white with a 0.5–3.5 mm awn. Both are widespread, particularly in disturbed wet areas, becoming weedy in various irrigated sites, especially in the Central Valley. Plants are salt tolerant and exude sodium chloride from glands on the leaves. A recent paper proposes to transfer most of our North American species into four segregate genera.

Plate 103. *Leptochloa fusca*

Melica   **Onion Grass, Melic**

Native caespitose perennials, sometimes rhizomatous. Stems to 2.5 m tall, bases sometimes enlarged into bulb-like corms. Leaf sheaths closed. Inflorescence an open to contracted panicle (pl. 104). Spikelets 1- to 7-flowered, bisexual, the upper 1–4 florets sterile, overlapping, and forming a knob-like or pointed cluster (rudiment); rounded to laterally compressed, breaking apart above the glumes and between the florets or below the glumes. Glumes 2, shorter than, equal to, or longer than the lowest floret, 1- to 11-veined, the margins membranous or parchment-

Plate 104. *Melica* inflorescence

like in texture; lemmas thin, 5- to several-veined, membranous to leathery in texture, their margins usually papery, awnless. Stamens [2] 3.

12 • 19 • 80. Temperate regions of both hemispheres, often in shady woodlands or on open, dry slopes. Of limited economic importance as forage.

1a   Bulb-like corms present (pl. 105)..**2**
1b   Bulb-like corms absent...**3**
2a   Lemma apex obtuse to acute, its base glabrous; rudiment not
       resembling bisexual florets...***M. bulbosa***
       ONION GRASS, WESTERN MELIC. Stems to 1 m tall. Panicles 5–30 cm
       long, branches appressed. Spikelets 6–15 [24] mm long, with [2]
       4–7 bisexual florets. Dry slopes, conifer forests, and along streams.
       Northern California through the Cascade Range and Sierra Nevada
       south to the edge of the Mojave Desert.
2b   Lemma apex strongly tapered, its base hairy; rudiment resembling
       bisexual florets..***M. subulata***
       ALASKA ONION GRASS, ROCK MELIC, TAPERED ONION GRASS. Stems to
       1+ m tall. Panicles 8–25 cm long, branches ascending to appressed.
       Spikelets 10–28 mm long with 2–5 bisexual florets. Meadows, stream
       banks, and conifer forests. Northern California through the Cascade Range and Sierra Nevada south to Monterey County.

Plate 105. *Melica* corms

3a Spikelets breaking apart below the glumes; pedicels bent sharply downward...**M. stricta**
    NODDING OR ROCK MELIC (pl. 106). (Fig. 17) Stems to 90 cm. Panicles 3–30 cm long, branches appressed. Spikelets 6–23 mm long, 1 or 2 per branch. Rocky, often dry sites in conifer forests to the alpine at 3,500 m. Northwest California, Sierra Nevada, South Coast, desert mountains. One variety is endemic to Southern California.

3b Spikelets breaking apart above the glumes; pedicels ± straight.......**4**

4a Spikelets 5–15 mm long; bisexual florets 2–6 ....**5**

Plate 106. *Melica stricta*

4b   Spikelets 3–7 mm long; bisexual florets [1] 2; palea almost as long as lemma...**6**

5a   Rudiment 1–3 mm long, not resembling the bisexual florets .... ***M. californica***
CALIFORNIA MELIC (pl. 107). Stems to 1.4 m tall. Panicles 4–34 cm long, branches appressed. Spikelets 5–15 mm long. Sea level to 2,100 m, from dry, open hillsides to moist pine forests. North Coast ranges, Sierra Nevada, Sacramento Valley, South Coast, Southern California.

5b   Rudiment 3–5 mm long, similar in shape to bisexual florets .... ***M. harfordii***
HARFORD'S MELIC. Plants to 1+ m tall. Panicles 6–25 cm long. Spikelets 7–20 mm long. Dry slopes, conifer forests. Northwest, Cascades, Sierra Nevada, San Francisco Bay Area, and South Coast Range.

6a   Upper glume 3- to 5-veined; stalk of the rudiment about 2.5 mm long..***M. torreyana***
TORREY'S MELIC. Stems to 1 m tall. Panicles 6–25 cm long, branches appressed. Spikelets 3.5–7 mm long. Common in chaparral and conifer forests and on serpentine soils, from sea level to 1,200 m; often abundant after fires. Endemic. North Coast ranges, Sierra Nevada, Sacramento Valley, South Coast ranges. A valuable forage grass.

Plate 107. *Melica californica*

Plate 108. *Melica imperfecta*

6b   Upper glume 1-veined; stalk of the rudiment about 0.5 mm long
....***M. imperfecta***
COAST RANGE OR LITTLE CALIFORNIA MELIC (pl. 108). Stems to 1+ m tall.
Panicles 5–36 cm long, branches appressed to spreading. Spikelets
3–7 mm long. Coastal dunes, open woods, and dry, rocky slopes.
North Coast ranges, Sierra Nevada foothills, Sacramento Valley,
Central Coast, and Southwest California. A valuable forage grass.

Plate 109. *Melinis repens*

Melinis **Molasses Grass, Ruby Grass, Natal Grass**

Annuals or perennials. Stems to 1.5 m tall. Inflorescence an open to contracted panicle. Spikelets 2-flowered (the lower staminate or sterile and the upper fertile), rounded to dorsally compressed, breaking apart below the glumes. Glumes 2 [1], the lower absent or shorter; upper glume 5- to 7-veined, similar to sterile lemma in size and texture; sterile lemma 3- to 5-veined; fertile lemma 1- to 5-veined, laterally compressed, awned or awnless; palea relatively long or absent in lower florets.

1 • 2 • 26. Savannas, grasslands, and disturbed areas of Africa and western Asia. A source of pasture and forage grasses. Ruby grass or Natal grass *(M. repens)* (pl. 109). Naturalized perennial. Stems to 1+ m tall.

Panicles 6–22 cm long. Spikelets 2–6 mm long. Lower glume 0–1.7 mm long; the upper glume 2–5 mm long, with conspicuous white, rose, or purple hairs. A common weed in much of the warmer parts of the world. Southwest California, mostly in Los Angeles and San Diego counties. I expect it to become more widespread.

Muhlenbergia   **Muhly, Nimblewill, Deer Grass**

Delicate, caespitose annuals to coarse, rhizomatous, stoloniferous perennials. Stems to 2 m tall, internodes solid or hollow. Ligule membranous. Inflorescence an open to contracted [spike-like] panicle. Spikelets small, 1-flowered [2-flowered and rarely keying properly!], bisexual, laterally compressed, breaking apart above the glumes. Glumes 2, equal or unequal, [0-] 1- [3-] veined, awnless to short-awned; lemmas 3-veined, typically with a single well-developed awn, occasionally mucronate or awnless.

22 • 71 • 155. Diverse habitats of both hemispheres, especially the New World. Ours of some value as forage grasses and in erosion control. The concept of *Muhlenbergia* has been expanded recently to include *Lycurus* and *Schedonnardus*. They were represented in our grass flora by wolf's-tail *(L. setaceus)* and tumble grass *(S. paniculatus)*, both of which appear to be known only from single collections.

1a   Plants annual **2**
1b   Plants perennial...**3**
2a   Lemma 2.5–4.5 mm long, its awn 1–3 cm long........***M. microsperma***
      LITTLE-SEEDED MUHLY (pl. 110). Native. Stems to 60 cm tall, typically purplish-red. Panicles 5–20 cm long, branches spreading to ascending. Spikelets 2.5–5.5 mm, florets readily deciduous. Moist to dry open, disturbed sites. Central and South coasts, desert mountains, Southern California.
2b   Lemma 1.5–2 mm long, awn 0–1 cm long........................***M. filiformis***
      PULL-UP OR SLENDER MUHLY (pl. 111). Native annual, but sometimes with short stolons and mat-forming. Stems to 30 cm tall. Panicles 1–6 cm long, branches appressed. Spikelets 1.5–3.2 mm long. Open moist meadows, seeps, along streams. Northern California, Sierra Nevada, Transverse ranges.
3a   Panicles 5–15 cm wide, its branches spreading **4**
3b   Panicles less than 4 cm wide, its branches typically ascending to appressed **5**
4a   Lemma awn 0–0.3 mm long...***M. asperifolia***
      SCRATCH GRASS, ALKALI MUHLY (pl. 112). Native. Plants rhizomatous-stoloniferous. Stems to 60 cm tall. Panicles 6–17 cm long, branches spreading. Spikelets 1–2 mm long, sometimes with 2 or 3 florets. Alkaline meadows, seeps, hot springs. Widespread. Grains often infected with a fungus that forms a **globose** structure filled with dark spores.

Plate 110. *Muhlenbergia microsperma*

Plate 111. *Muhlenbergia filiformis*

Plate 112. *Muhlenbergia asperifolia*

4b   Lemma awn 2–13 mm long...**M. porteri** **BUSHY MUHLY** (pl. 113). Native. Stems to 1 m tall. Panicles 4–15 cm long. Spikelets 3–4.5 mm long. Rocky slopes and cliffs, desert flats, often in and under shrubs. San Bernardino Mountains, Peninsular ranges, and Mojave Desert.

5a   Plants densely clumped, rhizomes absent.............................**M. rigens** **DEER GRASS, BASKET GRASS** (pl. 114). Native. Stems to 1.5 m tall, stiffly erect. Panicles 15–60 cm long, dense, spike-like. Spikelets 2.4–4 mm long. Its robust size and narrow panicles are diagnostic. Sandy to gravelly places along canyons, stream bottoms, and the edges of meadows and seeps. Cascades, Sierra Nevada, Central Valley, South Coast, Southern California. Native Americans mixed deer grass seeds with cornmeal to make bread or a mush, and also used its stems as the foundation around which coils were wrapped to make baskets. It is now a very popular ornamental.

5b   Creeping, scaly rhizomes present..**6**

6a   Plants with ascending stems, somewhat woody toward the base; glumes 2.5–4 mm long; lower lemma with short, soft hairs .... **M. californica** **CALIFORNIA MUHLY.** Native. Stems to 70 cm tall. Panicles 5–13 cm long. Spikelets 2.8–4 mm long. Streambanks, sandy slopes, and canyons. Transverse ranges.

6b   Plants forming mats or dense clumps; glumes 0.5–1.8 mm long; lower lemma glabrous or with short, stiff hairs .... **M. richardsonis** **MAT MUHLY.** Native. Stems to 40 cm tall, decumbent to erect. Panicles 1–12 cm long, branches appressed and partially concealing the main axis. Spikelets 1.7–3.1 mm long; lemmas short-awned. Dry to moist meadows, slopes, flats, and streambanks. Northwest California, Cascades, Sierra Nevada, South Coast ranges, Southwest California, desert mountains.

It is easy to confuse *Muhlenbergia* with *Agrostis* and *Sporobolus*, two other grasses with small, 1-flowered spikelets. Do not be discouraged. Several very famous botanists have had the same problem. See Table 44 for a comparison of the three genera.

(Key based largely on Peterson in Baldwin et al., pp. 1464, 1465.)

Plate 113. *Muhlenbergia porteri*

Plate 114. *Muhlenbergia rigens*

Neostapfia   Colusa Grass

Tufted, spreading, aromatic annual. Stems to 30 cm tall, ascending or decumbent; internodes solid. Leaves glandular-viscid, not clearly differentiated into blade and sheath. Inflorescence a dense, cylindrical spike-like raceme 2–8 cm long, often partially enclosed in dilated upper leaf sheaths, the spikelets spirally arranged. Spikelets 6–8 mm long, typically 5-flowered, bisexual, dorsally compressed, breaking apart above the glumes. Glumes 0; lemmas fan-shaped, prominently 7- to 11-veined, awnless; paleas much narrower than the lemmas.

1 • 1 • 1. Colusa grass (*Neostapfia colusana*) (pl. 115) is endemic to vernal pool margins in Colusa, Merced, Solano, Stanislaus, and Yolo counties. Do not collect! Listed: CDFG and USFSW.

Plate 115. *Neostapfia colusana*

Orcuttia   **Orcutt Grass**

Tufted annuals of vernal pool and similar habitats. Stems to 35 cm tall, erect to prostrate; internodes solid. Leaf blade and sheath not clearly differentiated. Inflorescence a spike-like raceme, 2–10 cm long. Spikelets 8–15 mm long, 4- to 40-flowered, bisexual, laterally compressed, breaking apart above the glumes and between the florets. Glumes 2, irregularly toothed, 5- to 9-veined; lemmas deeply-cleft, with 5 prominent awn-like teeth.

5 • 5 • 5. Four species are endemic to vernal pools in 5 to 8 California counties. Slender Orcutt grass *(O. tenuis)* (pl. 116) is the most-collected species; California Orcutt grass *(O. californica)* extends into Baja California, Mexico. Characters of lemma teeth are critical in distinguishing species. Do not collect! All are listed: CDFG and USFWS.

Plate 116. *Orcuttia tenuis*

Oryza   **Rice**

Annual or perennial herbs. Stems to 3 m tall. Inflorescence an open to contracted panicle. Spikelets appearing 1-flowered, bisexual, laterally compressed, breaking apart above the glumes. Glumes reduced to a 2-lobed cupule; lemmas 5-veined, awned or awnless. Stamens 6.

2 • 2 • 25. Moist, wet, shady regions of the Old and New World; none native to North America. Rice *(O. sativa)* (pls. 117 & 118). Annual [perennial]. Stems to 2 m tall (our cultivars shorter). Panicles 10–50 cm long. Spikelets 6–11 mm long. Escaped along roadsides in rice field areas, mostly Glenn and Butte counties south to Sacramento County. One of the world's principal cereals, with 696 million metric tons harvested in 2010, second only to

Plate 117. *Oryza sativa*

maize. It is widely cultivated in flooded fields or on dry land (upland rice). Annual production in California is more than 2 million tons, second only to Arkansas in the United States. Commercial production here began in 1912 in Richvale (Butte County), and today it is grown mostly in Central Valley.

Interpretation of the rice spikelet remains unsettled. A quick glance suggests a rather simple spikelet with two glumes and a single fertile floret. The opposing view is that the spikelet consists of a single fertile floret subtended by two sterile florets reduced to sterile lemmas that mimic glumes, and that the real glumes are reduced to a couple of inconspicuous lobes at the apex of the pedicel that are not at all glume-like. Recent developmental studies suggest that the latter view is correct. Where is Occam's Razor when you need it?

Plate 118. *Oryza sativa* (spikelets)

Panicum   **Panic Grass, Panicum, Rosette Grass**

Annuals or caespitose, rhizomatous or stoloniferous perennials. Stems to 4 m tall, herbaceous or woody, the internodes hollow or solid. Inflorescence an open to contracted terminal or axillary panicle [raceme]. Spikelets 1–8 mm long, 2-flowered, bisexual, generally dorsally compressed, breaking apart below the glumes. Lower floret sterile or sometimes staminate, its lemma similar in size and texture to the upper glume. Upper floret fertile, its lemma firm to indurate, awnless, and clasping the palea with its enrolled margins. Fertile lemma and palea of similar texture. Glumes 2, the lower much shorter than the upper, the lower 1- to 9-veined and the upper 3- to several-veined; sterile lemma 5- to 9-veined, awnless, similar to upper glume in size and texture; fertile lemma 3- to 11-veined, awnless, glabrous, firm to indurate at maturity; palea of fertile floret similar to lemma in texture, and tightly clasped by it.

14 • 71 • 500. Perhaps second only to the blue grasses *(Poa)* in number of species worldwide. Most are tropical, but many species are found in the warm, temperate parts of both hemispheres. Of considerable economic importance as a source of grains, pasture grasses, and weeds. The limits of the genus remain unsettled. Most of the genera in *Paniceae* were originally treated as species of *Panicum*. Dismemberment of the genus has accelerated in recent years. One of the segregates, *Dichanthelium*, enjoys wide acceptance. Caution! If you encounter a *Panicum* growing near geysers or other thermal sites in Sonoma, Nevada, or Shasta counties, do not collect it. It may be the endemic *P. acuminatum* var. *thermale*. Listed: CDFG.

1a   Plants of dunes and sandy soils; rhizomes or stolons present; glumes and lemmas with conspicuous white hairs
....***P. urvilleanum***
       DESERT OR SILKY PANIC GRASS (pl. 119). Native perennial. Stems to 1 m tall. Panicles 20–35 cm long. Spikelets 5–7.5 mm long. South Coast, desert mountains, Mojave and Sonoran deserts.
1b   Plants of moist sites, open fields, meadows, roadsides, and disturbed places; rhizomes or stolons absent; glumes and lemmas glabrous **2**
2a   Plants perennial; rosette of basal leaves present **3**
2b   Plants annual; rosette of basal leaves absent **4**

(account continued)

Plate 119. *Panicum urvilleanum*

3a Spikelet 2.7–3.5 mm; upper glume with a prominent orange to purplish spot at its base............. ***P. oligosanthes* var. *scribnerianum*** **SCRIBNER'S PANIC GRASS** (pl. 120). Native. Stems to 60 cm tall. Panicles 5–8 cm long. Meadows and forests. Northwest California and Cascades.

3b Spikelets 1.1–2.1 mm long; prominent spot at base of upper glume absent ....***P. acuminatum*** **HAIRY PANIC GRASS** (pl. 121). Native. Stems to 75 cm. Panicles 3–12 cm long. Mostly in moist habitats. Widespread. We have three, ques-

Plate 120. *Panicum oligosanthes* var. *scribnerianum*

tionably distinct varieties that differ in subtle details of pubescence on the leaf sheaths and blade surfaces.

4a   Stems and leaves mostly glabrous; lower glume apex rounded to truncate.. ***P. dichotomiflorum***
FALL PANIC GRASS. Naturalized. Stems to 1 m, erect or decumbent. Panicle 10–25 cm long. Spikelets 2–3 mm long. Waste areas, wet grounds, and fields. Cascades, Sierra Nevada foothills, Central Valley, South Coast.

4b   Stems and leaves hairy; lower glume apex pointed **5**

Plate 121. *Panicum acuminatum* var. *fasciculatum*

5a Spikelet 4.5–6 mm long..**_P. miliaceum_**
    PROSO, BROOM CORN, OR HOG MILLET (pl. 122). Naturalized. Stems to
    2 m tall. Panicles 10–40 cm long. Central Valley, San Francisco Bay
    Area, South Coast, Southern California. One of the oldest of the
    cereal grains, it is grown primarily to feed livestock and is one of the
    main ingredients in birdseed mixes.
5b Spikelets 2–4 mm long **6**
6a Palea of sterile floret 1.0–1.8 mm; lemma of upper floret with a
    crescent-shaped scar at its base..**_P. hillmanii_**

Plate 122. _Panicum miliaceum_

HILLMAN'S PANIC GRASS. Naturalized annual. Stems to 70 cm. Panicles 10–25 cm long. Spikelets 2–3 mm long. Disturbed areas, roadsides. North Coast ranges, Sierra Nevada, Central Valley, South Coast, Southern California.

6b Palea of sterile floret absent; upper lemma not scarred at base
.... ***P. capillare***

WITCH GRASS, TUMBLE GRASS (pl. 123). Native annual. Stems to 1 m tall, green or red-purple. Panicles 13–50 cm long, often about half the height of the plant. Spikelets 2–4 mm long. Fields, pastures, roadsides, ditches, and other disturbed areas. Widespread.

Plate 123. *Panicum capillare*

Parapholis   **Sickle Grass**

Caespitose annuals. Stems to 45 cm tall, erect to ± spreading, the internodes hollow. Inflorescence a single spike, 1–15 cm long, curved or
straight, twisted or not, the spikelets solitary at each node, ± embedded
in a thickened rachis. Spikelets 1-flowered, bisexual, cylindrical, breaking apart below the glumes with a rachis segment attached. Glumes 2, ±
equal, longer than the floret, 3- or 5-veined, leathery, their attachment
displaced so that they appear side-by-side in front; lemma hyaline, 1- to
3-veined; awnless; palea relatively long, tightly clasped by lemma.

2 • 2 • 6. Maritime soils and salt marshes from western Europe to India.
Curved sickle grass *(P. incurva)* (pl. 124). Naturalized. Stems to 35 cm

Plate 124. *Parapholis incurva*

tall. Spikes 1–15 cm long. Spikelets 4.5–7.5 mm long. Weedy on mud flats and in salt marshes from the North Coast through the Central Valley and along the South Coast to San Diego County. Its spikes are curved and twisted. European sickle grass *(P. strigosa)* was first found in North America around Humboldt Bay and is now known from Del Norte, Mendocino, and Sonoma counties. Its spikes are straight and not twisted.

Paspalum   **Dallis Grass, Knot Grass, Bahia Grass**

Caespitose, rhizomatous, or stoloniferous perennials [annuals]. Stems to 4 m tall, the internodes hollow or solid. Inflorescence a series of racemose [paired] branches, bearing subsessile spikelets. Spikelets 2-flowered, solitary or paired along a narrow or broadly winged rachis, bisexual, flat on one side and rounded on the other, breaking apart below the glumes. Lower floret sterile or staminate; upper floret fertile. Glumes 1 [2], the lower usually absent, the upper 3- to 6-veined, upper glume and sterile lemma of lower floret similar in size and texture; sterile lemma 3- to 5-veined, as long as the fertile lemma; fertile lemma 3- to 5-veined, rounded on the back, firm to indurate, awnless, its back facing toward the rachis; palea of the fertile floret broad, flat or slightly convex, its margins covered by the enrolled edges of the lemma.

9 • 45 • 400. Warmer regions of both hemispheres. A source of grains, pasture grasses, and weeds. Plants infected by the fungus *Claviceps paspali* are the cause of a neurological disorder called "paspalum staggers." See the discussion of toxic grasses for symptoms.

1a   Inflorescence racemose; spikelets 2 per node on an inflorescence branch, margins of upper glume and sterile lemma ciliate
....***P. dilatatum***

DALLIS GRASS (pls. 125 & 126). Naturalized perennial. Stems to almost 2 m tall; lower leaf sheaths hairy. Panicles branches [2] 3–5 [7], 1.5–12 cm long. Widespread in moist places, roadsides. Widely used for hay and pasture. Its common name is after A. T. Dallis of La Grange, GA.

(account continued)

Plate 125. *Paspalum dilatatum*

Plate 126. *Paspalum dilatatum*

Plate 127. *Paspalum distichum*

1b   Inflorescence digitate; spikelets 1 per node on an inflorescence branch, glabrous .... ***P. distichum***
KNOT GRASS, CROWN GRASS, THOMPSON GRASS (pl. 127). Rhizomatous native perennial. Stems to 60 cm tall; sheaths glabrous. Panicles with 2 [3] branches, these 1.4–7 cm long. Spikelets 2.4–3.2 mm long. (Fig. 14) Moist places, often in standing water. Widespread. Used in erosion control, but it can be weedy.

Phalaris   **Canary Grass**

Caespitose annuals or perennials, often rhizomatous. Stems to 2+ m tall. Inflorescence typically a cylindrical to ovoid, spike-like panicle. Spikelets with a single bisexual floret subtended by 2 [1] reduced (sometimes very small!) scale-like florets or reduced even further to bands or tufts of hairs, laterally compressed, breaking apart above or below the glumes or not breaking apart. Glumes 2, ± equal, 3- to 5-veined, as long as or longer than the fertile floret, usually with a winged dorsal keel; fertile lemma glabrous or hairy, inconspicuously 5-veined, awnless; palea 1- or 2-veined.

11 • 11 • 22. Temperate regions of Eurasia, Africa, and the New World; five are native to North America. Of economic importance for hay and fodder, grains in commercial birdseed mixtures, erosion control, and as ornamentals and in dried arrangements. Several are invasive weeds. The canary grasses contain various toxic principles that cause "phalaris staggers," a motor neuron dysfunction, in addition to a polio-like syndrome and cardiac failure in poisoned animals.

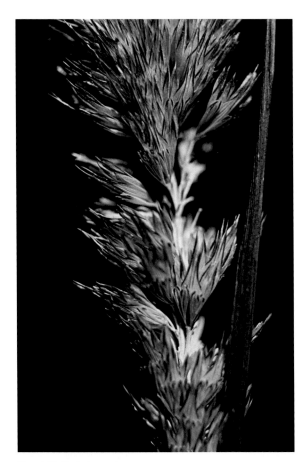

Plate 128. *Phalaris paradoxa*

1a   Spikelets dimorphic, in clusters of 4–7 lower staminate or sterile
      ones and a terminal pistillate or bisexual one; clusters typically
      breaking apart as a unit ....***Ph. paradoxa***
      HOOD CANARY GRASS (pl. 128). Naturalized annual. Stems to 1 m tall.
      Panicles 3–9 cm long. Sterile spikelets 4–6 mm long; fertile spikelets
      7–8 mm long. Disturbed areas, roadsides, cultivated fields. North
      Coast ranges, Sierra Nevada, Central Valley, Southern California.
1b   Spikelets similar, borne singly at a node; breaking apart above the
      glumes and beneath the florets **2**
2a   Glume keels with wings 0.2–1 mm wide...**3**
2b   Glume keels wingless 0–0.2 mm wide...**4**

3a   Plants annual; glume keel wings irregularly toothed or scalloped; sterile floret ± glabrous.. ***Ph. minor***
LESSER OR LITTLE-SEEDED CANARY GRASS. Naturalized. Stems to 1 m tall. Panicles 2–8 cm long. Spikelets 4–6.5 mm long. Disturbed areas. North Coast ranges, Sierra Nevada, Central Valley, Southern California. Common weed of alfalfa and sugar beet fields in the Imperial Valley. Consumption of plants, especially young ones, can lead to "phalaris staggers."

3b   Plants perennial, stems often swollen at base; glume keel wings usually entire; sterile floret(s) hairy .... ***Ph. aquatica***
HARDING GRASS, BULBOUS CANARY GRASS (pls. 129 & 130). Naturalized. Stems to 2 m tall. Panicles 1.5–15 cm long. Spikelets 4.5–7.5

Plate 129. *Phalaris aquatica*

mm long. Wet areas, ditches, and roadsides. Northwest California, Cascades, Sierra Nevada, Southern California. Introduced to provide additional forage. Escaping from pastures and rangelands. Named after R. R. Harding, an Australian botanist. Listed: Cal-IPC.

4a   Plants annual; bisexual floret beaked at its apex........... ***Ph. lemmonii***
      LEMMON'S CANARY GRASS. Endemic. Stems to 1.5 m tall. Panicles 4–20 cm long. Spikelets 5–7 mm long. Moist sites. Sierra Nevada, Central Valley, South Coast ranges, Southern California.

4b   Plants perennial; bisexual floret acute or acuminate, but not
      beaked **5**

Plate 130. *Phalaris aquatica*

Plate 131. *Phalaris arundinacea*

5a   Panicles 1.5–6 cm long, ovoid to cylindrical, branches not evident; rhizomes absent...**Ph. californica** **CALIFORNIA CANARY GRASS.** Native. Stems to 1.6 m tall. Panicles 1.5–5 cm long. Spikelets 5–8 mm long. Open moist fields, meadows, ravines, and woodlands. North, Central, and South Coast ranges. Reported for Oregon, but it has not been collected there since 1926.

5b   Panicles 5–40 cm long, elongate, branches evident; rhizomes present..**Ph. arundinacea** **REED CANARY GRASS** (pls. 131 & 132). Native. Stems to 2.5 m tall. Panicles 5–40 cm long. Spikelets 3.5–7.5 mm long. Moist areas, grasslands, and woodlands. North Coast, Sierra Nevada, Central Valley, Southern California.

Plate 132. *Phalaris arundinacea*

Phleum   **Timothy**

Caespitose annuals and perennials. Stems to 1.5 m tall, the bases sometimes tuberous. Inflorescence an ovoid to cylindrical, spike-like panicle, 1–10 cm long. Spikelets 1-flowered, bisexual, strongly laterally compressed, breaking apart above or below the glumes. Glumes 2, ± equal, longer than the floret, abruptly narrowed to an awn or mucro, 3-veined, keeled, the keels ciliate; lemma 5- to 7-veined, blunt, awnless.

2 • 2 • 15. Temperate regions of Eurasia and North America. Of economic importance as a source of hay and forage.

1b   Sheath of uppermost leaf not inflated; inflorescence cylindrical, generally 5 or more times longer than wide; lower internodes often enlarged or bulbous..***Ph. pratense***
TIMOTHY (pls. 133 & 134). (Fig. 16) Naturalized perennial. Stems to 1.5 m tall. Panicles 5–10+ cm long. Spikelets 3–4 mm long. Pastures, rangelands, and cooler mountain habitats. Widespread. Valuable hay and pasture grass, and a major cause of hay fever. The grass is named after Timothy Hansen, who introduced it to the American Colonies in 1720.

Plate 133. *Phleum pratense*

1b Sheath of uppermost leaf inflated; inflorescence ovoid, generally only 1.5–3 times longer than wide; lower internodes not enlarged or bulbous..***Ph. alpinum***
ALPINE TIMOTHY (pl. 134). Native perennial. Stems to 50 cm tall. Panicles 1–6 cm long. Spikelets 3–4 mm long. Meadows, bogs, and stream banks. Northern California, Sierra Nevada, Central Coast, mountains of Southern California.

Plate 134. *Phleum pratense* (left) and *Ph. alpinum* (right)

Phragmites   **Common Reed**

Robust rhizomatous or stoloniferous perennials. Stems herbaceous to woody, to 4 [10] m tall. Inflorescence a terminal, plumose panicle, 15–35 cm long. Spikelets 12–18 mm long, several-flowered, laterally compressed, the lower staminate or sterile, the middle florets bisexual, and the upper breaking apart above the glumes and between the florets; rachilla with long, silky hairs; callus also bearded. Glumes 2, pointed, awnless, the lower 1-veined and upper 3-veined; lemmas 3-veined, awnless.

1 • 1 • 4. Common reed *(Ph. australis)* (pls. 135 & 136). Native and naturalized. Widespread in marshes, around lakes and ponds, and along waterways over much of the continent; often considered the most widely

Plate 135. *Phragmites australis*

distributed vascular plant. Stems yield fibers used to make paper, cardboard, cellophane, fertilizer, and insulation material. Native Americans used it to make arrow shafts, tobacco pipes, splints, thatching, musical instruments, gambling sticks, mats, screens, baskets, cordage, snares, and they pulverized its stems for food and ate its young shoots as a potherb. I doubt that any other native California grass had such varied uses. Recent research suggests that we have three distinct genetic lineages present in North America, all of them reported for California. Two are native (one of them endemic), and the third is an invasive Eurasian introduction. The roots of common reed produce an acid that dissolves proteins in the roots of neighboring plants, thereby giving it a competitive advantage. I would class it as a transformative species in that it reduces biodiversity, has a

Plate 136. *Phragmites australis*

detrimental effect on the food supply for wildlife, and changes wetland hydrology. Pampas grass *(Cortaderia)*, a relative of poverty-oats, can be confused with *Arundo* and *Phragmites*. They are compared in Table 45.

Phyllostachys   **Fishpole or Timber Bamboo, Madake**
Shrubby to arborescent perennials. Stems woody, 3–20+ m tall. Main stems and branches with a distinctive groove on one side. Inflorescence a spike-like panicle, often subtended by a spathe. Spikelets large (to 8 cm!), several- to many-flowered, bisexual, laterally compressed, breaking apart above the glumes and between the florets, but rarely seen because flowering is so infrequent.

Plate 137. *Phyllostachys aurea*

2 • 12 • 60. Eastern Asia. Golden or fishpole bamboo *(Ph. aurea)* (pls. 137 & 138). Naturalized ornamental. Stems to 8 m tall. Spikelets 18–25 mm long. An extremely popular landscaping plant in California and the most commonly cultivated bamboo in the United States. Naturalized in the San Francisco Bay Area. There are also conspicuous stands of it along the Sacramento River in Shasta County and elsewhere. Young plants and those growing in shaded areas will not have the golden hue that gives this bamboo its common name. A helpful diagnostic feature is the shortening of the lower internodes in nature plants. This bamboo is more common than the limited number of herbarium specimens suggests.

The hedge bamboo *(Bambusa multiplex)*, Japanese bamboo *(Phyllostachys bambusoides)*, and metake or arrow bamboo *(Pseudosasa japonica)* are reported for California in the literature, but they have not been collected recently and are doubtfully naturalized.

Plate 138. *Phyllostachys aurea* (false petioles)

Annuals or perennials, caespitose or rhizomatous. Stems to 1+ m tall. Leaf sheaths closed to near the top. Inflorescence a single terminal raceme [panicle], 6–35 cm long. Spikelets large, linear, 5- to several-flowered, bisexual, laterally compressed, breaking apart above the glumes and between the florets. Glumes 2, unequal, shorter than the florets, the lower 1-veined and the upper 3-veined; lemmas 7- [9-] veined, the veins prominent, parallel, margins thin and membranous, apex entire or bifid, awned (ours) or awnless; palea winged on lower portion, awned or ours with a triangular appendage.

3 • 4 • 5. Wet sites. One species circumboreal in the Arctic; two native from British Columbia to California; two endemic to California. California semaphore grass *(P. californicus)* (pls. 139 & 140). The typical variety is an annual with stems to 1 m tall, racemes 6–35 cm long, and spikelets 15–60 mm long. It is endemic to moist sites, including vernal pools in Northern California, the Cascades and Sierra Nevada foothills, Sacramento Valley, and the San Francisco Bay Area. A second variety (var. *davyi*) is a perennial endemic to Mendocino and Lake counties. It has shorter lemma awns and palea appendages. Our two other species are rhizomatous, restricted to the coastal counties (Del Norte to Marin) and less frequently collected. The lemma awns of the North Coast semaphore grass *(P. hooverianus)* are 0.2–4 mm long, while those of the nodding semaphore grass *(P. refractus)* are 5–22 mm long.

Plate 139. *Pleuropogon californicus*

Plate 140. *Pleuropogon californicus*

Poa **Blue Grass, Mutton Grass, Spear Grass**

Perennials, many rhizomatous or stoloniferous; less often annuals. Stems to 1.5 m tall, the internodes hollow. Upper surface of the leaf blade with a groove on either side on the midvein; leaf tip often prow-shaped. Inflorescence an open to congested panicle, sometimes reduced to a raceme. Spikelets small, [1-] 2- to 10-flowered, bisexual or infrequently unisexual (species dioecious), laterally compressed, breaking apart above the glumes and between the florets. Glumes 2, ± equal, 1- or 3-veined; lemmas typically 5-veined, keeled, awnless, its base glabrous or with a web, tuft, or ring of fine, cottony hairs; palea distinctly 2-keeled.

37 • 67 • 500+. Cosmopolitan, probably the largest grass genus in the world; found typically in grasslands and meadows, but also in a variety of other habitats; many are weedy. Of considerable economic importance as a source of forage and pasture grasses, for lawns and sport fields, and for soil stabilization. Although the genus is relatively easy to recognize, species delimitation has been notoriously difficult because of rampant promiscuity—hybridization, backcrossing with parents, asexual reproduction that mimics sexual reproduction, and the formation of polyploids. This largest genus in our California grass flora can be recognized by its prow-shaped leaf tips, grooves on either side of the midvein on the upper leaf surface, and by its small, awnless spikelets with webbed calluses and keeled paleas. The concept of *Poa* has been expanded recently to include the genus *Dissanthelium*. It is represented in our flora by Catalina grass *(D. californicum),* endemic to the Channel Islands and adjacent Baja California, Mexico. It was thought to be extinct for several decades until its recent rediscovery. It has been renamed *Poa thomasii.*

1a   Stems with bulbous bases; florets often modified into leafy, tailed bulblets..***P. bulbosa***
       BULBOUS BLUE GRASS (pl. 141). Naturalized perennial. Stems to 60 cm. Sheaths with swollen bases. Panicles 3–12 cm long. Spikelets 3–5 mm, typically with the leafy tailed bulblets unique in our grass flora; callus webbed or glabrous. Disturbed places below 2,000 m. Widespread.

1b   Stem bases not bulbous; florets not so modified................................**2**
2a   Plants annual; anthers generally 0.2–1 mm long................................**3**
2b   Plants perennial; anthers generally 1.2–3.5 mm long........................**5**

(account continued)

Plate 141. *Poa bulbosa*

3a Callus glabrous .... **P. annua**
ANNUAL BLUE GRASS, WINTER GRASS (pl. 142). Naturalized annual [perennial]. Stems to 30 [45] cm. Panicles 1–8 cm long, erect. Spikelets 3–6 mm long; callus glabrous. This is one of the world's most cosmopolitan weeds and probably our earliest flowering grass each year.

3b Callus clothed in cobwebby hairs **4**

4a Lemmas glabrous; plants growing mostly at 1,500–3,000 m
.... **P. bolanderi**
BOLANDER'S BLUE GRASS. Stems 20–60 [70] cm tall. Panicles 10–15 [25] cm long. Spikelets 2.5–5 mm long. Openings in pine or fir forests. Northwestern California, Cascades, Sierra Nevada, and San Jacinto Mountains.

4b Lemmas with short hairs; plants growing mostly from sea level to 1,000 m .... **P. howellii**
HOWELL'S BLUE GRASS. Stems 30–80 cm tall. Panicles [10] 20–25 [30] cm long. Spikelets 4–6 mm long. Rocky banks, woodlands, chaparral. Widespread.

5a Rhizomes and/or stolons present [sometimes absent in *P. palustris*]
.... **6**

5b Rhizomes or stolons absent **9**

6a Stems, sheaths, and nodes strongly compressed .... **P. compressa**
CANADA BLUE GRASS, FLAT-STEMMED BLUE GRASS. Naturalized perennial. Stems to 60 cm. Panicles 3–8 cm long, branches roughened. Spikelets 3–7 mm; calluses webbed [glabrous]. Wet meadows and disturbed areas from the North Coast ranges, Cascades, Sierra Nevada, Southern California.

6b Stems, sheaths, and nodes not compressed or only slightly so **7**

(account continued)

Plate 142. *Poa annua*

7a Spikelets unisexual, the species dioecious; plants of coastal sand dunes ....***P. macrantha*** **SEASHORE BLUE GRASS** (pl. 143). Native. Rhizomes and stolons to 1 m. Aerial stems to 60 cm. Panicles 3–15 cm long, compacted, the branches smooth to somewhat scabrous. Spikelets 9–17 mm long. Coastal sand dunes of the North Coast. Douglas' blue grass *(P. douglasii)* has a similar appearance and occurs in the same habitat. It differs in having fewer spikelets per panicle and in its densely hairy inflorescence branches. It is endemic from Del Norte to San Diego counties.

7b Spikelets bisexual; plants of various habitats other than coastal dunes ***8***

Plate 143. *Poa macrantha*

8a Plants strongly rhizomatous; sheaths closed for up to ½ their
length .... ***P. pratensis***
KENTUCKY BLUE GRASS (pl. 144). Naturalized and possibly native.
Stems to 1 m. Panicles 6–15 cm long, loosely contracted to open, the
branches bearing spikelets mostly on the **distal** half. Spikelets 3–6
mm; calluses webbed. Highly variable, no doubt because it is both
asexually and sexually reproduced and it has the ability to hybridize
with closely related species. Its chromosome number ranges from 27
to 147, which may well be the world record. Naturalized throughout
the state. Important forage grass in mountain meadows; often used
with perennial rye grass in lawns. Listed: Cal-IPC.

Plate 144. *Poa pratensis*

8b Plants stoloniferous or caespitose; sheaths closed for up to ⅓ their length ....***Poa palustris***
FOWL BLUE GRASS. Naturalized. Stems to 1.5 m tall, erect or with spreading bases. Panicles 10–30 cm long. Spikelets 2–5 mm long. Of some importance for soil stabilization and food for waterfowl. Moist meadows, along streams, drier woods, and sagebrush scrub above 1,500 m. Cascades, Sierra Nevada, mountains in Southern California.

9a Spikelets broadly lanceolate to ± ovate, distinctly compressed ....***P. cusickii***
CUSICK'S BLUE GRASS, MOUNTAIN BLUE GRASS. Native. Plants dioecious or with female and bisexual florets. Stems to 70 cm tall; sheaths sometimes closed for ¾ their length. Panicles 2–10 cm long; branches ascending to erect. Spikelets 4–10 mm long; calluses glabrous or sparingly webbed. High mountain meadows, montane forests, sagebrush scrub. Northern California, Sierra Nevada, White and Inyo mountains.

9b Spikelets narrowly lanceolate, ± round in cross-section to weakly compressed...***P. secunda* complex**
PINE GRASS, NEVADA BLUE GRASS, SANDBERG'S BLUE GRASS (pl. 145). Natives, densely tufted. Stems to 1.2 m. Panicles 2–25 cm long, erect or lax, usually contracted, but more open when flowering. Spikelets 5–1 mm long, typically narrowly lanceolate; calluses glabrous or with a ring of hairs. Very common in a variety of habitats from sea level to about 4,000 m. Source of excellent fodder. *Poa secunda* is here very broadly defined, including up to 45 previously described species. It includes 11 species previously recognized in the California flora. Some of us see this as an improvement because so many of those species were ill-defined and identification was uncertain. Others have argued that this degree of conflation is unwise because it masks morphological and ecological differences.

(Key based in part on Soreng in Baldwin et al. 2012, pp. 1,476–1,478.)

Plate 145. *Poa secunda*

Polypogon   **Beard Grass, Rabbit's-foot Grass**

Annuals or perennials. Stems to 1+ m tall, often weak and decumbent and rooting at nodes. Inflorescence a soft, dense, contracted panicle, 1–30 cm long, sometimes lobed or interrupted. Spikelets small, 1-flowered, bisexual, ± laterally compressed, rachilla not extended, breaking apart below the glumes. Glumes 2, ± equal, longer than the floret, 1-veined, typically bearing a long awn from an entire or notched apex; lemma 5-veined, its apex typically toothed, awned or awnless. Stamens 1 or 3.

8 • 8 • 18. Pantropical and warm-temperate regions; all but one native to Europe, Africa, and South America. Of limited economic importance as forage, ornamentals, and invasive weeds.

1a   Glumes awnless .... ***P. viridis***
      WATER BEARD GRASS. Naturalized perennial. Stems to 1 m tall. Panicles 2–15 cm long, dense, often interrupted, pale green to purplish. Spikelets ± 2 mm long. Wet areas, ponds, irrigation ditches. Widespread. This species has also been included in *Agrostis*.

1b   Glumes awned **2**

2a   Lemma awnless ....***P. maritimus***
      MEDITERRANEAN BEARD GRASS. Naturalized. Stems to 50 cm. Panicles 2–8 cm long, dense, often purplish. Spikelets 2–2.5 mm long. Moist sites. North Coast ranges, Sierra Nevada foothills, Central Valley, Southwest California.

2b   Lemma awned...**3**

3a   Plants annual ....***P. monspeliensis***
      RABBIT'S-FOOT GRASS, ANNUAL BEARD GRASS (pl. 146). Naturalized. Stems to 80 cm. Panicles 2–17 cm long, dense, silky, bristly, yellowish-green to purplish. Spikelets 2–3 mm long. Moist to wet sites at low to medium elevations. Widespread. (Fig. 16)

3b   Plants perennial..**4**

4a   Glume awns 4–6 mm long; longest leaf blades 13–17 cm long
      .... ***P. australis***
      CHILEAN BEARD GRASS. Naturalized. Stems to 1 m tall. Panicles 6–16.5 cm long, dense, lobed or interrupted, purplish. Spikelets 1.8–3.5 mm long. Moist soils, especially at water's edge, at low elevations. North Coast ranges, Sierra Nevada foothills, Central Valley, Central Coast, Southwest California.

4b   Glume awns 1.5–3.2 mm long; longest leaf blades 5–9 cm long
      ....***P. interruptus***
      DITCH BEARD GRASS. Naturalized. Stems to 90 cm. Panicles 1.5–18 cm long, usually lobed or interrupted, pale green. Spikelets 2.5–3 mm long. Streambanks and ditches. Widespread.

Plate 146. *Polypogon monspeliensis*

Puccinellia   Alkali Grass

Caespitose annuals or perennials. Stems to 1 m tall. Leaf sheaths open. Inflorescence an open or congested panicle, 1–20 cm long. Spikelets small, several-flowered, bisexual, laterally compressed, breaking apart above the glumes and between the florets. Glumes 2, very unequal, shorter than the lowest floret, the lower generally 1-veined and the upper 3-veined; lemmas with 5 weak or strong, parallel veins, awnless; palea equaling or exceeding the lemma.

8 • 11 • 120. North temperate zone of both hemispheres, especially North America, typically of wet or marshy, especially alkaline and saline sites. A few species previously assigned to *Puccinellia* have been transferred to *Glyceria* and *Torreyochloa*. See Table 51 for a comparison. Two of our California species are known from a single county. One of them, Howell's alkali grass *(P. howellii)* (pl. 147) is known from just one site in Shasta County. Two others are relatively widespread, but not much collected. Both grow in saline meadows and flats, typically below about 2,500 m.

1a   Plants annual .... ***P. simplex***
        WESTERN ALKALI GRASS. Stems 2–25 cm tall. Panicles 1–18 cm long, compact, the lower branches erect. Spikelets 3.5–8 mm long, several-flowered. Lemma rounded to weakly keeled, apex acute. Saline soils. Central Valley, San Francisco Bay, and the Mojave Desert.
1b   Plants perennial...**2**
2a   Lowest lemma 1.5–2 mm long, its tip obtuse to truncate
        ....***P. distans***
        EUROPEAN ALKALI GRASS. Naturalized perennial. Stems to 60 cm. Panicles 2.5–20 cm long. Spikelets 2.5–7 mm long. (Fig. 17) Saline meadows and flats. Widespread.

(account continued)

Plate 147. *Puccinellia howellii*

Plate 148. *Puccinellia lemmonii*

2b Lowest lemma 2.2–4.5 [5] mm long, its tip acute to obtuse
.... ***P. nuttalliana***
NUTTALL'S ALKALI GRASS. Native perennial. Stems to 1 m tall. Panicles
5–30 cm long. Spikelets 3.5–9 mm long; its upper lemma margins
toothed. Saline meadows and flats. Widespread. A similar grass, but
less frequently encountered grass is *P. lemmonii* (Lemmon's alkali
grass) (pl. 148). It has entire upper lemma margins.

Rostraria   **Mediterranean Hair Grass, Cat-tail Grass**
Plants annual. Stems to 70 cm tall. Leaves mostly cauline. Inflorescence
a dense, spike-like panicle, 1.5–12 cm long. Spikelets 3–4.5 mm long, 3-

Plate 149. *Rostraria cristata*

to 6-flowered, bisexual, laterally compressed, breaking apart above the glumes and between the florets. Glumes 2, the lower 1.8–3.5 mm long and the upper 2–4.5 mm long, shorter than the lowest floret; lemmas 3–4 mm long, ciliate on keels, the lower lemmas with a 1–3 mm awn, the uppermost lemma awnless or short-awned; palea about as long as the lemma, its apex toothed or awned.

1 • 1 • 10. Mediterranean, Europe, and western Asia. Mediterranean hair grass *(R. cristata)* (pl. 149). Open disturbed sites. North Coast ranges, Cascades, Sierra Nevada foothills, Central Valley, South Coast ranges. This species has been assigned traditionally to *Koeleria*.

RYTIDOSPERMA   **Wallaby Grass**

Caespitose perennials, sometimes with short rhizomes. Stems to 1 m tall, erect to nodding. Leaf sheaths glabrous or hairy; blades flat or inrolled, glabrous or hairy; ligule a ring of hairs. Inflorescence a panicle or raceme. Spikelets 3- to 10-flowered, bisexual, laterally compressed, breaking apart above the glumes and between the florets. Glumes 2, ± equal, typically enclosing the florets; lemmas ovate to lanceolate, 5- to 9-veined, with two complete or incomplete rows or tufts of hairs, 2-lobed with awn-like bristles and a central awn to 16 mm long.

Plate 150. *Rytidosperma penicillatum*

4 • 5 • 45. Southeast Asia, Oceania, and South America. Of some economic importance as forage. The wallaby grasses have escaped from experimental plots and forage trials in California and Oregon. They differ from species of *Danthonia* in having a transverse rows or tufts of hairs on their lemmas and in lacking the self-pollinated spikelets in the lower sheaths. Hairy poverty grass (***R. penicillatum***) (pls. 150 & 151). Naturalized. Stems to 90 cm tall; rhizomes present. Panicles or racemes 5–15 cm long. Spikelets 9–15 mm long. Well established in pastures and disturbed areas. North and Central coasts, Transverse ranges.

Plate 151. *Rytidosperma penicillatum*

Schismus   **Arabian Grass, Mediterranean Grass**

Annuals or weak perennials, caespitose or decumbent. Stems 2–30 cm tall. Leaf blades short, with flat or rolled margins when dry; ligule a fringe of hairs. Inflorescence a contracted or loosely spike-like panicle, 2–7 cm long. Spikelets 5- to 7-flowered, bisexual, slightly laterally compressed, breaking apart above or below the glumes, rachilla extended beyond uppermost floret. Glumes 2, 3- to 7-veined, ± equal, shorter than or equaling the enclosed florets; lemmas similar to glumes, 7- to 9-veined, its apex bifid or emarginate, awnless, mucronate, or awned.

1 • 1 • 3. Africa, and from the Mediterranean to India. Mediterranean grass *(S. barbatus)* (pls. 152 & 153). Naturalized annual. Stems to 20 cm

Plate 152. *Schismus barbatus*

tall, erect to prostrate. Panicles 1–6 cm long. Spikelets 4–6.5 mm long. Arabian grass (var. *arabicus*) and Mediterranean grass (var. *barbatus*) have become major weeds in Southern California, especially in the deserts. They range from the central San Joaquin Valley south to San Diego County and then east into the Sonoran and Mojave deserts. They have traditionally been treated as separate species. In *S. barbatus* var. *arabicus*, the lower glume is as long or longer than the upper florets and the palea is shorter than the lemma. These grasses were not shown as occurring in California in the first edition of Hitchcock's *Manual of the Grasses of the United States* (1935); both appeared in the 1951 edition. There are 978 specimens of *Schismus* in the Consortium of California Herbaria, the oldest dating to 1935. Eleven more were collected in the 1930s, 20 in the 1940s, and 52 in the 1950s. Then came the explosion. It is startling and depressing to see the extent to which these grasses have invaded and replaced native species, and thereby transformed the natural landscape. Listed: Cal-IPC.

Plate 153. *Schismus barbatus*

Scribneria   **Scribner's Grass**

Low, tufted annual. Stems to 30 cm tall. Inflorescence a slender spike, 4–
11 cm long; spikelets 1 per node (sometimes with 2 at some nodes) inserted
flatwise against the rachis. Spikelets 4–7 mm long, 1-flowered, bisexual,
laterally compressed, breaking apart above the glumes and between the
florets; rachilla extended as a tiny, hairy bristle. Glumes 2, ± equal, lower
2-veined and the upper 4-veined, awnless; lemma membranous, inconspicuously 3- to 5-veined, minutely 2-toothed, the midvein extended as a
short, straight awn. Palea about as long as lemma. Stamen 1.

1 • 1 • 1. The genus is usually considered endemic to North America,
ranging from Washington to California, but it has not been collected

Plate 154. *Scribneria bolanderi*

in Washington for many years and there is a single collection from Baja California, Mexico. Scribner's grass *(S. bolanderi)* (pl. 154). Variety of habitats, from dry rocky soils to seeps and vernal pools. Widespread, except for the desert areas. Inconspicuous and easily overlooked. I once walked through a large population in Lake County before realizing what was beneath my feet. See Table 43 for a comparison of grasses of a similar inflorescence.

Secale   Rye

Annuals, sometimes perennials. Stems to 1+ m tall. Auricles usually present. Inflorescence a balanced, often nodding, spike, 4–15 cm long, the spikelets solitary at the node, strongly ascending, and placed flatwise to the rachis. Spikelets typically 2-flowered, bisexual, laterally compressed, breaking apart below the glumes or not in domesticated forms. Glumes 2, narrow, 1-veined, tapering to a point; lemmas sharply keeled, ciliate, 5-veined, tapering to a long awn.

1 • 1 • 3. Eurasia. Rye *(S. cereale)* (pls. 155 & 156). Naturalized. Stems to 1.5 m tall. Spikes 5–15 cm long. Spikelets 12–15 mm long. Weed in barley and wheat fields and along roadsides. Also planted as a cover crop and for erosion control. Of considerable economic importance in making bread, beer, gin, whisky, and vodka. Plants can be infected by the ergot fungus. See the earlier discussion of toxic grasses for more details and Table 52 for a comparison of barley, rye, and wheat.

Plate 155. *Secale cereale*

Plate 156. *Secale cereale*

TABLE 52. A comparison of *Hordeum*, *Secale*, and *Triticum*

Characteristic	Hordeum	Secale	Triticum
Spikelets per node	3	1	1
Florets per spikelet	1	2 [3]	2–9
Glumes	awn-like	linear to tapering to point	ovate
Glumes	1-veined	1-veined	3- to 9-veined
Lemma margins ciliate	no	yes	no

Setaria   **Foxtail, Bristle Grass**

Annuals or caespitose perennial. Stems to 6 m tall, the internodes hollow or solid. Inflorescence a dense, spike-like panicle, sometimes open and branching more evident. Spikelets 1–5 mm long, awnless, but subtended by 1 to several bristles (sterile branches), 2-flowered (the lower sterile and the upper fertile), dorsally compressed, bisexual, breaking apart below the glumes but above the bristle(s). Glumes 2, the lower broad, typically about half the length of the upper, upper glume and sterile lemma similar in size and texture; sterile lemma 5-veined, as long as or longer than the fertile one; fertile lemma 1- to 5-veined, indurate, rounded at its apex, with fine to coarse transverse wrinkles; palea relatively long.

10 • 28 • 140. Warmer regions of both hemispheres. A source of grains, a minor cereal (foxtail or Italian millet, which we have consumed for about 8,000 years), pasture grasses, and weeds. Most U. S. species are aggressive annual weeds in maize and bean fields. Seven of our ten California species are weedy, naturalized annuals.

1a   Spikelet bristles downwardly barbed, often causing panicles to become intertangled.. **S. verticillata**
    BUR OR HOOKED BRISTLE GRASS. Naturalized annual. Stems to 1 m tall. Panicles 5–13 cm long. Spikelets 1.5–2.5 mm long, subtended by 1 or 2 purple-tipped bristles. Fields and roadsides; an aggressive weed in vineyards. Central Valley, South Coast, Southern California.
1b   Spikelet bristles upwardly barbed **2**
2a   Spikelets subtended by 1–3 bristles...**S. viridis**
    GREEN BRISTLE GRASS. Naturalized annual. Stems erect to decumbent, to 1 m tall. Panicles 2–15 cm long, densely spike-like. Spikelets ± 2 mm long, subtended by 1–3 green [purple] bristles. Moist roadsides, stream banks, agricultural areas. Widespread.
2b   Spikelet subtended by 4–12 bristles...**3**

Plate 157. *Setaria pumila*

3a Plants annual. ....**S. pumila**
    YELLOW BRISTLE GRASS, SUMMER GRASS, PIGEON GRASS (pls. 157 &
    158). Naturalized. Stems to 1.3 m tall. Panicles 3–15 cm long, erect,
    densely spike-like. Spikelets 2–3.5 mm long, subtended by 4–12 yel-
    low bristles. (Fig. 14) Moist disturbed sites. Widespread.
3b Plants perennial; knot-like rhizomes present...................**S. parviflora**
    MARSH OR KNOT ROOT BRISTLE GRASS. Native. Stems to 1.2 m tall. Pan-
    icles 3–8 cm long, densely spike-like. Spikelets 2–3 mm long, sub-
    tended by 4–12 yellow to purple bristles. Moist sites and disturbed
    places, where the plant can be weedy. Sierra Nevada foothills, Cen-
    tral Valley, Central and South coasts, Southern California. This spe-
    cies was often called *S. gracilis* and *S. geniculata* in our older floras.

Plate 158. *Setaria pumila*

Sorghum

Sorghum, Johnson Grass, Milo, Broomcorn, Kaffir

Stout annuals or caespitose-stoloniferous-rhizomatous perennials. Stems to 3 m tall, the internodes solid. Inflorescence a large, open to contracted panicle, 5–60 cm long. Spikelets 2-flowered, dorsally compressed, in pairs (one sessile and fertile; the other pedicellate and usually staminate) or in trios at branchlet tips (the laterals pedicellate and sterile). Sessile spikelets breaking apart with a rachis segment. Glumes 2, ± equal, 3- to several-veined, leathery, awnless; sterile lemma membranous, awnless; fertile lemma membranous, 1- to 3-veined, with a bent and twisted awn (deciduous in *S. halepense*).

2 • 2 • 35. Tropical and subtropical regions of the Old World; one native to Mexico. Of considerable economic importance as a source of grains, fodder, sugar, and weeds. Hybrids between the two species discussed below are common.

1a   Plants annual [perennial]; caryopses often visible at maturity
....***S. bicolor***
      SORGHUM, SORGHO, MILO, BROOMCORN, SUDAN GRASS (pl. 159). Natu-
      ralized. Stems to 2.5 m tall. Panicles 10–60 cm long. Spikelets 3–9
      mm long; typically not breaking apart at maturity. Roadsides and
      in disturbed areas. North Coast, North Coast Ranges, Central Val-
      ley, Central and South Coast, Southern California. Domesticated

Plate 159. *Sorghum bicolor*

about 3,000 years ago in Africa, this is now the world's fourth most important cereal, after maize, wheat, and rice. Its many cultivars are the source of food (grains), sweet syrup (stems), fodder, and brooms and brushes (panicle branches). Traditional brooms are made from the panicles of a variety called broomcorn. Look carefully and you may find spikelets. Sorghum plants, under certain environmental conditions, may produce toxins leading to muscular incoordination, sensitivity to sunlight, nitrate poisoning, and cyanide poisoning.

1b Plants perennial from stout rhizomes; caryopses not exposed at maturity .... ***S. halepense***
JOHNSON GRASS (pls. 160 & 161). Naturalized. Stems to 2 m tall. Panicles 10–50 cm long. Spikelets 4–9 mm long. Disturbed areas,

Plate 160. *Sorghum halepense*

especially along roadsides. Widespread. Plants typically infected by a rust *(Puccinia purpurea)* that causes the red, purple, or tan spots so commonly found on the leaves. Named after William Johnson, an American agriculturalist who introduced the grass into Alabama. Listed: CDFA; also on the list of the ten most noxious weeds in the world.

Plate 161. *Sorghum halepense*

Spartina   **Cord Grass, Marsh Grass**

Mostly stoloniferous-rhizomatous perennials. Stems to 2 m tall, internodes solid or hollow. Inflorescence a panicle of few to many short, often appressed, racemose branches. Spikelets 1-flowered, strongly overlapping on one side of rachis, bisexual, conspicuously laterally compressed, breaking apart below the glumes. Glumes 2, unequal, the lower 1-veined and the upper 1- to 3-veined, the upper as long or longer than the floret, awned or awnless; lemma 1- or 3-veined, keeled, awnless; palea relatively long, with membranous margins. (Fig. 13)

6 • 13 • 16. All but one New World. Mostly grasses of coastal salt marshes and alkaline-saline interior sites. Vegetative reproduction is common. Of economic importance as food for livestock and erosion control; several are aggressive invaders of tidal marshes and mud flats.

1a   Plants of alkaline meadows, marshes, lake shores, and stream
      banks above 1,000 m. ....**S. gracilis**
      ALKALI CORD GRASS. Native. Stems to 1 m tall, strongly rhizomatous.
      Panicles 8–25 cm long, with 3–12 branches. Spikelets 6–11 mm long.
      East of the Sierra Nevada, White and Inyo mountains, and northern
      Mojave Desert. Our only interior cord grass.
1b   Plants of coastal salt marshes below 10 m **2**
2a   Rhizomes present; stems 7–12 mm wide at base, internodes fleshy;
      leaf blades 5–17 mm wide at base; glumes generally curved
      ....**S. foliosa**
      CALIFORNIA CORD GRASS. Native. Stems to 1+ m tall. Panicles 12–25
      cm long, with 3–25 branches. Spikelets 8–25 mm long. Reproduces
      mainly by means of its rhizomes. Typically dominant in the coastal
      salt marshes of the San Francisco Bay Area and the South Coast.
      Smooth or salt water cord grass *(S. alterniflora)*, a highly aggressive
      species native to eastern North America, was accidentally introduced in the marshes of the San Francisco Bay region in the 1970s.
      Smooth cord grass crosses with the native California cord grass to
      create an invasive hybrid that may eventually replace it.

(account continued)

Plate 162. *Spartina densiflora*

2b   Rhizomes absent; stems 3–6 mm wide at base, internodes firm; leaf
blades 4–8 mm wide at base; glumes generally straight
....***S. densiflora***
CHILEAN OR DENSE-FLOWERED CORD GRASS (pls. 162 & 163). Natural-
ized. Stems to 1.5 m tall. Panicles 10–30 cm long, with 2–20 branches.
Spikelets 8–14 mm long. Introduced to Humboldt Bay marshes dur-
ing lumber trade with Chile via ship ballast in the 1870s and to the
San Francisco Bay marshes in 1974 as part of a restoration project.
Listed: Cal-IPC. The State Coastal Conservancy and the Humboldt
Bay National Wildlife Refuge have begun a major eradication effort,
using mechanical removal techniques.

Plate 163. *Spartina densiflora*

Sporobolus   Dropseed, Sacaton

Caespitose annuals or perennials (ours), a few rhizomatous. Stems to 2 m tall, internodes usually solid. Leaf sheaths often ciliate at the apex; ligules ciliate. Inflorescence an open or contracted panicle. Spikelets small, 1-flowered, bisexual, rounded to laterally compressed, breaking apart above the glumes. Glumes 2, unequal, 1-veined, shorter than the floret; lemma 1- [3-] veined, its texture similar to the glumes, awnless; palea shorter or longer than the lemma, sometimes splitting at maturity and thereby resembling an extra lemma. Fruit an achene, with its wall free from the seed (hence the common name).

8 • 33 • 160+. Diverse habitats in the warm-temperate, subtropical, and tropical regions of both hemispheres. One of only three genera of California grasses (the others being *Crypsis* and *Swallenia*) with seeds that fall from or are forcibly ejected from the drying pericarp. A source of edible grains, materials for basketry, fodder, and plants for revegetation. See Table 44 for a comparison with two other grasses with frustratingly small, 1-flowered florets.

1a   Inflorescence a dense spike-like panicle **2**
1b   Inflorescence an open panicle with evident branching....................**3**
2a   Sheath apex glabrous; spikelets and upper leaves often blackened
       by a fungal infection...*S. indicus*
       SMUT GRASS. Naturalized. Stems to 1 m tall. Panicles 20–35 cm long.
       Spikelets 1.5–2.5 mm long. The fungal infection is the basis of the common name. Lawns, roadsides, irrigated pastures, and other disturbed sites. Central Valley, Central and South coasts, Southwest California.
2b   Sheath apex with hairs to 4 mm long; plants not blackened
       ....*S. contractus*
       SPIKE DROPSEED (pl. 164). Native. Stems to 1+ m tall. Panicles 15–45 cm long. Spikelets 1.7–3 mm long. Sandy soils, washes, scrub, woodlands. White and Inyo mountains and the desert.

(account continued)

Plate 164. *Sporobolus contractus*

3a Sheath apex with conspicuous tuft of white hairs; mature sheath bases dull .... **S. cryptandrus**
SAND DROPSEED. Native. Stems to 1 m tall. Panicles 15–40 cm long. Spikelets 1.5–2.5 mm long. Rocky slopes to light sandy soils, and roadsides. Cascades, Sierra Nevada foothills, Sacramento Valley, South Coast, Southern California.

3b Sheath apex glabrous or with a few scattered hairs; mature sheath bases glossy ....**S. airoides**
ALKALI SACATON (pl. 165). Native. Stems to 1+ m tall. Panicles 15–45 cm long. Spikelets 1.3–2.8 mm long. Dry, sandy, gravelly, seasonally moist sites, usually on alkaline soils. Sierra Nevada foothills, Central Valley, Southern California. An important component of the origi-

Plate 165. *Sporobolus airoides*

nal California grassland. Grains were eaten by Native Americans who also used stems as the foundation material for coiled baskets.

Stipa   **Needle Grass, Rice Grass, Porcupine Grass**
Caespitose perennials [annuals]. Stems to 2 m tall, herbaceous or woody, the internodes hollow or solid. Leaves often in a basal clump; abortive self-pollinated spikelets often present within sheaths. Inflorescence an open to contracted panicle, the branches sometimes delicate (pl. 166). Spikelets 1- [2–6] flowered, bisexual, terete to laterally compressed, breaking apart above the glumes. Glumes 2, 1- to 7-veined, as long or longer than the floret; lemmas long, narrow, firm to indurate at maturity, 3- to

Plate 166. *Stipa arida*

5-veined, often tightly wrapped around palea and caryopsis, terminating in a conspicuous persistent or deciduous awn; lemma base short and blunt or forming a sharp-pointed callus, this usually clothed in stiff hairs; palea relatively long, similar to lemma in texture, sometimes with a deep groove.

35 • 54 • ± 300. Temperate, subtropical, and tropical regions of both hemispheres. Of economic significance as a source of pasture grasses, fibers for cordage and mats, and weeds. As treated here the genus includes species also assigned to a number of segregate genera, notably *Achnatherum* (pubescent paleas), *Hesperostipa* (glabrous paleas with prow-shaped or pinched tips), *Nassella* (lemma margins strongly overlapping), *Oryzopsis* (deciduous awns), and *Piptochaetium* (palea longitudinally grooved). Their circumscription remains unsettled. The sharp-pointed florets of several species can cause mechanical injury to domesticated and wild animals and have been known to provide rambunctious children with some amusement.

1a   Awns generally curved [straight], falling early from the floret........**2**
1b   Awns twisted below and bent once or twice above, generally persistent **3**
2a   Lemma densely hairy; glumes 5–9 mm long; callus sharp .... **S. hymenoides**
       INDIAN RICE GRASS, SAND GRASS (pl. 167). Native. Stems to 70 cm tall. Leaf blades mostly basal, sharp-pointed. Panicles 9–20 cm long. Spikelets 5–8 mm long. Arid and semiarid sites. Cascades and Sierra Nevada foothills, South Coast, warm deserts. Its roots are surrounded by a distinctive mucilaginous sheath that harbors nitrogen-fixing bacteria. One of our most palatable native grasses for livestock, which has led to serious overgrazing in some areas. Native Americans consumed the grains. Increasingly popular as an ornamental.

(account continued)

Plate 167. *Stipa hymenoides*

2b   Lemma glabrous; glumes 2.5–3.5 mm long; callus blunt
....**S. miliacea**
SMILO, MILLET MOUNTAIN GRASS (pl. 168). Naturalized. Stems to 1.5 m
tall. Cauline leaves well developed. Panicles 10–40 cm long. Spikelets
± 3 mm long. Disturbed sites, where it is often weedy in vacant lots
and along roadsides and creeks, at low elevations. It has been used
as a pasture grass and for erosion control. North Coast, Sacramento
Valley, Central and South coasts. Listed: Cal-IPC.

3a   Awns hairy to pilose **4**

3b   Awns glabrous or with minute somewhat rigid hairs, but not obviously hairy..**5**

Plate 168. *Stipa miliacea*

4a Stem bases green or straw-colored; awns twice-bent, the lower segments hairy and the uppermost hairy or glabrous ....**S. occidentalis**
WESTERN NEEDLE GRASS, CALIFORNIA NEEDLE GRASS (pl. 172). Native. Stems to 1+ m tall. Panicles 5–30 cm long. Spikelets 7–15 mm long; callus sharp. In *S. o.* var. *occidentalis*, the terminal awn segment is densely hairy and the glumes purple; in var. *pubescens*, the two upper segments are densely hairy and the glumes typically green; in var. *californica*, the two upper segments may also be hairy, but with hairs of mixed lengths. Open woods, flats, and ridges, elevation mostly 1,400–4,000 m. North Coast Ranges, Cascades, Sierra Nevada, higher mountains of Southern California.

4b Stem bases orange-brown; awns once-bent, the lower segment pilose and the upper glabrous ....**S. speciosa**
DESERT NEEDLE GRASS (pls. 169 & 170). Native. Stems to 60 cm tall. Panicles 10–15 cm long. Spikelets 25–40 mm long; callus sharp. Arid and semiarid canyons and mountain slopes, mostly below 2,000 m, primarily in the southern half of the state. Three subspecies in California, differing in lengths of lemma hairs and hairiness of the terminal awn segment.

5a Lemma margins strongly overlapping through their entire length **6**

5b Lemma margins not overlapping or only scarcely so **8**

Plate 169. *Stipa speciosa*

Plate 170. *Stipa speciosa*

6a Lemmas less than 7 mm long; awns generally 1–5 cm long
    ....**S. lepida**
    FOOTHILL NEEDLE GRASS. Native. Stems to 1 m tall. Panicles 9–55 cm
    long. Spikelets 6–10 mm long; lemma apex forming a ciliate crown;
    callus sharp. Dry hillsides in chaparral. Northwest California, Cen-
    tral and South coasts, Southwest California.
6b Lemmas more than 7 mm long; awns generally 5–11 cm long..........**7**

Plate 171. *Stipa pulchra*

7a   Upper lemma glabrous at maturity...**S. cernua**
      NODDING NEEDLE GRASS. Native. Stems to 1 m tall. Panicles 15–80 cm
      long. Spikelets 12–19 mm long; lemma apex forming a crown; callus
      sharp. Grasslands, juniper woodlands, and chaparral. North Coast
      ranges, Cascade and Sierra Nevada foothills, Central Valley, South
      Coast ranges, Southwest California.

7b   Lemma uniformly hairy ....**S. pulchra**
      PURPLE NEEDLE GRASS (pl. 171). Native. Stems to 1 m tall. Panicles
      18–60 cm long. Spikelets 15–25 mm long. Chaparral and grasslands.
      North Coast, Sierra Nevada foothills, Central Valley to Southern
      California. Once thought to be a major element in the pre-European
      grassland of the Central Valley. Declared official state grass in 2004.

8a   Callus 1.7–6 mm long .... **S. comata**
      NEEDLE-AND-THREAD GRASS. Native. Stems to 1+ m tall. Panicles
      dense, 7–32 cm long, fully exserted or partially enclosed in the
      uppermost sheaths. Spikelets 15–25 mm long. Florets narrow; lemma
      white-hairy, callus sharp; awn twice-bent or straight, 12–15 cm long.
      We have two varieties that differ in the degree of exsertion of the
      panicles from their sheaths and the length of terminal awn segment.
      Grasslands, sagebrush scrub, and piñon-juniper woodlands. Edge of
      the Mojave Desert north to the Sierra Nevada and Cascades.

8b   Callus 0.1–2 mm long..**9**

9a   Lemma tip hairs 0–2.2 mm long..**S. lemmonii**
LEMMON'S NEEDLE GRASS. Native. Stems to 1 m tall. Panicles 7–21 cm long. Spikelets 7–12 mm long. Sagebrush and coniferous forests. Northern California, Sierra Nevada, Southern California. The two varieties in California (one of them endemic) differ in degree of hairiness of the lower stems and sheaths.

9b   Lemma tips hairs 2–7 mm long **10**

10a Awn bent twice; stems to 2 m tall, 3–6 mm in diameter
....**S. coronata**
GIANT OR CRESTED NEEDLE GRASS. Native. Panicles 15–60 cm long. Spikelets ± 20 mm long; callus blunt to acute; awn 25–45 mm long.

Plate 172. *Stipa occidentalis*

Mostly on gravel and rocky slopes in chaparral. South Coast Range, Southwest California.

10b Awn bent once; stems to 80 cm tall, 0.8–2 mm in diameter
.... ***Stipa parishii* var. *parishii***
PARISH'S NEEDLE GRASS. Native. Panicles 11–15 cm long. Spikelets 12–14 mm long; callus acute; awn 15–35 mm long. Dry, rocky slopes in scrub and piñon-juniper woodlands. Desert, Transverse, and Peninsular ranges.

(Key based in part on Columbus et al. in Baldwin et al. 2012, pp. 1,491, 1,492.)

Swallenia   **Eureka Valley Dune Grass**

Coarse, rhizomatous, perennial. Stems to 1.5 m tall, herbaceous to woody. Leaf blades distichous, narrow, stiff, sharp-pointed. Inflorescence a contracted panicle, 4–10 cm long. Spikelets 10–15 mm long, 3- to 7-flowered; bisexual, laterally compressed, persistent on the rachis. Glumes 2, ± equal, the lower 5- to 7-veined and the upper 7- to 11-veined; lemmas 5- to 7-veined, awnless, densely hairy on lower margins. Seed falling free from the pericarp. This is one of the three grass genera endemic to California.

1 • 1 • 1. Eureka Valley dune grass *(S. alexandrae)* (pls. 173 & 174) is endemic to dunes in Inyo County. The scientific name commemorates Jason Swallen, a grass expert at the U.S. National Herbarium, who first recognized that this plant belongs to a new genus; and Annie Montague Alexander, who, along with her field companion Louise Kellogg, first collected the plant in 1949. Their field book noted bunches of a scraggly coarse grass growing on the dunes in Eureka Valley. Now threatened by off-highway vehicles, sand boarding activity, and Russian thistle. Do not collect! Listed: CDFG and USFWS.

Plate 173. *Swallenia alexandrae* (Eureka Valley sand dune, Inyo Co.)

Plate 174. *Swallenia alexandrae*

Torreyochloa   **False Manna Grass**

Rhizomatous perennials. Stems to 1.5 m tall. Leaf sheaths open. Inflorescence a terminal panicle, 5–25 cm long. Spikelets 2- to 8-flowered, bisexual, laterally compressed to terete, breaking apart above the glumes and below the florets. Glumes 2, unequal, shorter than the florets, lower lower 1- [3-] veined and the upper [1-] 3- [5-] veined; lemmas prominently [5-] 7- to 9-veined, the veins ± parallel, awnless; palea and lemma ± equal in length.

Plate 175. *Torreyochloa pallida*

2 • 2 • 4. Colder, wet, freshwater sites of North America and Asia. Pale false manna grass *(T. pallida* **var.** *pauciflora)* (pl. 175). (Fig. 17) Native. Stems to 1.5 m tall. Panicles 5–25 cm long. Spikelets 4–7 mm long. Wet places, margins of lakes, bogs, marshes, and streams, from about 200 to 3,500 m. Well grazed because of its succulence. North Coast, Cascades, Sierra Nevada, mountains of Southern California. See Table 51 for a comparison with alkali grass and manna grass.

Tridens   **Purpletop, Tridens**

Erect, caespitose perennials. Stems to 1 m tall. Inflorescence an open or contracted panicle. Spikelets 3- to 12-flowered, bisexual, laterally compressed, breaking apart above the glumes and between the florets. Glumes 2, ± equal, the lower 1-veined and the upper 1- to 3-veined, shorter than the florets; lemmas broad, 3-veined, typically hairy below, the apex notched or 2-lobed, the mid-vein usually extending between the teeth as a mucro or short awn.

1 · 10 · 16-18. Eastern and southern United States and adjacent Mexico. Slim tridens *(T. muticus)* (pl. 176). Native, densely tufted. Stems to 50 cm. Panicles 4–20 cm, branches appressed. Spikelets 8–13 mm long, often purple tinged. Dry, often limestone soils. Great Basin and desert mountains.

Plate 176. *Tridens muticus*

Mostly caespitose perennials. Stems to 1.5 m tall. Inflorescence a con-tracted panicle. Spikelets 2- to 5-flowered, laterally compressed, bisexual, breaking apart above or below the glumes or not breaking apart, the rachilla hairy, prolonged above the uppermost floret. Glumes 2, equal or unequal, the lower 1- to 3-veined and the upper 1- to 5-veined; lemmas 5- to 7-veined, its apex bifid, the teeth awned, with a straight or bent awn from the base of the cleft or awnless; palea veins extended as bristle-like teeth. (Fig. 15) You may confuse this genus with *Deschampsia*. See Table 49 for a comparison.

5 • 7 • 75. Temperate, subarctic, and alpine regions of both hemispheres. Of economic importance as a source of pasture and fodder grasses.

1a   Inflorescence a more open panicle; upper glumes at least twice as wide as the lower; spikelets pedicellate; leaves both basal and cauline.. ***T. canescens***

       TALL TRISETUM (pl. 177). Native. Stems to 1+ m tall. Panicles 6–25 cm long, loose to contracted or sometimes spike-like, erect or nodding. Spikelets 7–9 mm long. Meadows and wooded areas, especially coni-fer forests, often along stream banks. North Coast ranges, Cascades, Sierra Nevada, Central Coast, South Coast ranges.

1b   Inflorescence a spike-like panicle; upper glumes less than twice as wide as the lower; spikelets ± sessile; leaves mostly basal
                                                                              T. spicatum

       SPIKE TRISETUM (pl. 178). Native. Stems to 40 cm tall. Panicles 2.5–10 cm long. Spikelets 5–8 mm long. Moist meadows, forests, ledges, and flats at higher elevations. North Coast ranges, Cascades, Sierra Nevada to mountains in Southern California.

Plate 177. *Trisetum canescens*

Plate 178. *Trisetum spicatum*

Triticum **Wheat**

Caespitose annuals. Stems to 1.5 m tall, the internodes hollow or solid. Inflorescence a thick, balanced spike 6–18 cm long, the spikelets solitary at each node and attached flatwise to the rachis. Spikelets 10–15 mm long, 2- to 5-flowered, bisexual, laterally compressed or rounded, generally breaking apart below the glumes along with a segment of the rachis or remaining intact in domesticated forms. Glumes 2, ± equal, shorter than the florets, 5- to 11-veined, mucronate or with 1 or more awns at its apex; lemmas keeled or rounded, glabrous or pubescent, several-veined, awned (bearded wheat) or awnless; palea entire or notched at apex.

Plate 179. *Triticum aestivum*

1 • 3 • 8-20. Eurasia. Wheat, common wheat, or bread wheat *(T. aestivum)* (pls. 179 & 180). Naturalized. Stems to 1.5 m tall, our cultivars typically shorter. Spikes 6–18 cm long. Spikelets 10–15 mm long. It escapes from fields where it is being grown throughout much of the state. Of inestimable economic importance. The most widely planted world crop and third, after maize and rice, in annual production (653 million metric tons in 2010), providing us with 20 percent of our calories and as much as 14 percent of our protein. Its 30,000 cultivars supply us with food, fermented and distilled beverages, cosmetics, and health products. See Table 52 for a comparison with barley and rye, two other cereal grasses with spikes as their inflorescence type.

Plate 180. *Triticum aestivum*

Ventenata   North Africa Grass

Plants annual. Stems to 75 cm tall; nodes purple-black. Leaves mostly on lower half of plants. Inflorescence an open to contracted panicle, 15–20 cm long, the spikelets more or less at the ends of branches. Spikelets 10–15 mm long, 2- or 3-flowered, the lowest staminate, the others bisexual, laterally compressed, breaking apart above the staminate floret. Glumes 2, the lower 3- to 7-veined, the upper 3- to 9-veined, longer, both shorter than adjacent lemmas. Lemmas 5-veined, the lowest with a straight awn

Plate 181. *Ventenata dubia*

from its tip, the upper with a bent, twisted awn to 16 mm arising from its midpoint.

1 · 1 · 5. Eurasia. Dry, open habitats. Several of my recent collections have been from vernal pools. Of no economic importance. North Africa grass or ventenata *(V. **dubia**)* (pls. 181 & 182). Disturbed sites, mainly in Northern California. Introduced into Washington 60 years ago and into California in the early 1980s. I have included it because of its aggressive weediness. Caution! Mature spikelets with only the lowest staminate floret present can be difficult to identify.

Plate 182. *Ventenata dubia*

Zizania   **Wild-rice**

Plants annual, aquatic, monoecious. Stems to 3 m tall and 1 cm in diameter. Leaf blades to 60 cm long and 2.5 cm wide. Inflorescence a conspicuous, attractive panicle of unisexual spikelets; the staminate on lower spreading to ascending branches and the pistillate on upper ascending to erect branches. Glumes vestigial or absent. Pistillate spikelet terete, angled at maturity, its lemma 3-veined and tapering to a slender awn; caryopsis purplish black. Staminate spikelet terete, its lemma 5-nerved, stamens 6.

1 • 3 • 4. North America and Asia. Marshes and flooded agricultural fields. It is, in my opinion, our most distinctive and handsome cereal crop. Economically important as a source of food for animals and humans. Wild-rice (*Z. palustris* var. *interior*) (pls. 183 & 184) has been grown in California since 1972 from seed collected in Minnesota, where it is native. Today California is the world's leading producer. Much of the operation is centered in the Sacramento Valley. It can escape from paddies into roadside ditches, but farmers have told me that it does not persist. Wild-rice is neither a wild form of cultivated rice nor its ancestor.

Plate 183. *Zizania palustris* (paddy in Shasta Co.)

Plate 184. *Zizania palustris*

APPENDIX
A CHECKLIST OF CALIFORNIA GRASSES

This checklist is my attempt to account for all of the native and naturalized grasses found in California, including crops, ornamentals, and lawn grasses that have escaped from cultivation and persist without our assistance. It includes historical collections, but it does not include several grasses that have been cited in the literature but for which proper documentation, especially herbarium specimens, is lacking. Grasses that have not been found in several decades or only once are shown with the symbol † and the date of the most recent collection. They are presumed extinct or extirpated.

Acrachne racemosa, monsoon grass (Naturalized (?) annual †: 1991)
Aegilops cylindrica, jointed goat grass (Naturalized annual)
Aegilops geniculata, ovate goat grass (Naturalized annual)
Aegilops neglecta, three-awned goat grass (Naturalized annual)
Aegilops tauschii, Tausch's goat grass (Naturalized annual)
Aegilops triuncialis, barbed goat grass (Naturalized annual)
X *Agropogon lutosus*, perennial beard grass, water beard grass (Naturalized perennial)
Agropyron cristatum, crested wheat grass, Fairway wheat grass (Naturalized perennial)
Agrostis avenacea, Pacific bent grass (Naturalized annual-perennial)
Agrostis blasdalei var. *blasdalei*, Blasdale's bent grass (Endemic perennial)
Agrostis blasdalei var. *marinensis*, Marin bent grass (Endemic perennial)
Agrostis capillaris, colonial bent grass (Naturalized perennial)
Agrostis clivicola var. *clivicola*, coastal bent grass (Endemic perennial)
Agrostis clivicola var. *punta-reyesensis*, Point Reyes bent grass (Endemic perennial)
Agrostis densiflora, California bent grass (Native perennial)
Agrostis elliottiana, Elliott's bent grass, Sierra bent grass (Native annual)
Agrostis exarata, spike bent grass (Native perennial)
Agrostis filiformis, Pacific bent (Naturalized perennial)
Agrostis hallii, Hall's bent grass (Native perennial)
Agrostis hendersonii, Henderson's bent grass (Native annual)
Agrostis hooveri, Hoover's bent grass (Endemic perennial)
Agrostis humilis, alpine bent grass, mountain bent grass (Native perennial)
Agrostis x *idahoensis*, Idaho bent grass (Native perennial)

Agrostis microphylla, small-leaved bent grass (Native annual)

Agrostis nebulosa, cloud grass (Naturalized annual)

Agrostis oregonensis, Oregon redtop, Oregon bent grass (Native perennial)

Agrostis pallens, dune bent grass, seashore bent grass, leafy bent grass, thin grass (Native perennial)

Agrostis perennans, upland bent grass, autumn bent (Naturalized (?) perennial †: 1992)

Agrostis scabra, tickle grass, rough bent grass (Native annual-perennial)

Agrostis stolonifera, creeping bent grass (Naturalized perennial)

Agrostis tandilensis, Kennedy's bent grass (Naturalized (?) annual †: 1998)

Agrostis variabilis, mountain bent grass (Native perennial)

Aira caryophyllea var. *capillaris*, elegant, fine, or awned hair grass (Naturalized annual)

Aira caryophyllea var. *caryophyllea*, silver hair grass (Naturalized annual)

Aira caryophyllea var. *cupaniana*, silver hair grass (Naturalized (?) annual †: 1995)

Aira praecox, little, early, or yellow hair grass, shiver grass (Naturalized annual)

Alopecurus aequalis var. *aequalis*, short-awned foxtail, little meadow foxtail (Native perennial)

Alopecurus aequalis var. *sonomensis*, Sonoma foxtail (Endemic perennial)

Alopecurus carolinianus, Carolina foxtail (Native annual)

Alopecurus geniculatus var. *geniculatus*, water foxtail (Native perennial)

Alopecurus myosuroides, slender meadow foxtail (Naturalized annual)

Alopecurus pratensis subsp. *pratensis*, meadow foxtail (Naturalized perennial)

Alopecurus saccatus, Pacific meadow foxtail (Native annual)

Ammophila arenaria subsp. *arenaria*, European beach grass, marram (Naturalized perennial)

Ammophila breviligulata subsp. *breviligulata*, American beach grass (Naturalized (?) perennial †: 1967)

Amphibromus nervosus, Australian wallaby grass (Naturalized (?) perennial †: 1996)

Andropogon glomeratus var. *pumilus*, bushy bluestem (Native perennial †: 1962)

Andropogon glomeratus var. *scabriglumis*, bushy bluestem, bushy beard grass (Native perennial)

Andropogon virginicus var. *virginicus*, broom sedge, yellow sedge bluestem (Naturalized perennial)

Anthoxanthum aristatum subsp. *aristatum*, small sweet vernal grass (Naturalized annual)

Anthoxanthum hirtum, hairy sweet grass (Naturalized perennial)

Anthoxanthum nitens, sweet grass (Naturalized (?) perennial)

Anthoxanthum occidentale, vanilla grass (Native perennial)

Anthoxanthum odoratum subsp. *odoratum*, sweet vernal grass (Naturalized annual-perennial)

Apera interrupta, dense silky-bent (Naturalized annual)

Apera spica-venti, silky-bent grass, loose bent grass (Naturalized annual)

Aristida adscensionis, six-weeks three-awn (Native annual)

Aristida californica var. *californica*, California three-awn, Mojave three-awn (Native perennial)

Aristida dichotoma var. *dichotoma*, church mouse three-awn (Naturalized annual)

Aristida divaricata, poverty three-awn (Native perennial)

Aristida oligantha, prairie three-awn, old field three-awn (Naturalized (?) annual)

Aristida purpurea var. *fendleriana*, Fendler's three-awn (Native perennial)

Aristida purpurea var. *longiseta*, purple three-awn, red three-awn (Native perennial)

Aristida purpurea var. *nealleyi*, Nealley's three-awn (Native perennial)

Aristida purpurea var. *parishii*, Parish's three-awn (Native perennial)

Aristida purpurea var. *purpurea*, purple three-awn (Native perennial)

Aristida purpurea var. *wrightii*, Wright's three-awn (Native perennial)

Aristida scheideana var. *orcuttiana*, beggar tick grass, single-awn grass (Native perennial)

Aristida ternipes var. *gentilis*, hook three-awn, spider grass (Native perennial)

Arrhenatherum elatius, tall oat grass (Naturalized perennial)

Arundo donax, giant reed grass, carrizo (Naturalized perennial)

Avena barbata, slender wild oat (Naturalized annual)

Avena fatua, wild oat (Naturalized annual)

Avena occidentalis, western oat (Naturalized (?) annual)

Avena sativa, cultivated oat (Naturalized annual)

Avena sterilis, animated oat (Naturalized annual)

Axonopus fissifolius, carpet grass (Naturalized (?) perennial †: 1958)

Bambusa multiplex, hedge bamboo (Naturalized (?) perennial †: 1961)

Beckmannia syzigachne, American slough grass (Native annual)

Blepharidachne kingii, King's eyelash grass (Native annual-perennial)

Bothriochloa barbinodis var. *barbinodis*, cane bluestem, cane beard grass (Native perennial)

Bothriochloa exaristata, awnless bluestem (Naturalized perennial)

Bothriochloa ischaemum, yellow bluestem, King's Ranch bluestem (Naturalized perennial)

Bothriochloa laguroides subsp. *torreyana*, plumed beard grass, silver bluestem (Naturalized perennial)

Bouteloua aristidoides var. *aristidoides*, needle grama (Native annual)

Bouteloua barbata var. *barbata*, six-week's grama, annual grama (Native annual)

Bouteloua curtipendula var. *caespitosa*, sideoats grama (Native perennial)

Bouteloua eriopoda, black grama (Native perennial)

Bouteloua gracilis var. *gracilis*, blue grama, eyelash grass (Native perennial)

Bouteloua trifida var. *trifida*, red grama (Native perennial)

Brachypodium distachyon, false brome, purple-brome, stiff-brome (Naturalized annual)

Brachypodium phoenicoides, perennial false brome, Mediterranean false brome (Naturalized perennial)

Brachypodium pinnatum, heath false brome (Naturalized perennial)

Brachypodium rupestre subsp. *caespitosum*, false brome (Naturalized perennial)

Brachypodium sylvaticum subsp. *sylvaticum*, slender false brome (Naturalized perennial)

Briza maxima, rattlesnake grass, large quaking grass (Naturalized annual)

Briza media, perennial quaking grass (Naturalized (?) perennial †: 1994)

Briza minor, small quaking grass, annual quaking grass (Naturalized annual)

Bromus arenarius, Australian chess (Naturalized annual)

Bromus arizonicus, Arizona brome (Native annual)

Bromus arvensis subsp. *arvensis*, field brome (Naturalized annual)

Bromus berteroanus, Chilean brome (Naturalized annual)

Bromus brizaeformis, rattlesnake brome (Naturalized annual)

Bromus carinatus, California brome, large-flowered brome, mountain brome (Native annual-perennial)

Bromus caroli-henrici, weedy brome (Naturalized annual)

Bromus catharticus var. *catharticus*, rescue grass (Naturalized annual-perennial)

Bromus catharticus var. *elatus*, rescue grass (Naturalized perennial)

Bromus ciliatus, fringed brome (Native perennial)

Bromus commutatus, hairy chess, meadow brome (Naturalized annual)

Bromus diandrus, ripgut, ripgut brome, great brome, needle brome (Naturalized annual)

Bromus erectus, English brome, upright brome (Naturalized annual)

Bromus frondosus, weeping brome (Native perennial)

Bromus grandis, tall brome (Native perennial)

Bromus hallii, Hall's brome (Endemic perennial)

Bromus hordeaceus subsp. *hordeaceus*, soft brome, lop grass (Naturalized annual)

Bromus hordeaceus subsp. *molliformis*, soft brome (Naturalized annual)

Bromus hordeaceus subsp. *thominei*, soft brome (Naturalized annual)

Bromus inermis subsp. *inermis*, smooth brome (Naturalized perennial)

Bromus japonicus subsp. *japonicus*, Japanese brome (Naturalized annual)

Bromus laevipes, Chinook brome, woodland brome (Native perennial)

Bromus madritensis subsp. *madritensis*, Spanish brome, compact brome (Naturalized annual)

Bromus madritensis subsp. *rubens*, foxtail brome, red brome (Naturalized annual)

Bromus orcuttianus, Orcutt's brome (Native perennial)

Bromus porteri, Porter's brome, nodding brome (Native perennial)

Bromus pseudolaevipes, Coast Range brome (Endemic perennial)

Bromus racemosus, smooth brome, bald brome (Naturalized annual)

Bromus richardsonii, Richardson's brome, fringed brome (Native perennial)

Bromus scoparius, broom brome (Naturalized (?) annual †: 1892)

Bromus secalinus var. *decipiens*, rye brome (Naturalized annual)

Bromus secalinus var. *secalinus*, rye brome (Naturalized annual)

Bromus sitchensis, Alaska brome, Sitka brome (Native perennial)

Bromus squarrosus, squarrose brome, corn brome (Naturalized annual)

Bromus sterilis, poverty brome, sterile brome, barren brome (Naturalized annual)

Bromus suksdorfii, Suksdorf's brome (Native perennial)

Bromus tectorum, downy brome, cheat grass, bronco grass (Naturalized annual)

Bromus vulgaris, narrow-flowered brome, Columbia brome (Native perennial)

Calamagrostis bolanderi, Bolander's reed grass (Endemic perennial)

Calamagrostis breweri, Brewer's reed grass (Native perennial)

Calamagrostis canadensis var. *canadensis*, bluejoint (Native perennial)

Calamagrostis canadensis var. *langsdorffii*, Langsdorff's bluejoint (Native perennial)

Calamagrostis foliosa, leafy reed grass (Endemic perennial)

Calamagrostis koelerioides, tufted pine grass, fire reed grass (Native perennial)

Calamagrostis muiriana, Muir's reed grass (Endemic perennial)

Calamagrostis nutkaensis, Pacific reed grass, Nootka reed grass (Native perennial)

Calamagrostis ophitidis, serpentine reed grass (Endemic perennial)

Calamagrostis purpurascens var. *purpurascens*, purple reed grass, pine grass (Native perennial)

Calamagrostis rubescens, pine reed grass, pine grass (Native perennial)

Calamagrostis stricta subsp. *inexpansa*, California reed grass (Native perennial)

Calamagrostis stricta subsp. *stricta*, northern reed grass (Native perennial)

Catapodium rigidum subsp. *rigidum*, fern grass (Naturalized annual)

Cenchrus advena, fountain grass (Naturalized perennial)

Cenchrus americanus, pearl millet (Naturalized annual)

Cenchrus ciliaris var. *ciliaris*, buffel grass (Naturalized perennial)

Cenchrus echinatus, southern sandbur (Naturalized annual)

Cenchrus incertus, coastal sandbur, bur grass (Naturalized annual-perennial)

Cenchrus latifolius, Uruguayan fountain grass (Naturalized (?) perennial †: 1969)

Cenchrus longispinus, mat sandbur, innocent weed (Naturalized annual)

Cenchrus macrourus, African feather grass, waterside reed (Naturalized perennial)

Cenchrus nervosus, bent spike fountain grass (Naturalized perennial)

Cenchrus purpureus, Napier grass, elephant grass (Naturalized perennial)

Cenchrus setaceus, crimson fountain grass, tender fountain grass (Naturalized annual-perennial)

Cenchrus villosus, feathertop (Naturalized perennial)

Chloris gayana, Rhodes grass (Naturalized perennial)

Chloris truncata, weeping windmill grass, Australian finger grass (Naturalized perennial)

Chloris verticillata, tumble windmill grass, finger grass (Naturalized perennial)

Chloris virgata, feather finger grass (Naturalized annual)

Cinna bolanderi, Bolander's reed grass (Endemic perennial)

Cinna latifolia, wood reed grass, sweet reed grass, drooping wood reed (Native perennial)

Cortaderia jubata, jubata grass, purple pampas grass, Andean pampas grass (Naturalized perennial)

Cortaderia selloana, Uruguayan pampas grass (Naturalized perennial)

Crypsis alopecuroides, foxtail prickle grass (Naturalized annual)

Crypsis schoenoides, prickle grass, swamp-timothy (Naturalized annual)

Crypsis vaginiflora, African crypsis, sharp-leaved crypsis, modest prickle grass (Naturalized annual)

Cynodon dactylon var. *dactylon*, Bermuda grass, devil grass (Naturalized perennial)

Cynodon plectostachyus, star grass (Naturalized (?) perennial †: 1957)

Cynodon transvaalensis, Florida grass (Naturalized (?) perennial †: 2003)

Cynosurus cristatus, crested dogtail (Naturalized perennial)

Cynosurus echinatus, dogtail, bristly dogtail, hedgehog dogtail (Naturalized annual)

Dactylis glomerata subsp. *glomerata*, orchard grass (Naturalized perennial)

Dactyloctenium aegyptium, crowfoot, Durban crowfoot, Egyptian grass (Naturalized annual-perennial)

Danthonia californica, California oat grass (Native perennial)

Danthonia decumbens, common heath grass (Naturalized perennial)

Danthonia intermedia, timber oat grass, wild mountain oat grass (Native perennial)

Danthonia unispicata, one-spike oat grass, few-flowered wild oat grass (Native perennial)

Dasyochloa pulchella, fluff grass (Native perennial)

Deschampsia atropurpurea, mountain hair grass (Native perennial)

Deschampsia caespitosa subsp. *beringensis*, Bering tufted hair grass, coast hair grass (Native perennial)

Deschampsia caespitosa subsp. *caespitosa*, tufted hair grass, mountain hair grass (Native perennial)

Deschampsia caespitosa subsp. *holciformis*, Pacific hair grass (Native perennial)

Deschampsia danthonioides, annual hair grass (Native annual)

Deschampsia elongata, slender hair grass (Native perennial)

Digitaria bicornis, yellow-green crab grass (Naturalized (?) annual-perennial †: 1926)

Digitaria californica, cottontop, Arizona cottontop (Native perennial)

Digitaria ciliaris var. *ciliaris*, southern crab grass, summer crab grass (Naturalized annual)

Digitaria eriantha, Pangola grass (Naturalized (?) perennial †: 1939)

Digitaria ischaemum var. *ischaemum*, smooth crab grass (Naturalized annual)

Digitaria sanguinalis, hairy crab grass (Naturalized annual)

Dinebra retroflexa var. *retroflexa*, viper grass (Naturalized annual)

Distichlis littoralis, shore grass, salt-cedar (Native perennial)

Distichlis spicata, salt grass (Native perennial)

Echinochloa colona, jungle-rice, shama millet, shanwa millet (Naturalized annual)

Echinochloa crus-galli, large barnyard grass, water grass (Naturalized annual)

Echinochloa crus-pavonis var. *crus-pavonis*, gulf cockspur grass (Naturalized annual)

Echinochloa crus-pavonis var. *macera*, gulf cockspur grass (Naturalized annual)

Echinochloa esculenta, Japanese water grass (Naturalized annual)

Echinochloa frumentacea, Siberian millet, Japanese millet, billion-dollar grass (Naturalized annual)

Echinochloa oryzoides, early water grass (Naturalized annual)

Echinochloa phyllopogon, rice field grass (Naturalized annual)

Ehrharta calycina, perennial veldt grass (Naturalized perennial)

Ehrharta erecta, upright veldt grass (Naturalized perennial)

Ehrharta longiflora, annual veldt grass, long-flowered veldt grass (Naturalized annual)

Eleusine coracana subsp. *africana*, African finger millet (Naturalized annual)

Eleusine indica var. *indica*, goose grass, Indian goose grass (Naturalized annual)

Eleusine tristachya, three-spike goose grass (Naturalized annual)

X *Elyhordeum californicum*, California wild rye (Native perennial)

X *Elyhordeum macounii*, Macoun's wild rye (Native perennial)

X *Elyhordeum stebbinsianum*, Stebbins' wild rye (Native perennial)

Elymus x *aristatus*, purple wheat grass (Native perennial)

Elymus arizonicus, Arizona wild-rye (Naturalized perennial)

Elymus californicus, California bottlebrush grass (Endemic perennial)

Elymus canadensis var. *canadensis*, Canada wild-rye (Naturalized perennial)

Elymus caput-medusae subsp. *caput-medusae*, medusa head grass (Naturalized annual)

Elymus cinereus, ashy wild-rye, Great Basin wild-rye (Native perennial)

Elymus condensatus, giant wild-rye (Native perennial)

Elymus elymoides subsp. *brevifolius*, short-leaved squirreltail (Native perennial)

Elymus elymoides subsp. *californicus*, California squirreltail (Native perennial)

Elymus elymoides subsp. *elymoides*, squirreltail (Native perennial)

Elymus elymoides subsp. *hordeoides*, western bottlebrush grass (Native perennial †: 1980)

Elymus glaucus subsp. *glaucus*, blue wild-rye, western wild-rye (Native perennial)

Elymus glaucus subsp. *virescens*, Virginia wild-rye (Naturalized perennial)

Elymus x *gouldii*, Gould's wild-rye (Endemic perennial)

Elymus x *hansenii*, Hansen's squirreltail (Native perennial)

Elymus hispidus, intermediate wheat grass (Naturalized perennial)

Elymus interruptus, Texas wild-rye (Native perennial)

Elymus lanceolatus subsp. *lanceolatus*, thick spike wild-rye, stream side wild-rye (Native perennial)

Elymus mollis subsp. *mollis*, American dune grass, sea lyme grass (Native perennial)

Elymus multinodus, Russian quack grass (Naturalized perennial)

Elymus multisetus, big squirreltail (Native perennial)

Elymus pacificus, Pacific wild-rye (Endemic perennial)

Elymus ponticus, tall wild-rye, Eurasian quack grass (Naturalized perennial)

Elymus repens subsp. *repens*, quack grass, couch grass, creeping wild-rye (Naturalized perennial)

Elymus salina, saline wild-rye (Native perennial)

Elymus x *saundersii*, Saunder's wild-rye (Native perennial)

Elymus x *saxicolus*, rock wild-rye (Native perennial)

Elymus scribneri, Scribner's wild-rye (Native perennial)

Elymus sierrae, Sierra wild-rye (Native perennial)

Elymus smithii, western wheat grass (Native perennial)

Elymus spicatus subsp. *spicatus*, blue bunch wheat grass (Native perennial)

Elymus stebbinsii, Stebbins' wild-rye (Endemic perennial)

Elymus trachycaulus, slender wheat grass, bearded wheat grass (Native perennial)

Elymus triticoides, beardless wild-rye (Native perennial)

Elymus x *vancouverensis*, Vancouver wild-rye (Native perennial)

Enneapogon desvauxii, feather pappus grass, nine-awned pappus grass (Native annual-perennial)

Eragrostis barrelieri, Mediterranean love grass (Naturalized annual)

Eragrostis capillaris, lace grass (Naturalized annual)

Eragrostis cilianensis, stink grass, candy grass (Naturalized annual)

Eragrostis curvula, weeping love grass (Naturalized perennial)

Eragrostis hypnoides, teal love grass, creeping love grass, creeping meadow grass (Native annual)

Eragrostis lehmanniana, Lehmann's love grass (Naturalized perennial)

Eragrostis lutescens, six weeks love grass, viscid love grass (Native annual)

Eragrostis mexicana subsp. *mexicana*, Mexican love grass (Native annual)

Eragrostis mexicana subsp. *virescens*, Chilean love grass (Native annual)

Eragrostis minor, little love grass, candy grass (Naturalized annual)

Eragrostis pectinacea var. *miserrima*, Gulf love grass, desert love grass (Native annual)

Eragrostis pectinacea var. *pectinacea*, Carolina love grass, tufted love grass (Native annual)

Eragrostis pilosa var. *pilosa*, Indian love grass (Naturalized annual)

Eragrostis secundiflora var. *oxylepis*, sand love grass, red love grass (Native perennial)

Eragrostis superba, Massai love grass, superb love grass (Naturalized perennial)

Eremochloa ciliaris, fringed centipede grass (Naturalized (?) perennial †: 1862)

Eriochloa acuminata var. *acuminata*, southwestern cup grass, summer grass (Native annual)

Eriochloa aristata var. *aristata*, awned cup grass, bearded cup grass (Native (?) annual)

Eriochloa contracta, prairie cup grass (Naturalized annual)

Eriochloa villosa, hairy cup grass (Naturalized annual)

Erioneuron avenaceum var. *avenaceum*, short-leaved woolly grass (Native perennial †: 1880)

Erioneuron pilosum var. *pilosum*, hairy-tridens, hairy woolly grass (Native perennial)

Eustachys distichophylla, weeping finger grass (Naturalized (?) perennial †: 1941)

Festuca altaica, northern rough fescue, altai fescue (Native (?) perennial †: 1977)

Festuca arundinacea subsp. *arundinacea*, alta, tall, reed, or meadow fescue (Naturalized perennial)

Festuca brachyphylla subsp. *breviculmis*, alpine fescue (Endemic perennial)

Festuca bromoides, brome six-weeks fescue (Naturalized annual)

Festuca californica var. *californica*, California fescue (Native perennial)

Festuca californica var. *hitchcockiana*, Hitchcock's California fescue (Endemic perennial)

Festuca californica var. *parishii*, Parish's California fescue (Endemic perennial)

Festuca elmeri, Elmer's fescue, coast fescue (Native perennial)

Festuca idahoensis, Idaho fescue, blue bunch fescue (Native perennial)

Festuca kingii, spiked fescue (Native perennial)

Festuca microstachys , small, Pacific, or Eastwood's six-weeks grass (Native annual)

Festuca minutiflora, small-flowered annual fescue (Native perennial)

Festuca myuros, rat-tail fescue, rat-tail six-weeks grass (Naturalized annual)

Festuca occidentalis, western fescue (Native perennial)

Festuca octoflora, six-weeks fescue (Native annual)

Festuca perennis, perennial rye grass, English rye grass (Naturalized annual-perennial)

Festuca pratensis, meadow fescue, English blue grass (Naturalized perennial)

Festuca rubra, red fescue (Native-naturalized perennial)

Festuca saximontana var. *purpusiana*, Rocky Mountain fescue (Native perennial)

Festuca saximontana var. *saximontana*, Rocky Mountain fescue (Native perennial)

Festuca subulata, bearded fescue, nodding fescue (Native perennial)

Festuca subuliflora, coast range fescue, crinkle-awned fescue (Native perennial)

Festuca temulenta, darnel, flax darnel, poison darnel (Naturalized annual)

Festuca trachyphylla, hard fescue, sheep fescue (Naturalized perennial)

Festuca viridula, green-leaved fescue, mountain bunch grass (Native perennial)

Gastridium phleoides, nit grass (Naturalized annual)

Gaudinia fragilis, French oat grass, fragile oat (Naturalized (?) annual †: 2002)

Glyceria borealis, northern manna grass (Native perennial)

Glyceria davyi, Davy's manna grass (Endemic perennial; status uncertain)

Glyceria declinata, waxy manna grass (Naturalized perennial)

Glyceria elata, tall manna grass (Native perennial)

Glyceria fluitans, water manna grass (Naturalized perennial)

Glyceria grandis var. *grandis*, American manna grass, reed manna grass (Native perennial)

Glyceria leptostachya, Davy's manna grass (Native perennial)

Glyceria x *occidentalis*, northwestern manna grass (Native (?) perennial)

Glyceria striata, fowl manna grass (Native perennial)

Hainardia cylindrica, thintail, barb grass (Naturalized annual)

Heteropogon contortus, twisted tanglehead (Naturalized perennial)

Hilaria jamesii, galleta, James' galleta (Native perennial)

Hilaria rigida, big galleta, woolly grass (Native perennial)

Holcus lanatus, velvet grass (Naturalized perennial)

Holcus mollis subsp. *mollis*, creeping velvet grass (Naturalized perennial)

Hordeum arizonicum, Arizona barley (Native annual-perennial)

Hordeum brachyantherum subsp. *brachyantherum*, meadow barley (Native perennial)

Hordeum brachyantherum subsp. *californicum*, California barley (Endemic perennial)

Hordeum bulbosum, bulbous barley (Naturalized (?) perennial †: 1946)

Hordeum depressum, alkali barley, dwarf barley, low barley (Native annual)

Hordeum intercedens, bobtail barley (Native annual)

Hordeum jubatum subsp. *jubatum*, foxtail barley, squirreltail grass (Native annual-perennial)

Hordeum marinum subsp. *gussoneanum*, Mediterranean barley (Naturalized annual)

Hordeum marinum subsp. *marinum*, sea barley (Naturalized annual)

Hordeum murinum subsp. *glaucum*, glaucous barley, blue foxtail (Naturalized annual)

Hordeum murinum subsp. *leporinum*, hare barley, mouse barley, farmer's foxtail (Naturalized annual)

Hordeum murinum subsp. *murinum*, wall barley, mouse barley (Naturalized annual)

Hordeum pusillum, little barley (Native annual †: 1965)

Hordeum vulgare var. *vulgare*, barley, cultivated barley (Naturalized annual)

Hyparrhenia hirta, thatching grass (Naturalized perennial)

Imperata brevifolia, California satintail (Native perennial)

Kikuyuochloa clandestina, kikuyu grass (Naturalized perennial)

Koeleria macrantha, June grass, crested Koeler's grass, prairie June grass (Native perennial)

Lagurus ovatus, hare's tail (Naturalized annual)

Lamarckia aurea, goldentop (Naturalized annual)

Leersia hexandra, southern cut grass (Naturalized perennial)

Leersia oryzoides, rice cut grass (Native perennial)

Leptochloa dubia, green sprangletop (Naturalized perennial)

Leptochloa fusca subsp. *fascicularis*, bearded sprangletop, clustered salt grass (Native annual)

Leptochloa fusca subsp. *fusca*, bearded sprangletop (Native annual †: 1983)

Leptochloa fusca subsp. *uninervia*, Mexican sprangletop, dense-flowered sprangletop (Native annual)

Leptochloa panicea subsp. *brachiata*, sprangletop (Native annual-perennial)

Leptochloa viscida, sticky sprangletop, Sonoran sprangletop (Native annual)

Lolium rigidum, Wimmera rye grass, Swiss rye grass (Naturalized annual)

Melica aristata, awned melic grass, bearded melic grass (Native perennial)

Melica bulbosa, onion grass, western melic (Native perennial)

Melica californica, California melic (Native perennial)

Melica frutescens, woody melic (Native perennial)

Melica fugax, little onion grass (Native perennial)

Melica geyeri var. *aristulata*, Geyer's onion grass (Endemic perennial)

Melica geyeri var. *geyeri*, Geyer's onion grass (Native perennial)

Melica harfordii, Harford's melic (Native perennial)

Melica imperfecta, Coast Range melic, slender melic, small-flowered melic (Native perennial)

Melica spectabilis, purple onion grass, showy onion grass (Native perennial)

Melica stricta var. *albicaulis*, nodding onion grass (Endemic perennial)

Melica stricta var. *stricta*, nodding onion grass, rock melic (Native perennial)

Melica subulata, Alaska onion grass, rock melic (Native perennial)

Melica torreyana, Torrey's melic grass (Endemic perennial)

Melinis repens subsp. *repens*, Natal grass, ruby grass, pink crystals grass (Naturalized annual)

Miscanthus sinensis, eulalia, Chinese silver grass, maiden grass (Naturalized (?) perennial †: 1970)

Muhlenbergia alopecuroides, bristly wolftail (Native perennial)

Muhlenbergia andina, foxtail muhly, hairy muhly (Native perennial)

Muhlenbergia appressa, Devil's Canyon muhly (Native annual)

Muhlenbergia arsenei, tough muhly, Navajo muhly (Native perennial)

Muhlenbergia asperifolia, scratch grass, alkali muhly (Native perennial)

Muhlenbergia californica, California muhly (Native perennial)

Muhlenbergia dumosa, bamboo muhly (Native perennial)

Muhlenbergia filiformis, pull-up muhly, slender muhly (Native annual-perennial)

Muhlenbergia fragilis, delicate muhly (Native annual)

Muhlenbergia jonesii, Jones' muhly, Modoc muhly (Endemic perennial)

Muhlenbergia mexicana, slender muhly, pull-up muhly (Native annual-perennial)

Muhlenbergia microsperma, annual muhly, little-seeded muhly (Native annual-perennial)

Muhlenbergia minutissima, least muhly (Native annual)

Muhlenbergia montana, mountain muhly (Native perennial)

Muhlenbergia paniculata, tumble grass (Native perennial †: 1980)

Muhlenbergia pauciflora, New Mexican muhly, few-flowered muhly (Native perennial)

Muhlenbergia porteri, bush muhly, mesquite muhly (Native perennial)

Muhlenbergia richardsonis, mat muhly (Native perennial)

Muhlenbergia rigens, basket grass, deer grass (Native perennial)

Muhlenbergia schreberi, nimblewill (Naturalized perennial)

Muhlenbergia thurberi, Thurber's muhly (Native perennial)

Muhlenbergia utilis, Aparejo grass (Native perennial)

Munroa squarrosa, false buffalo grass (Native annual)

Neostapfia colusana, Colusa grass (Endemic annual)

Orcuttia californica, California Orcutt grass (Native annual)

Orcuttia inaequalis, San Joaquin Valley Orcutt grass (Endemic annual)

Orcuttia pilosa, hairy Orcutt grass (Endemic annual)

Orcuttia tenuis, slender Orcutt grass (Endemic annual)

Orcuttia viscida, Sacramento Orcutt grass (Endemic annual)

Oryza rufipogon, wild red rice, brown-bearded rice (Naturalized (?) annual-perennial †: 1922)

Oryza sativa var. *sativa*, rice, cultivated rice (Naturalized annual)

Panicum acuminatum var. *fasciculatum*, Pacific panic grass (Native perennial)

Panicum acuminatum var. *lindheimeri*, Lindheimer's panic grass (Native perennial †: 1972)

Panicum acuminatum var. *thermale*, Geyser's panic grass, hot springs Panicum (Endemic perennial)

Panicum antidotale, blue panic grass (Naturalized perennial)

Panicum capillare, witch grass (Native annual)

Panicum coloratum, Klein grass (Naturalized perennial)

Panicum dichotomiflorum var. *dichotomiflorum*, fall panic grass (Naturalized annual)

Panicum hillmanii, Hillman's panic grass (Naturalized annual)

Panicum hirticaule var. *hirticaule*, rough stalk, Mexican witch grass (Native annual)

Panicum maximum, Guinea grass, guinea liver-seed grass (Naturalized perennial)

Panicum miliaceum, broom corn millet, hog millet (Naturalized annual)

Panicum oligosanthes var. *scribnerianum*, Scribner's panic grass (Native perennial)

Panicum repens, torpedo grass (Naturalized (?) perennial †: 1975)

Panicum rigidulum var. *rigidulum*, red-top panic grass (Naturalized perennial)

Panicum urvilleanum, desert panic grass, silky panic grass (Native perennial)

Panicum virgatum, switch grass (Naturalized perennial)

Parapholis incurva, curved sickle grass (Naturalized annual)

Parapholis strigosa, European sickle grass, sea hard grass (Naturalized annual)

Paspalum boscianum, bull paspalum (Naturalized (?) annual †: 1934)

Paspalum dilatatum, Dallis grass (Naturalized perennial)

Paspalum distichum, knot grass, crown grass, Thompson grass (Native perennial)

Paspalum notatum, Pensacola bahia grass (Naturalized perennial)

Paspalum pubiflorum, hairy-seeded paspalum (Naturalized perennial)

Paspalum quadrifarum, tussock paspalum (Naturalized perennial)

Paspalum urvillei, Vasey's grass (Naturalized perennial)

Paspalum vaginatum, seashore paspalum (Naturalized perennial)

Paspalum virgatum, upright paspalum (Naturalized perennial)

Phalaris angusta, timothy canary grass (Native annual)

Phalaris aquatica, Harding grass, bulbous canary grass (Naturalized perennial)

Phalaris arundinacea subsp. *arundinacea*, reed canary grass (Native perennial)

Phalaris brachystachys, short-spiked canary grass (Naturalized annual)

Phalaris caerulescens, sunol grass (Naturalized (?) perennial †: 1999)

Phalaris californica, California canary grass (Native perennial)

Phalaris canariensis, common canary grass, annual canary grass (Naturalized annual)

Phalaris caroliniana, Carolina canary grass (Naturalized annual)

Phalaris lemmonii, Lemmon's canary grass (Endemic annual)

Phalaris minor, little-seeded canary grass (Naturalized annual)

Phalaris paradoxa, hood canary grass (Naturalized annual)

Phleum alpinum subsp. *alpinum*, mountain timothy, alpine timothy (Native perennial)

Phleum pratense subsp. *pratense*, timothy (Naturalized perennial)
Phragmites australis subsp. *americanus*, common reed (Native perennial)
Phragmites australis subsp. *australis*, common reed (Naturalized perennial)
Phragmites australis subsp. *berlandieri*, Berlandier's reed (Naturalized (?) perennial)
Phyllostachys aurea, timber bamboo, golden bamboo, madake (Naturalized perennial)
Phyllostachys bambusoides, Japanese timber bamboo (Naturalized (?) perennial †; 1989)
Pleuropogon californicus var. *californicus*, California semaphore grass (Endemic annual-perennial)
Pleuropogon californicus var. *davyi*, Davy's semaphore grass (Endemic perennial)
Pleuropogon hooverianus, Hoover's or North Coast semaphore grass (Endemic perennial)
Pleuropogon refractus, nodding semaphore grass (Native perennial)
Poa abbreviata subsp. *marshii*, Marsh's blue grass (Native perennial)
Poa abbreviata subsp. *pattersonii*, Patterson's blue grass (Native perennial)
Poa annua, annual blue grass, winter grass (Naturalized annual-perennial)
Poa atropurpurea, San Bernardino blue grass (Endemic perennial)
Poa bigelovii, Bigelow's blue grass (Native annual)
Poa bolanderi, Bolander's blue grass (Native annual)
Poa bulbosa, bulbous blue grass (Naturalized perennial)
Poa compressa, Canada blue grass, flat-stemmed blue grass (Naturalized perennial)
Poa confinis, dune blue grass, coastline blue grass (Native perennial)
Poa cusickii subsp. *cusickii*, Cusick's blue grass (Native perennial)
Poa cusickii subsp. *epilis*, skyline blue grass, mountain blue grass (Native perennial)
Poa cusickii subsp. *pallida*, Cusick's blue grass (Native perennial)
Poa cusickii subsp. *purpurascens*, purple blue grass (Native perennial)
Poa diaboli, Diablo Canyon blue grass (Endemic perennial)
Poa douglasii, seashore blue grass, sand blue grass, Douglas' blue grass (Endemic perennial)
Poa fendleriana subsp. *fendleriana*, mutton grass (Native perennial)
Poa fendleriana subsp. *longiligula*, long-tongue mutton grass (Native perennial)
Poa glauca subsp. *rupicola*, timberline blue grass (Native perennial)
Poa howellii, Howell's blue grass (Native annual)
Poa infirma, weak blue grass (Naturalized annual)
Poa keckii, Keck's blue grass (Endemic perennial)
Poa kelloggii, Kellogg's blue grass (Endemic perennial)
Poa leptocoma subsp. *leptocoma*, bog blue grass, marsh blue grass (Native perennial)
Poa lettermanii, Letterman's blue grass (Native perennial)
Poa x *limosa*, Lassen County blue grass (Native perennial)

Poa macrantha, large-flowered seashore blue grass (Native perennial)

Poa napensis, Napa blue grass (Endemic perennial)

Poa nemoralis, wood blue grass, forest blue grass (Naturalized perennial)

Poa palustris, fowl blue grass (Naturalized perennial)

Poa piperi, Piper's blue grass (Native perennial)

Poa pratensis, Kentucky blue grass (Naturalized perennial)

Poa pringlei, Pringle's blue grass (Native perennial)

Poa rhizomata, timber blue grass (Native perennial)

Poa secunda subsp. *juncifolia*, alkali blue grass (Native perennial)

Poa secunda subsp. *secunda*, Nevada blue grass, Sandberg's blue grass (Native perennial)

Poa sierrae, Sierra blue grass (Endemic perennial)

Poa stebbinsii, Stebbins' blue grass, subalpine blue grass (Endemic perennial)

Poa tenerrima, delicate blue grass (Endemic perennial)

Poa thomasii, Catalina grass (Native annual)

Poa trivialis subsp. *trivialis*, rough blue grass, rough-stalked meadow grass (Naturalized perennial)

Poa unilateralis subsp. *unilateralis*, San Francisco blue grass (Native perennial)

Poa wheeleri, Wheeler's blue grass (Native perennial)

Polypogon australis, Chilean beard grass, Chilean rabbit's-foot grass (Naturalized perennial)

Polypogon elongatus, stream bank beard grass (Naturalized perennial)

Polypogon fugax, Asian beard grass (Naturalized (?) annual †: 1879)

Polypogon imberbis, rabbit's-foot grass, beard grass (Naturalized (?) perennial †: 1948)

Polypogon interruptus, ditch beard grass (Naturalized perennial)

Polypogon maritimus, Mediterranean beard grass, maritime beard grass (Naturalized annual)

Polypogon monspeliensis, rabbit's-foot grass, tawny rabbit's-foot grass (Naturalized annual)

Polypogon viridis, water beard grass (Naturalized perennial)

Pseudosasa japonica, arrow bamboo, hardy bamboo, metake (Naturalized (?) perennial †: 1946)

Puccinellia distans subsp. *distans*, European alkali grass, spreading alkali grass (Naturalized perennial)

Puccinellia howellii, Howell's alkali grass (Endemic perennial)

Puccinellia lemmonii, Lemmon's alkali grass (Native perennial)

Puccinellia nutkaensis, Alaska alkali grass, Nootka alkali grass (Native perennial)

Puccinellia nuttalliana, Nuttall's alkali grass (Native perennial)

Puccinellia parishii, Parish's alkali grass, bog alkali grass (Native annual)

Puccinellia pumila, dwarf alkali grass (Native perennial)

Puccinellia simplex, western alkali grass, California alkali grass (Native annual)

Rostraria cristata, bristly koeleria, Mediterranean hair grass (Naturalized annual)

Rottboellia cochinchinensis, itch grass (Naturalized (?) annual)

Rytidosperma caespitosum, wallaby grass (Naturalized perennial)

Rytidosperma penicillatum, hairy poverty grass (Naturalized perennial)

Rytidosperma racemosum, wallaby grass (Naturalized perennial)

Rytidosperma richardsonii, Straw wallaby grass (Naturalized perennial)

Saccharum ravennae, Ravenna grass (Naturalized perennial)

Schismus barbatus var. *arabicus*, Arabian schismus (Naturalized annual)

Schismus barbatus var. *barbatus*, Mediterranean schismus (Naturalized annual)

Schizachyrium scoparium var. *scoparium*, little bluestem, little false bluestem (Naturalized (?) perennial)

Sclerochloa dura, common hard grass (Naturalized annual)

Scleropogon brevifolius, burro grass (Native perennial)

Scribneria bolanderi, Scribner's grass (Native annual)

Secale cereale, rye, cultivated rye (Naturalized annual)

Setaria adhaerans, bur bristle grass, tropical barbed bristle grass (Naturalized annual)

Setaria faberi, Japanese bristly foxtail (Naturalized annual)

Setaria italica, foxtail millet, Italian foxtail millet (Naturalized (?) annual †: 1921)

Setaria megaphylla, big-leaved bristle grass (Naturalized perennial)

Setaria parviflora, marsh bristle grass, knot root bristle grass (Native perennial)

Setaria pumila subsp. *pumila,* yellow foxtail, yellow bristle grass (Naturalized annual)

Setaria sphacelata, golden-timothy, African bristle grass (Naturalized perennial)

Setaria verticillata, bur bristle grass, hooked bristle grass, pigeon grass (Naturalized annual)

Setaria verticilliformis, barbed bristle grass (Naturalized annual)

Setaria viridis var. *viridis*, green bristle grass (Naturalized annual)

Sorghum bicolor subsp. *bicolor,* sorghum, milo, sorgo, broomcorn, grain sorghum (Naturalized annual)

Sorghum bicolor subsp. x *drummondii,* Sudan grass (Naturalized annual)

Sorghum bicolor subsp. *verticilliforum*, wild sorghum (Naturalized (?) annual †: 1959)

Sorghum halepense, Johnson grass (Naturalized perennial)

Spartina alterniflora, smooth cord grass, saltwater cord grass (Naturalized (?) perennial)

Spartina x *anglica*, common cord grass (Naturalized (?) perennial)

Spartina densiflora, Chilean cord grass, dense-flowered cord grass (Naturalized perennial)

Spartina foliosa, California cord grass (Native perennial)

Spartina gracilis, alkali cord grass (Native perennial)

Spartina patens, salt meadow cord grass (Naturalized (?) perennial)

Sphenopholis obtusata, prairie wedge-scale, early bunch grass (Native perennial)

Sporobolus airoides var. *airoides*, alkali sacaton, alkali dropseed (Native perennial)

Sporobolus contractus, spike dropseed, narrow-spiked dropseed (Native perennial)

Sporobolus creber, slender dropseed (Naturalized perennial)

Sporobolus cryptandrus, sand dropseed (Native perennial)

Sporobolus flexuosus, mesa dropseed (Native perennial)

Sporobolus indicus var. *indicus*, smut grass (Naturalized perennial)

Sporobolus vaginiflorus var. *vaginiflorus*, poverty dropseed (Naturalized (?) annual †: 1949)

Sporobolus wrightii, Wright's sacaton, Wright's dropseed, big alkali sacaton (Native perennial)

Stenotaphrum secundatum, St. Augustine grass (Naturalized (?) perennial)

Stipa arida, Mormon needle grass, funeral grass (Native perennial)

Stipa x *bloomeri*, Bloomer's mountain-rice (Native perennial)

Stipa brachychaeta, puna grass, aracauria needle grass (Naturalized perennial)

Stipa capensis, Mediterranean needle grass (Naturalized annual)

Stipa cernua, nodding needle grass (Native perennial)

Stipa chaetophora, purple spear grass, stipoid rice grass (Naturalized perennial)

Stipa comata var. *comata*, needle-and-thread grass (Native perennial)

Stipa comata var. *intermedia*, Tweedy's needle-and-thread grass (Native perennial)

Stipa coronata, giant stipa (Native perennial)

Stipa diegoensis, San Diego needle grass (Native perennial)

Stipa divaricata, small-flowered rice grass, little-seeded rice grass (Native perennial)

Stipa exigua, little rice grass, little mountain-rice (Native perennial)

Stipa hymenoides, Indian rice grass, sand grass (Native perennial)

Stipa kingii, King's mountain-rice (Endemic perennial)

Stipa x *latiglumis*, Yosemite needle grass, Sierra needle grass (Endemic perennial)

Stipa lemmonii var. *lemmonii*, Lemmon's needle grass (Native perennial)

Stipa lemmonii var. *pubescens*, Crampton's needle grass (Endemic perennial)

Stipa lepida var. *lepida*, foothill needle grass, small-flowered needle grass (Native perennial)

Stipa lettermanii, Letterman's needle grass (Native perennial)

Stipa manicata, Andean tussock grass (Naturalized perennial)

Stipa mauritanica, dis grass, Mauritanian grass (Naturalized perennial)

Stipa miliacea subsp. *miliacea*, smilo, smilo grass, millet mountain grass (Naturalized perennial)

Stipa nelsonii subsp. *dorei*, mountain needle grass, Dore's needle grass (Native perennial)

Stipa nevadensis, Sierra needle grass, Nevada needle grass (Native perennial)

Stipa occidentalis var. *californica*, California needle grass (Native perennial)

Stipa occidentalis var. *occidentalis*, western needle grass (Native perennial)

Stipa occidentalis var. *pubescens*, Elmer's needle grass (Native perennial)

Stipa parishii var. *parishii*, Parish's needle grass (Native perennial)

Stipa pinetorum, pine needle grass, pine woods needle grass (Native perennial)

Stipa plumosa, South American rice grass, plumose needle grass (Naturalized (?) perennial †: 1983)

Stipa pulchra, purple needle grass, nodding needle grass (Native perennial)

Stipa purpurata, rice grass, bristly spear grass (Naturalized perennial)

Stipa scribneri , Scribner's needle grass (Native (?) perennial †: 1982)

Stipa speciosa, desert needle grass (Native perennial)

Stipa stillmanii, Stillman's needle grass (Endemic perennial)

Stipa tenuissima, fine-stem tussock grass, Mexican feather grass (Naturalized perennial)

Stipa thurberiana, Thurber's needle grass (Native perennial)

Stipa viridula, green needle grass (Native perennial)

Stipa webberi, Webber's needle grass (Native perennial)

Swallenia alexandrae, Eureka Valley dune grass (Endemic perennial)

Torreyochloa erecta, spike false manna grass (Native perennial)

Torreyochloa pallida var. *pauciflora*, few-flowered or pale false manna grass (Native perennial)

Tribolium obliterum, Capetown grass (Naturalized perennial)

Tridens muticus var. *muticus*, slim tridens, awned fluff grass (Native perennial)

Trisetum canescens, tall false oat, silvery oat grass (Native perennial)

Trisetum cernuum, nodding trisetum (Native perennial)

Trisetum flavescens, yellow-oat (Naturalized (?) perennial †: 1917)

Trisetum spicatum, spike trisetum, narrow false oat (Native perennial)

Trisetum wolfii, Wolf's false oat, beardless false oat (Native perennial)

Triticum aestivum subsp. *aestivum*, wheat, bread wheat, common wheat (Naturalized annual)

Tuctoria greenei, awnless Orcutt grass, awnless spiral grass (Endemic annual)

Tuctoria mucronata, Crampton's tuctoria, prickly spiral grass (Endemic annual)

Urochloa arizonica, Arizona signal grass (Native annual)

Urochloa texana, Texas signal grass, Texas millet (Naturalized (?) annual †: 1992)

Ventenata dubia, North Africa grass, venenata grass (Naturalized annual)

Zoysia japonica, zoisia, Japanese lawn grass (Naturalized (?) perennial †: 1976)

GLOSSARY, ABBREVIATIONS, AND SYMBOLS

When I use a word . . . it means just what I choose it to mean— neither more nor less.

Lewis Carroll, Through the Looking Glass, 1872

Abbreviations & Symbols

Cal-IPC California Invasive Plant Council
CDFA California Department of Food and Agriculture
CDFG California Department of Fish and Game
CNPS California Native Plant Society
USFWS United States Fish and Wildlife Service
cm = centimeter
m = meter
mm = millimeter
mmt = million metric tons
TJM2 = *The Jepson Manual,* second edition
± = more or less
† = presumed extinct, extirpated, or doubtfully naturalized
[−] = unusual or rare condition or measurement

Glossary

achene a dry, single-seeded fruit whose seed coat and fruit wall are separate from one another, as in the sedges
acuminate gradually tapering to an extended point
acute sharp-pointed
adventitious originating from mature tissues, as in aerial roots or bulbs that arise from a location other than the primary root system
aerial growing above ground rather than in the soil
androecium the male portion of a flower, consisting of one or more stamens
annual living for a single growing season; see also "perennial"
anther the sac-like, pollen-producing part of a stamen
anthesis the phase during which a flower is fully opened and pollination occurs
apex the upper or distal end of a structure; plural, apices
apomixis a type of reproduction that involves the organs and processes typically associated with sexual reproduction but that does not involve the actual

fusion of egg and sperm nuclei; used more loosely as a synonym for asexual reproduction

appressed lying against a surface or, in the case of inflorescence branches, against a central or principal axis

ascending growing upward, obliquely at first and then erect, as in certain grass stems

asexual any form of reproduction that does not involve the union of egg and sperm

attenuate gradually narrowed to a slender point

auricles the paired, ear-shaped appendages at the apex of the sheath in some grasses

awl-shaped the leaf or bract shape characterized by a gradual taper from the base to a sharp point; an awl is a tool for punching holes in leather or wood

awn a substantial hair or bristle that arises from the apex or back of glumes or lemmas [very rarely paleas]; awned, having awns

axile the interior angle formed by a stem and the petiole or pedicel that it bears

axillary inflorescence an inflorescence that arises from a lateral position on a culm, as opposed to one that is terminal

axis the central stem of an inflorescence

balanced having spikelets ± equally inserted on both sides of a central axis

beak a prominent sterile elongation of a caryopsis

beard a line or tuft of hairs

bifid two-cleft or two-lobed, as in the apex of a lemma or glume

bisexual a flower, floret, or spikelet that bears both male and female reproductive structures; the term "perfect" is also used for this condition

blade the flattened, expanded portion of a leaf

body the membranous portion of a glume, lemma, or palea, exclusive of awns or teeth

both hemispheres the Old World and the New World

bract a reduced leaf; glumes, lemmas, and paleas are also bracts

bristle a short, stiff hair; a sterile branch

bulb an underground plant structure consisting of a series of overlapping leaf bases attached to a much-reduced stem axis; many bulbs are actually corms

bulbils small axillary bulbs that replace more typical florets or spikelets, as in *Poa bulbosa*

bulblet a small bulb

caespitose occurring in clumps or tufts; also spelled "cespitose"

callus a hardened, often pointed, base of a lemma or floret

capillary hair-like, as in delicate panicle branches or awns

capitate aggregated into a dense, head-like cluster, as in an arrangement of spikelets

capsule a dry, dehiscent fruit that opens by means of slits, lids, pores, or teeth as in the rush family

caryopsis a dry, single-seeded fruit whose seed coat and fruit wall are inseparable; the fruit type of the vast majority of grasses

cauline pertaining to a stem, as in cauline leaves that are inserted along a stem as opposed to the base of the plant

ciliate fringed with marginal hairs

closed sheath a sheath in which the two edges are fused with one another to form a continuous cylinder around the culm, as in brome grasses and orchard grass

column the lower, sometimes twisted portion of an awn; the fused bases of awns, as in *Aristida*

complex a group of closely related and often difficult to distinguish taxa, as in the *Festuca microstachys* complex

compressed flattened, as if pressure had been applied to a sheath, spikelet, or bract

continuous not breaking apart; remaining intact, as in the central axis of an inflorescence at maturity

contracted narrowed, as opposed to open or spreading

convolute rolled longitudinally, with one edge completely within the other, as in a rolled up leaf blade

corm a dense, vertical, underground stem surrounded by dry, papery leaf bases; often loosely called a bulb

corrugated wrinkled

cosmopolitan common to all or to most of the world

culm the stem of a grass plant

cultivar a cultivated variety

dead metabolically disadvantaged

deciduous falling from a plant at the end of a season

decumbent said of stems that lie on the ground, but whose ends are upturned

depauperate not fully developed, stunted; often as the result of growing on an impoverished site

diffuse widely or loosely spreading, as in inflorescence branches

digitate having parts that arise from an apex, as in inflorescence branches or the fingers of your hand

dimorphic having two different shapes, as in the glumes of *Koeleria* or the general appearance of certain fertile and sterile spikelets

dioecious a species in which staminate and pistillate flowers or spikelets occur on separate plants, as in pampas grass

diploid the chromosome complement found in vegetative cells of the plant body; typically expressed in terms of "2n," as in 2n = 14

disarticulation the separating or disjoining of spikelet parts from one another or of portions of an inflorescence axis from one another

distal at the end opposite the point of attachment, as opposed to proximal

distichous attached in two vertical rows, as in leaves on a stem or spikelet bracts on a rachilla

divergent spread apart from one another

dorsal relating to or attached to the back of an organ, the side that is turned away from the axis

dorsally compressed flattened, as if pressure had been brought to bear on the back of a bract; also referred to as "dorsiventrally compressed"

elliptical in the form of a flattened circle

endemic confined to a particular region, applied especially when the area is relatively small

endosperm the nutritive tissue within the seed that originates from the fusion of polar nuclei and sperm nucleus

entire said of a margin of a leaf or bract that lacks lobes or teeth

erose said of a margin that appears to have been gnawed or worn away

exserted protruding beyond or out of another structure, as in an inflorescence from a sheath

fascicle a tight cluster or clump, as in leaves, axillary stems, or spikelets

fertile lemma a lemma that encloses a flower

filament the delicate stalk that supports an anther

filiform thread-like

floret a subunit of a spikelet, consisting of a lemma, palea, and flower; incorrectly defined as only the flower itself

forb any herbaceous plant that is not a grass or does not appear grass-like

gamete a sex cell; the egg or sperm

genome all of the genetic information found in a single complete set of chromosomes in an organism

genus a group of related species; the first component of a scientific name

glabrous without hairs

gland a secretory structure; used more broadly for any warty protuberance; glandular, having or bearing glands

glaucous having a blue-gray or sea-green color; also used for a whitish waxy covering that can be easily rubbed off

globose almost spherical

glume a sterile bract at the base of a spikelet; most grasses have two such structures, some have one, a few have none

glutinous covered with a sticky exudate

grain the fruit of the grass family; see "caryopsis"

gynoecium the female portion of a flower, consisting of the seed-producing components

habit the general appearance of a plant

haploid the chromosome complement found in the nuclei of gametes; often expressed by the letter "n," as in n = 7

herb an annual, biennial, or perennial plant whose stems die back to the ground at the end of the growing season because they lack the firmness of sufficient secondary growth

herbaceous having the features of an herb

hirsute having coarse, ± erect hairs

hispid having long, rigid, bristly hairs; hispidulous, minutely hispid

hyaline having a colorless, thin, translucent or transparent texture

hybrid a plant or animal that is the offspring of a cross between two or more strains, breeds, varieties, species, or genera; hybrids occur spontaneously in nature and they are created in the garden and laboratory

hybridization the natural or artificial processes by which hybrids are created

indigenous native to a region

indurate hard, as in texture

inflorescence the flowering portion of a grass plant; the arrangement of spikelets on a culm

innovation a basal, typically vigorous offshoot

inserted joined to or placed on, as in leaves on a stem or bracts on the spikelet axis

internode the region between two consecutive nodes on a stem

introduced purposefully brought into a region, as in the case of a crop plant or an ornamental

involucre an organized set of bracts or of branchlets that surrounds or forms a series or set beneath a spikelet, group of spikelets, or floret

involute with both edges rolled longitudinally inward toward the midpoint of a leaf or bract

joint the node of a grass stem or inflorescence axis; a point where articulation or disarticulation occurs

keel a prominent ridge or rib, as seen in some glumes, lemmas, or paleas

lanceolate a leaf blade or bract that is narrow and tapers on both ends and that is widest above the middle (not to be confused with Lancelot, the most famous of King Arthur's knights)

laterally compressed flattened, as if pressure had been brought to bear on the sides of a bract, as opposed to the back (dorsally compressed)

lemma one of the two bracts enclosing the grass flower, the other being the palea; the lemma is typically the larger bract

ligule the membranous flap or series of hairs at the junction of the sheath and blade of the grass leaf

locule a chamber within an ovary

linear several to many times longer than wide, as in the typical blade of a grass leaf

lodicule the reduced perianth of the grass flower; these tiny, mitten-shaped structures are all that remains of the calyx

membranous soft, thin, and pliable, as in the texture of a glume or lemma

meristem the region of actively dividing cells of the stem or root apex; the meristematic region of the grass leaf occurs at its base, thereby permitting the plants to survive grazing, fires, and lawn mowers

microhair any of the ± microscopic hairs that occur on the surface of plant parts; in the grasses, they are of diagnostic significance

midrib the central rib of a leaf or bract

minute small, as in the size of your vocabulary if you had to use the glossary for this term

monoecious said of a species in which the staminate and pistillate flowers or spikelets occur on the same plant, as in maize or Job's tears

mucro a short, sharp point or extension, as seen at the tip of lemma or glume; mucronate bearing a mucro

n the number of chromosomes found in the nuclei of sex cells; in diploid organisms, n equals the haploid chromosome number

native originating naturally in a particular region; occurring in an area before the arrival of humans, especially European explorers, traders, etc.

naturalized not native to a particular area, but now well established and maintaining itself without human assistance

neuter lacking reproductive structures; sterile

node the point or region on a stem where a leaf or bract is attached

nut a dry, hard, indehiscent, 1-seeded fruit

oblique slanting or unequal-sided

oblong much longer than broad, with the sides ± parallel, as in the shape of certain leaf blades

obtuse having a blunt or rounded trip

open sheath a sheath in which the two edges touch one another or overlap, but are not fused to form a collar or cylinder

ours the grasses as represented in California

ovary the seed-bearing portion of a flower

ovate egg-shaped

palea one of two bracts enclosing the grass flower, the other being the lemma; typically the smaller and more delicate of the two

panicle an elongate or rounded, much-branched inflorescence in which the spikelets are attached on the outermost branchlets

parallel extending in the same direction and equidistant, as in the veins of most grass blades

pedicel the stalk that supports a spikelet; see also "peduncle"

pedicellate borne on a stalk (pedicel)

peduncle the stalk that supports an inflorescence of spikelets; see also "pedicel"

pendent hanging down

perennial living for several to many years, often blooming and dying back at the end of each growing season; see also "annual"

perianth the calyx and corolla collectively

pericarp the fruit wall

persistent not breaking apart, as in an inflorescence axis or rachilla that remains intact at maturity

petiolate having a petiole

petiole the stalk that supports a leaf blade

pilose covered with soft distinct hairs

pistil the female component of a flower, consisting of an ovary, style, and one or more stigmas

pistillate a flower, floret, spikelet, or plant that bears only female reproductive structures

pitted having small cavities or depressions; also referred to as "punctate"

plumose feather-like, as in the awn of certain needle-grasses with prominent hairs

polyploid an organism whose nuclei contain three or more sets of chromosomes

p. p. the abbreviation of the Latin phrase *pro parte*, meaning "in part"; often used to mean some, but not all, species in a genus, as in *Panicum* p. p.

proliferated the term applied to a spikelet or an inflorescence when some portion has been modified into bulblets or other vegetative structures

prop roots the aerial roots at the base of a maize plant that provide mechanical support for the stem

prostrate lying flat on the ground

puberulent minutely pubescent; downy, the hairs soft, straight, and erect

pubescent said of any plant structure that is hairy, especially if the hairs are short and soft

raceme an elongate arrangement of stalked spikelets attached along an unbranched central axis

racemose an inflorescence that is raceme-like in general form

rachilla the unbranched central axis of a spikelet; not the central axis of an inflorescence of spikelets

rachilla extension the portion of a rachilla that extends beyond the insertion of the uppermost floret; often appearing as a bristle

rachis the unbranched central axis of a spike, raceme, or rame; the primary axis of a panicle

rame an elongate arrangement of stalked and unstalked spikelets borne in repeating pairs or trios along an unbranched axis; the inflorescence type characteristic of the bluestem grasses and their relatives

rank a vertical row, as seen when looking down on a plant; often expressed in terms of 2-ranked, 3-ranked, etc., which would indicate the number of rows

reflexed turned or bent abruptly downward or backward

rhizomatous rhizome-bearing

rhizome an underground, horizontal stem that bears reduced, scaly leaves

rosette a dense, circular cluster of basal leaves

rudiment a small, very poorly developed floret

rugose wrinkled, as in the surface of a bract

runner a stolon, especially a slender one

scabrous covered with short, stiff hairs, so as to be rough to the touch

scutellum the specialized tissue thought to represent the single cotyledon of the grass plant

secund with florets or spikelets turned toward one side only, usually as a result of torsion along an axis

serpentine a group of rocks or soils, often greenish or brownish, that is rich in magnesium, nickel, and asbestos but poor in calcium and other nutrients; the term is also applied to plants that grow on this substrate

sessile not stalked; seated on or attached directly to another plant part

sheath the lower portion of a grass leaf that surrounds the stem

silica bodies crystals of silicon dioxide that occur in specialized epidermal cells of the grass leaf; their shape is of diagnostic significance

silica cells the shorter epidermal cells of the grass leaf and stem that contain silica deposits

sp. species, in the singular

spathe a large bract that is attached beneath and often ± surrounds an inflorescence, as in the bracts of certain bluestems; spathulate, having a spathe

species a kind of plant or animal whose distinctiveness is seen in morphological, anatomical, cytological, chemical, and genetic discontinuities presumably brought about by reproductive isolation

species name a binomial consisting of the genus and the specific epithet, as in *Zea mays*

specific epithet the second element of a binomial (the *mays* of *Zea mays*)

spike an elongate arrangement of sessile spikelets borne on an unbranched central axis

spikelet the basic unit of the grass inflorescence, typically consisting of two glumes and one or more florets

spp. species, in the plural

spreading oriented outward and ± diverging from the point of origin

stamen the pollen-producing organ of a flower, consisting of an anther and a filament

staminate said of a flower, floret, spikelet, or plant that bears only stamens

stem the plant axis that bears leaves, flowers, and fruits; principally aerial, but sometimes subterranean in the form of rhizomes, bulbs, etc.

sterile lacking reproductive parts

sterile lemma a lemma that does not enclose a flower; often all that remains of a reduced floret

stigma the region of the female reproductive structure that is receptive to pollen; in grasses, the feathery portion that sits atop the ovary

stipe a stalk; stipitate stalked, as in the florets of certain grasses

stolon an aerial, horizontal stem, often rooting at the nodes, that bears ordinary foliage leaves, as in Bermuda grass; often called "runners"

stoloniferous stolon-bearing

striate marked with fine, longitudinal, parallel lines, grooves, or ridges

style the elongated portion of a pistil arising from the ovary

subsp. abbreviation for subspecies; sspp., plural

subtend to be below another plant part in point of attachment, as in a set of bracts attached beneath a spikelet

sucker a vegetative shoot that originates from below ground

taxon a taxonomic group of any rank—species, genus, family, etc.; plural, taxa

terete round, as seen in cross-section; "spherical" is not a synonym

terminal uppermost, as in a floret in a spikelet or an inflorescence on a stem

throat the adaxial surface at the junction of the sheath and blade of the grass leaf

tiller a ± erect basal branch or sucker shoot

transverse in a cross-wise direction, as across the face or surface of a plant part

truncate with a squared-off or chopped-off apex or base, as in the appearance of certain leaves or bracts

tufted in bunches or clumps

turgid swollen

unilateral one-sided; situated on one side only, as in spikelets on one side of a rachis or branch

unisexual a flower, spikelet, or plant that bears either stamens or carpels but not both

var. variety

venation the arrangement of veins on a leaf or bract

ventral pertaining to or attached to the inner side of an organ; the side that faces toward a central axis

verrucose a surface, as on a lemma, covered by warty protuberances

verticil a whorl or circular arrangement of parts around a central axis; verticillate, whorled

vestigial rudimentary, poorly developed, much-reduced in size

villous covered with shaggy, soft, but unmatted hairs

viscid sticky, gummy

weed an undesirable, aggressive kind of plant that has a set of biological features that often allows it to out-compete native species and crop plants in a particular area

winged having a membranous lateral extension of an organ, as in a winged glume or inflorescence branch

x the designation of the number of chromosomes that constitutes the basic set for a particular organism, as in x = 5

Selected References

Chapman, G. P. 1996. "A Critical Glossary of the Grasses." *In The Biology of Grasses.* Wallingford, UK: CAB International. Pp. 237–249.

Harrington, H. D. 1977. "Chapter XI: Illustrated Glossary." *In How to Identify Grasses & Grasslike Plants.* Chicago: The Swallow Press. Pp. 85–142.

Jackson, B. D. 1928. *A Glossary of Botanic Terms with Their Derivation and Accent.* Fourth edition. London: Duckworth & Co., Ltd. [A wonderful reference!]

Smith, J. P., Jr. 1977. *Vascular Plant Families.* Eureka, CA: Mad River Press. Pp. 288–312.

Stearn, W. T. 1992. "Glossary." *In Botanical Latin.* Fourth edition. Devon, UK: David & Charles. [The standard reference.]

INDEX

described, 7, 29, 30
of grasses compared to rushes and
sedges, 13
Shiver Grass, 170
Shore Grass, 249–251
Short-Awned Foxtail, 172
Showy Chloris, 223
Sickle Grass, 324–325
Sierran Wood Reed, 225
Silk Panic Grass, 318–319
Silver Hair Grass, 170
Silver Pampas Grass, 230
Six-Weeks Fescue, 272
Six-Weeks Grama, 199
Six-Weeks Grass, 270
Six-Weeks Three-Awn, 180
Slender Hair Grass, 243
Slender Muhly, 308, 310
Slender Oat/Slender Wild Oat, 192
Slender Wheat Grass, 264
Slender Wood Reed, 225
Slough Grass, 194
Small Fescue, 273
Small-Leaved Bent Grass, 169
Smilo, 378
Smooth Barley, 288
Smooth Brome, 212
Smooth Crab Grass, 246–247, 248
Smut Grass, 372
Soft Brome, 214
Soft Chess, 214
Sorgho, 366–367
Sorghum, **365–368**
bicolor, 366–367
halepense, 365, 367–368
Southern Sandbur, 219
Southwestern Cup Grass, 269
Spanish Brome, 210
Spartina, **369–371**
densiflora, 370–371
foliosa, 369
gracilis, 369
Spear Grass, 342–349
species
grass family rank, 6, 7
hybrid percentage, 10
numerical overview, 46–52
specimen collection, 116–120
Spider Grass, 182
Spike Bent Grass, 169
Spike Dropseed, 372–373
Spike Trisetum, 387, 389

spikelet structure
arrangement, 7, 41–44
components, 35–40
compression, 38
described, 7
disarticulation, 39
dissection, 122–123
of grasses compared to rushes and
sedges, 13
models, 40
sexuality, 39
spikes, 7, 35, 41, 43–44
Sporobolus, **372–375**
airoides, 374–375
contractus, 372–373
cryptandrus, 374
indicus, 372
Muhlenbergia and *Agrostis* compared
to, 165
Sprangletop, 300–301
Squirreltail, 100, 261
Squirreltail Barley, 290
stamen
described, 33
of grasses compared to rushes and
sedges, 13
typical temperate, 7
Stebbins, G. Ledyard, 123, 132, 135
Stebbins' Wild-Rye, 264
stem system, 7, **28–32**
of grasses compared to rushes and
sedges, 13
reproduction by segments, 9
Sterile Brome, 208
stigma, 33
described, 7, 36
of grasses compared to rushes and
sedges, 13
Stink Grass, 266
Stipa, **375–383**
arida, 375
cernua, 381
comata, 381
coronata, 382–383
hymenoides, 376–377
lemmonii, 382
lepida, 380
miliacea, 378
occidentalis, 379
parishii var. *parishii*, 383
pulchra, 381
speciosa, 379–380

stolon, described, 7, 29, 30
subalpine meadows, 76
subfamilies of California grasses
   Aristidoideae, 126–127
   Arundinoideae, 127, 128
   Bambusoideae, 128–129
   Chloridoideae, 127, 129–130
   Danthonioideae, 127, 130–131
   Ehrhartoideae, 127, 131–132
   numerical overview, 47–48
   Panicoideae, 132–134
   Poöideae, 134–140
subtropical regions, photosynthetic
   pathway, 9
Sudan Grass, 366–367
Summer Grass, 269, 364–365
Swallenia, **383–384**
   alexandrae, 383–384
Swamp-Timothy, 230–233
Sweet Grass, 176–179
Sweet Vernal Grass, 176–179

Tall Fescue, 274–275
Tall Manna Grass, 280–281
Tall Oat Grass, 99, 184–186
Tall Trisetum, 387–388
Tapered Onion Grass, 303
Tares, 270, 271
taxa, numerical overview, 46–52
taxonomic philosophy, 3–4
taxonomy, related families, 12
Tender Fountain Grass, 220–221
tetany, 106
Thintail, 282–283
Thompson Grass, 328
threatened grasses, 89–91
Three-Awn Grass, 180–182
Three-Awned Goat Grass, 99, 163
Tickle Grass, 165–169
Timber Bamboo, 338–339
Timber Oat Grass, 237
Timothy, **333–335**
   Alpine Timothy, 335
Tobosa, 283–285
Torreyochloa, **384–385**
   Glyceria and *Puccinellia* compared to, 280
   pallida, 385
Torrey's Melic, 305
toxic grasses, 102–107
tribes, numerical overview, 47
Tribolium obliterum, 100
Tridens, **386**
   muticus, 386

Trisetum, **387–389**
   canescens, 387–388
   Deschampsia compared to, 246
   spicatum, 387, 389
Triticum, **390–391**
   aestivum, 100, 390–391
   Hordeum and *Secale* compared to, 363
tropical regions, photosynthetic pathway, 9
Tufted Hair Grass, 244–245
Tufted Love Grass, 267
Tufted Pine Grass, 215
Tumble Grass, 323
Typhaceae, 12

Uruguayan Pampas Grass, 230
uses, 11, 109–112

valley grassland, 59–63
Vanilla Grass, 179
vegetative reproduction, 9
vegetative structure, 28–32
veldt grasses, **254–256**
   Annual Veldt Grass, 254
   Long-Flowered Veldt Grass, 254
   Panic Veldt Grass, 254
   Perennial Veldt Grass, 254, 255–256
Velvet Grass, 286–287
Ventenata, **392–393**
   dubia, 100, 392–393
vernacular names, 15–16
vernal pools, 68, 69
Vulpia, Festuca compared to, 270

Wall Barley, 288
Wallaby Grass, 356–357
Water Beard Grass, 350
Water Grass, 251–253
Waxy Manna Grass, 279
weedy grasses
   biological features, 93
   defining, 92–93
   economic importance, 92
   miscellaneous, 99–100
   noxious, 95–99
   positive aspects, 93
   roadside, 93
Weeping Love Grass, 265
Western Alkali Grass, 353
Western Fescue, 277
Western Melic, 303
Western Needle Grass, 379
Western Wild-Rye, 262
Wheat, 390–391

ABOUT THE AUTHOR

James P. Smith, Jr., is Professor of Botany, Emeritus, and Curator of the Herbarium at Humboldt State University where he taught courses in plant taxonomy, agrostology, poisonous plants, and economic botany; he also served in various administrative capacities. He is the author of *Vascular Plant Families* and a *Key to the Genera of Grasses of the Conterminous United States*. He was a co-editor of three editions of the California Native Plant Society's rare plant inventories, and editor and contributor to the treatment of the grass family in both editions of *The Jepson Manual*.